ALEX GRAHAM'S FRED BASSET

2008

Orion Books Ltd
Orion House
5 Upper St Martin's Lane
London WC2H 9EA

First published by Orion in 2008

Drawings by Michael Martin

Cover illustrations by Alex Graham

© Associated Newspapers plc 2008

ISBN 978 0 7528 9385 3

Printed in the UK by CPI William Clowes,
Beccles, NR34 7TL

www.orionbooks.co.uk

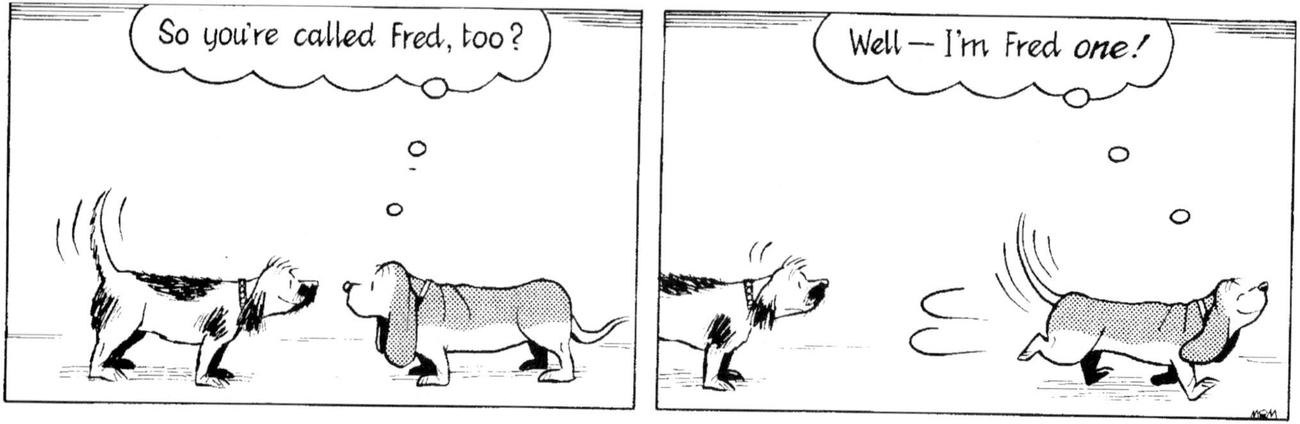
So you're called Fred, too?
Well — I'm Fred one!

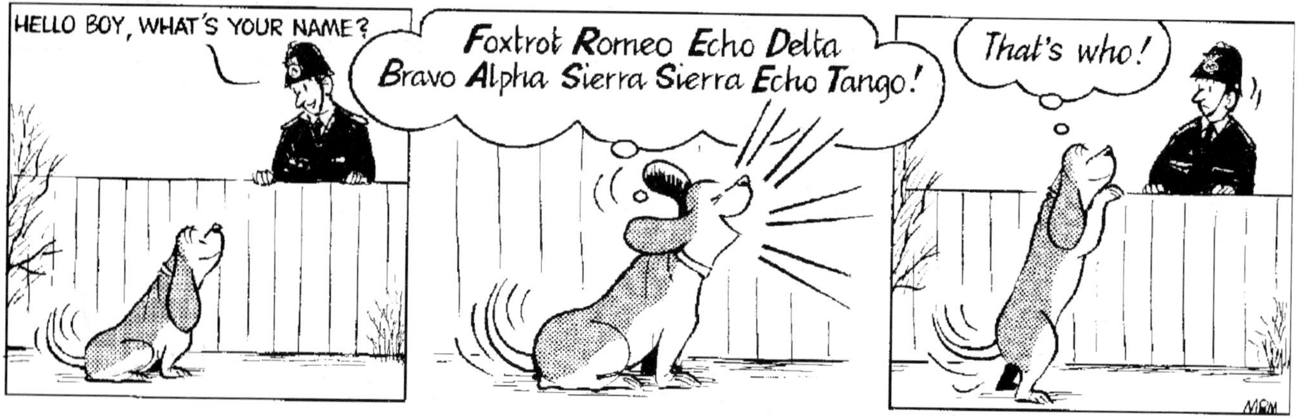
HELLO BOY, WHAT'S YOUR NAME?
Foxtrot Romeo Echo Delta Bravo Alpha Sierra Sierra Echo Tango!
That's who!

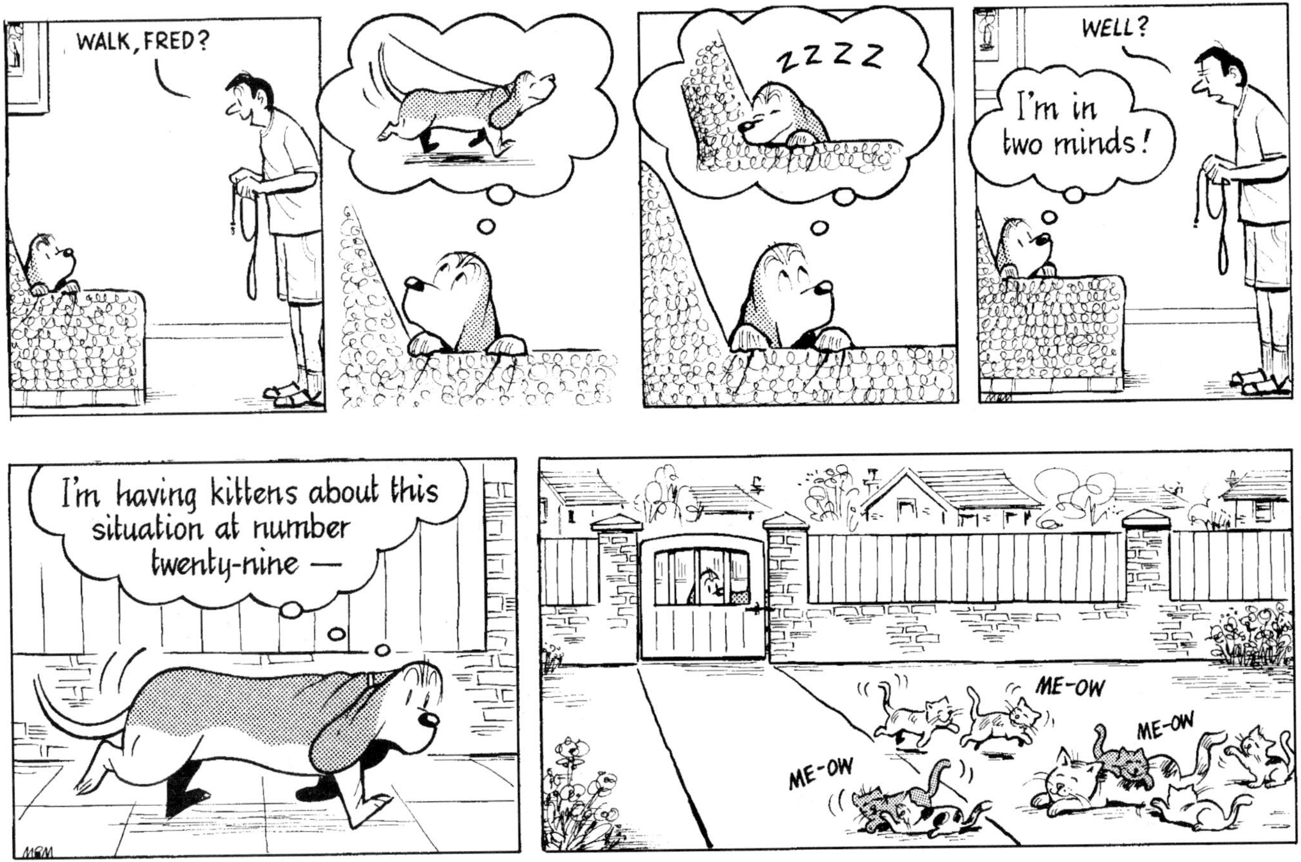

WALK, FRED?
ZZZZ
WELL?
I'm in two minds!
I'm having kittens about this situation at number twenty-nine —
ME-OW
ME-OW
ME-OW

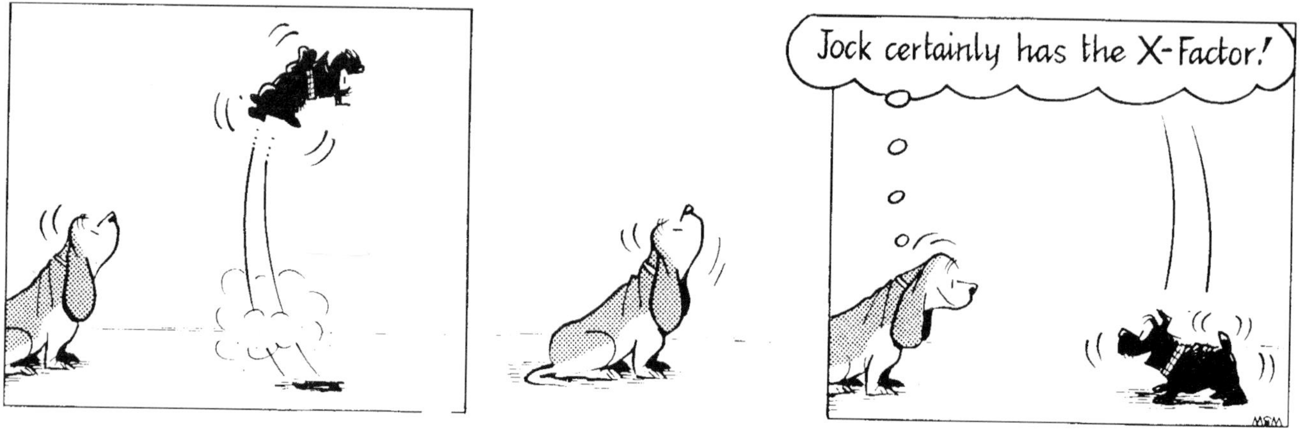
Jock certainly has the X-Factor!

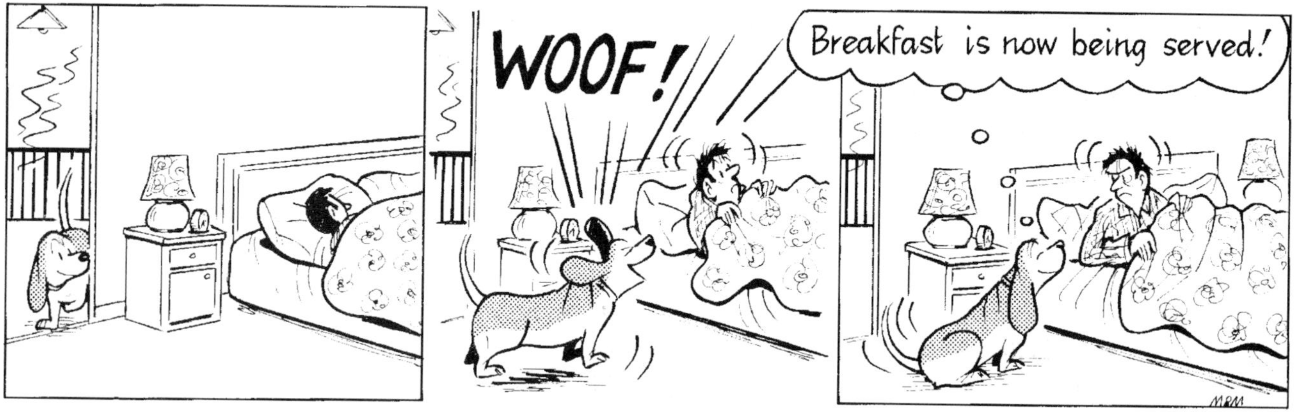
WOOF!
Breakfast is now being served!

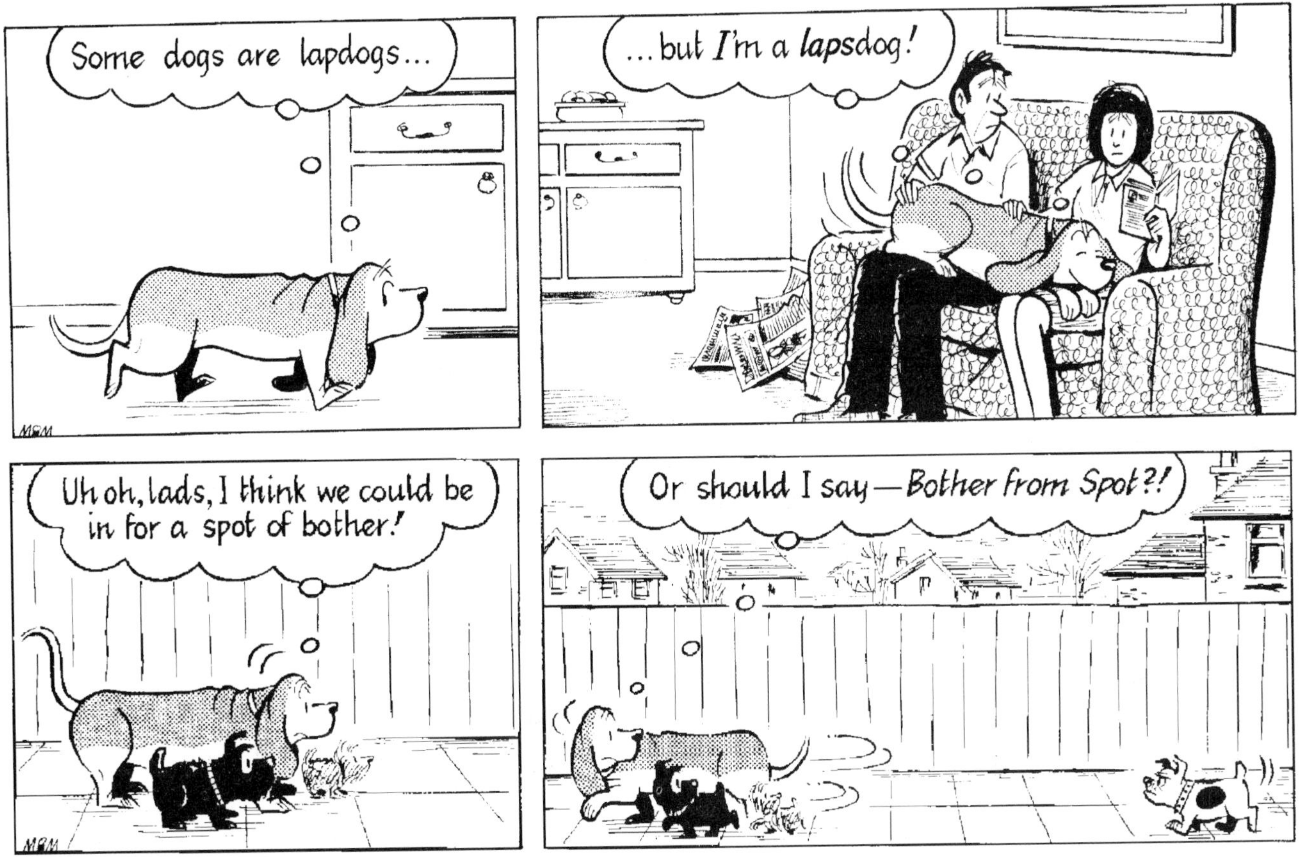
Some dogs are lapdogs...
...but I'm a lapsdog!
Uh oh, lads, I think we could be in for a spot of bother!
Or should I say—Bother from Spot?!

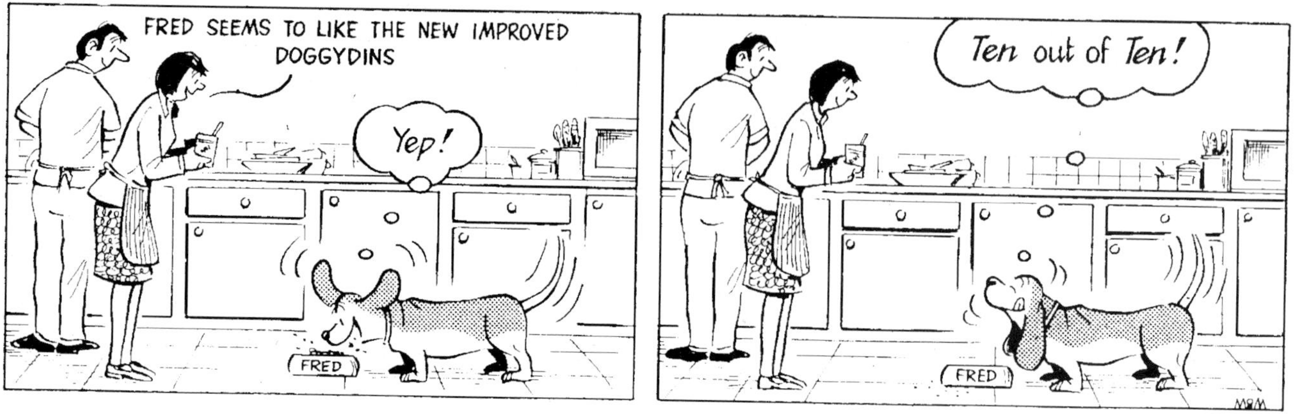
FRED SEEMS TO LIKE THE NEW IMPROVED DOGGYDINS
Yep!
FRED
Ten out of Ten!
FRED

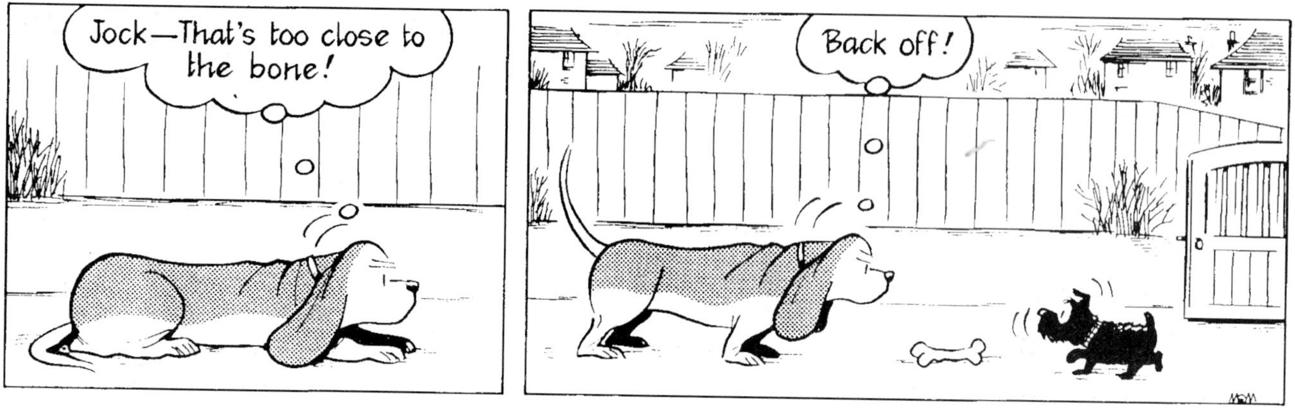
Jock—That's too close to the bone!
Back off!

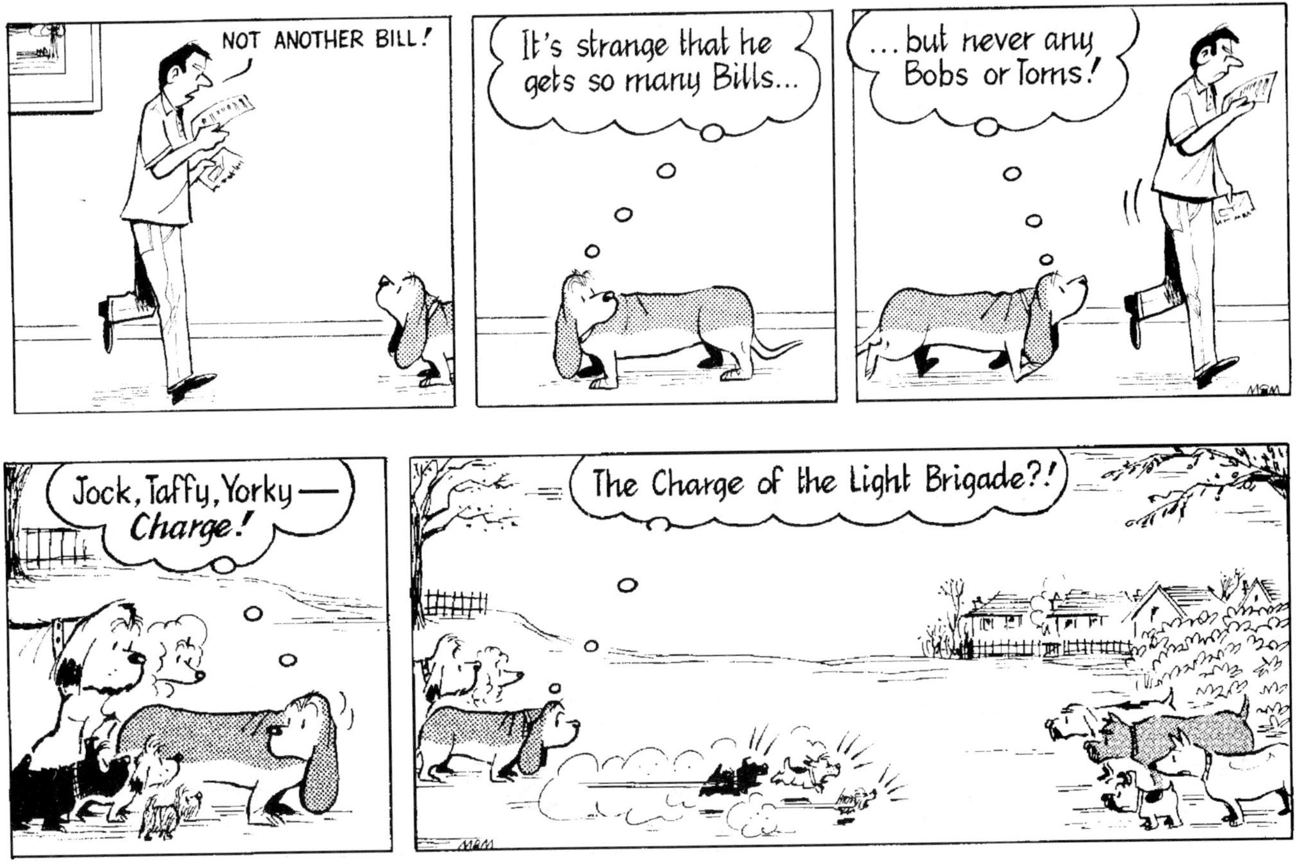
NOT ANOTHER BILL!
It's strange that he gets so many Bills...
...but never any Bobs or Toms!
MGM
Jock, Taffy, Yorky—Charge!
The Charge of the Light Brigade?!
MGM

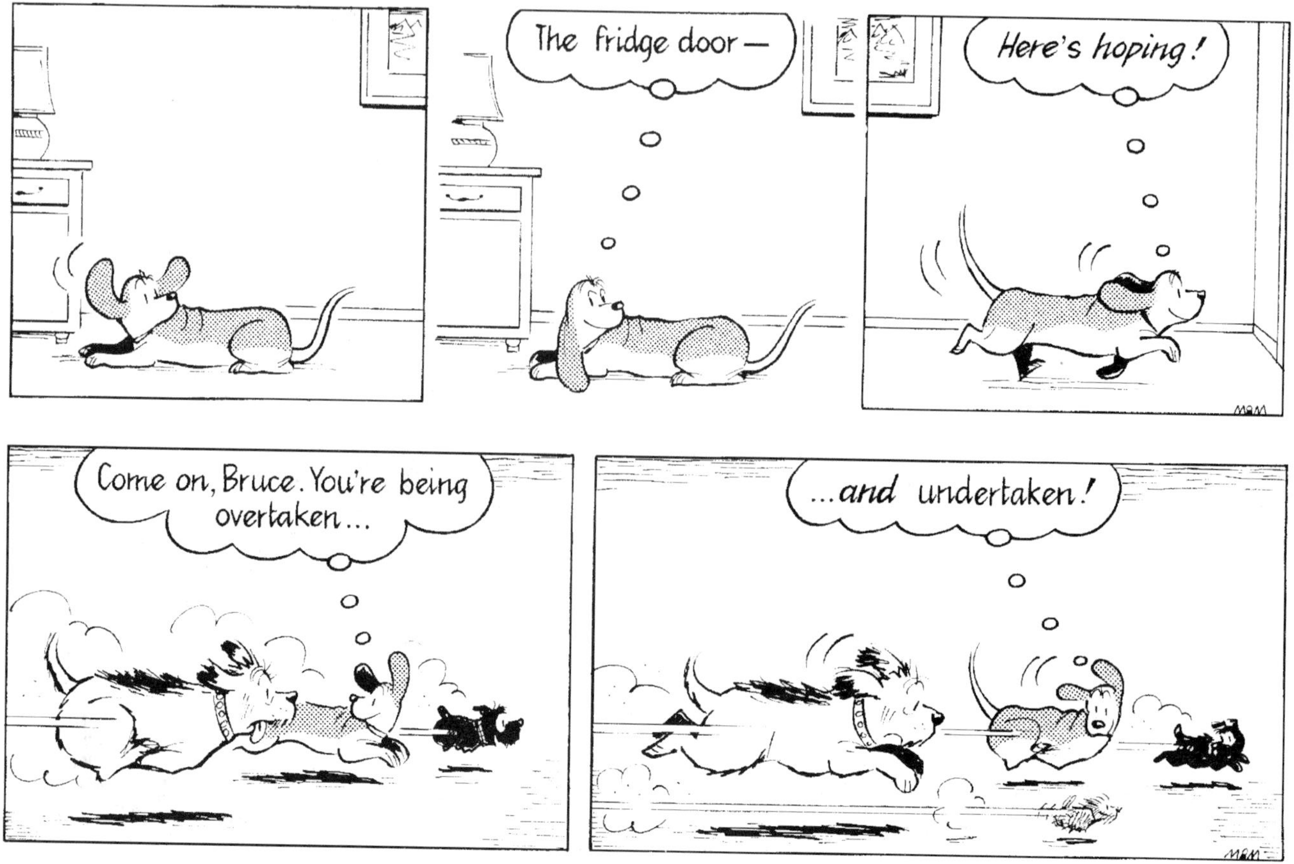
The fridge door —
Here's hoping!
MGM
Come on, Bruce. You're being overtaken...
...and undertaken!
MGM

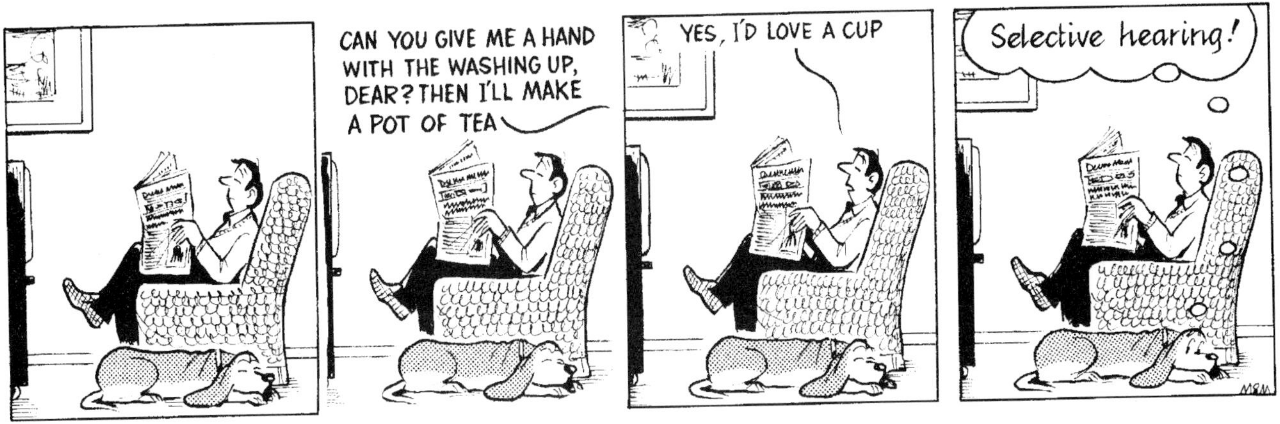
CAN YOU GIVE ME A HAND WITH THE WASHING UP, DEAR? THEN I'LL MAKE A POT OF TEA
YES, I'D LOVE A CUP
Selective hearing!

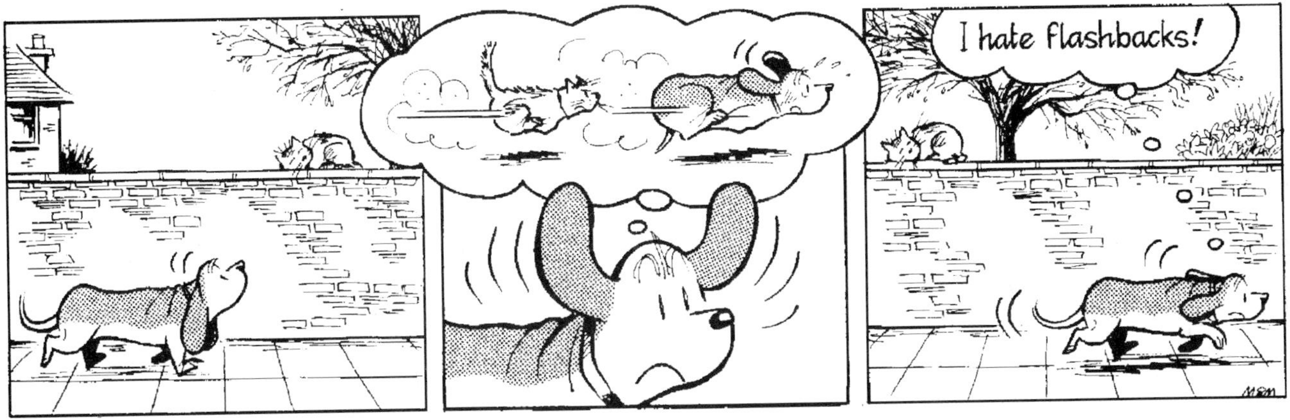
I hate flashbacks!

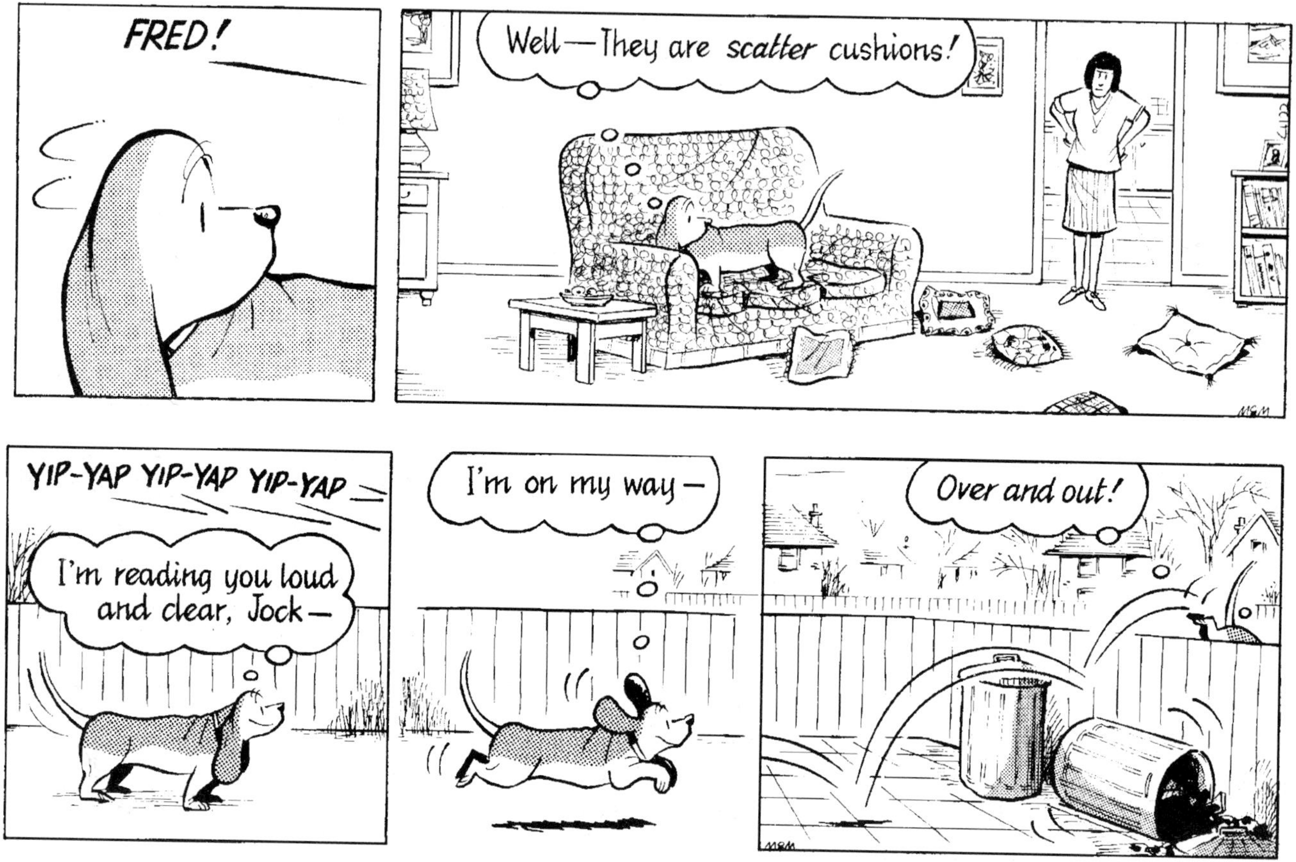
FRED!
Well—They are scatter cushions!
YIP-YAP YIP-YAP YIP-YAP
I'm reading you loud and clear, Jock—
I'm on my way—
Over and out!

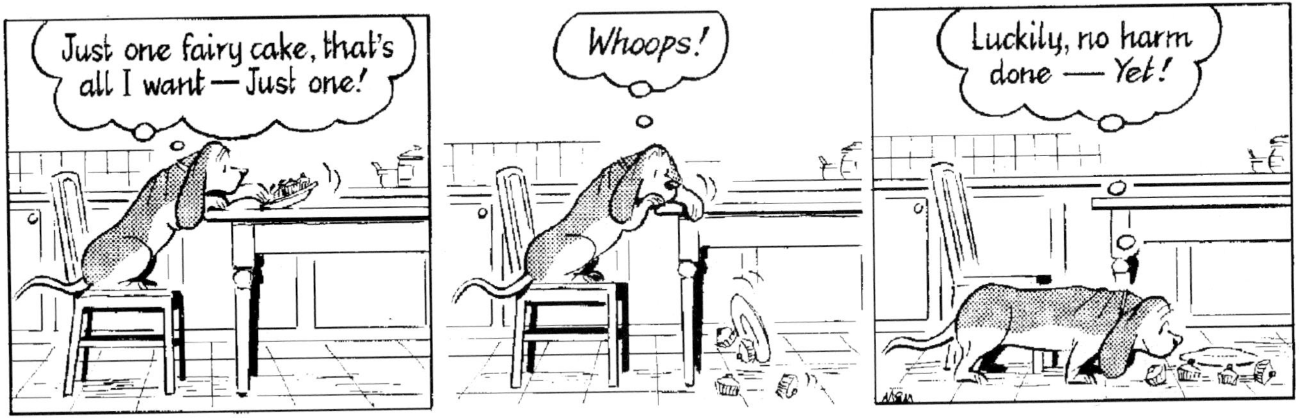
Just one fairy cake, that's all I want — Just one!
Whoops!
Luckily, no harm done — Yet!

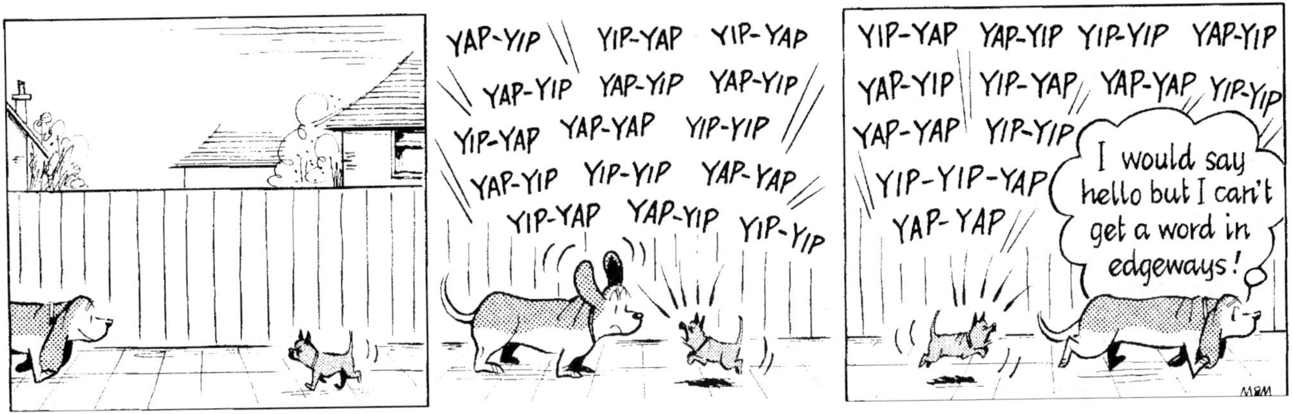
YAP-YIP YIP-YAP YIP-YAP
YAP-YIP YAP-YIP YAP-YIP
YIP-YAP YAP-YAP YIP-YIP
YAP-YIP YIP-YIP YAP-YAP
YIP-YAP YAP-YIP YIP-YIP
YIP-YAP YAP-YIP YIP-YIP YAP-YIP
YAP-YIP YIP-YAP YAP-YAP YIP-YIP
YAP-YAP YIP-YIP
YIP-YIP-YAP
YAP-YAP
I would say hello but I can't get a word in edgeways!

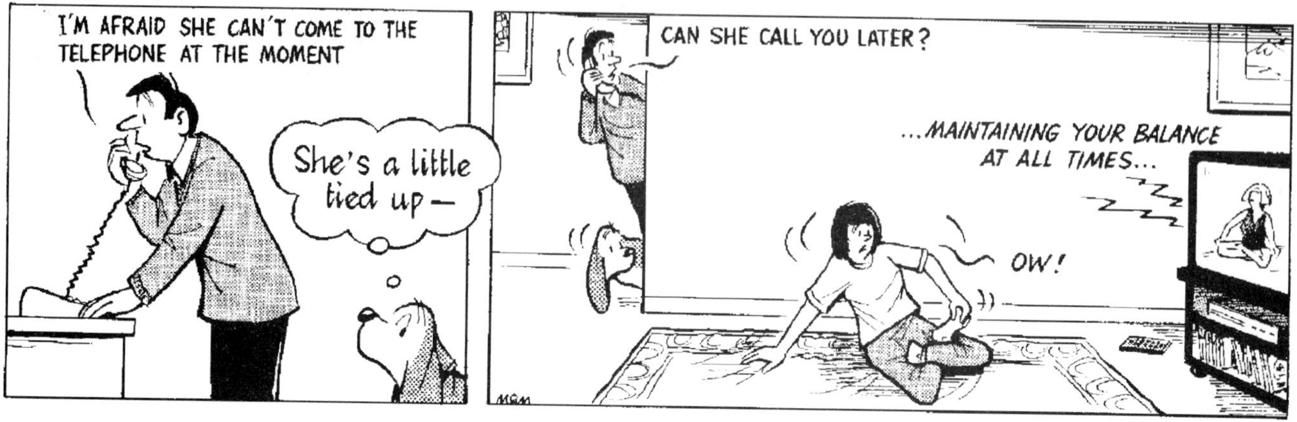
I'M AFRAID SHE CAN'T COME TO THE TELEPHONE AT THE MOMENT
She's a little tied up —
CAN SHE CALL YOU LATER?
...MAINTAINING YOUR BALANCE AT ALL TIMES...
OW!

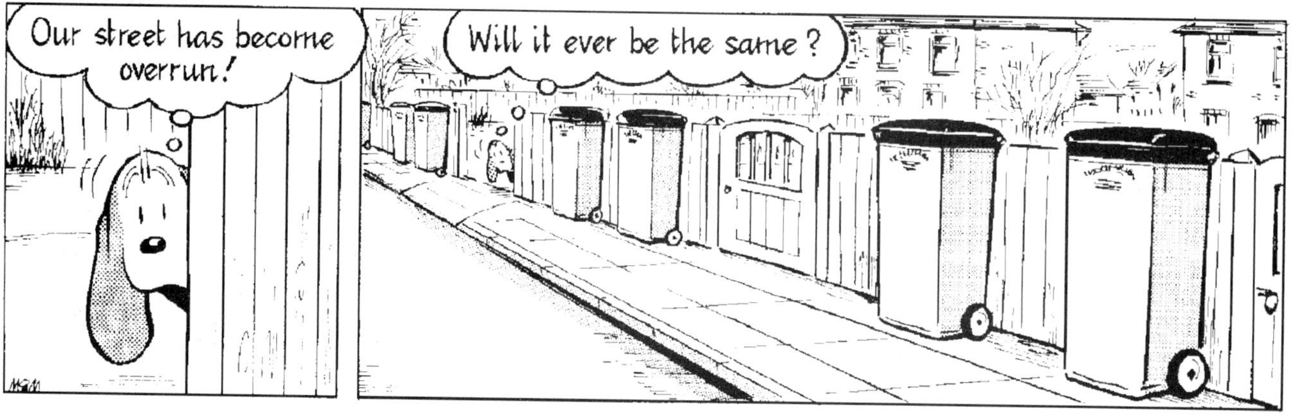
Our street has become overrun!
Will it ever be the same?

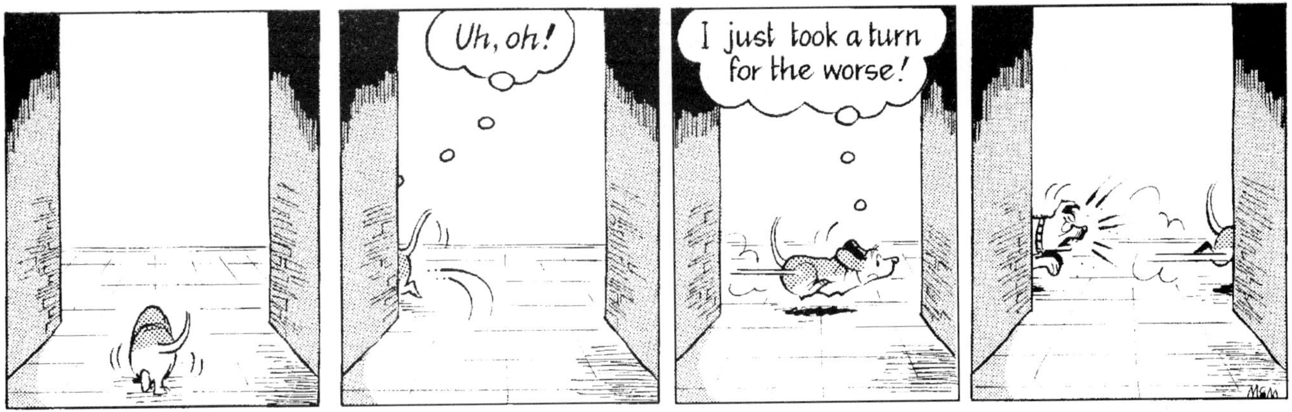
Uh, oh!
I just took a turn for the worse!

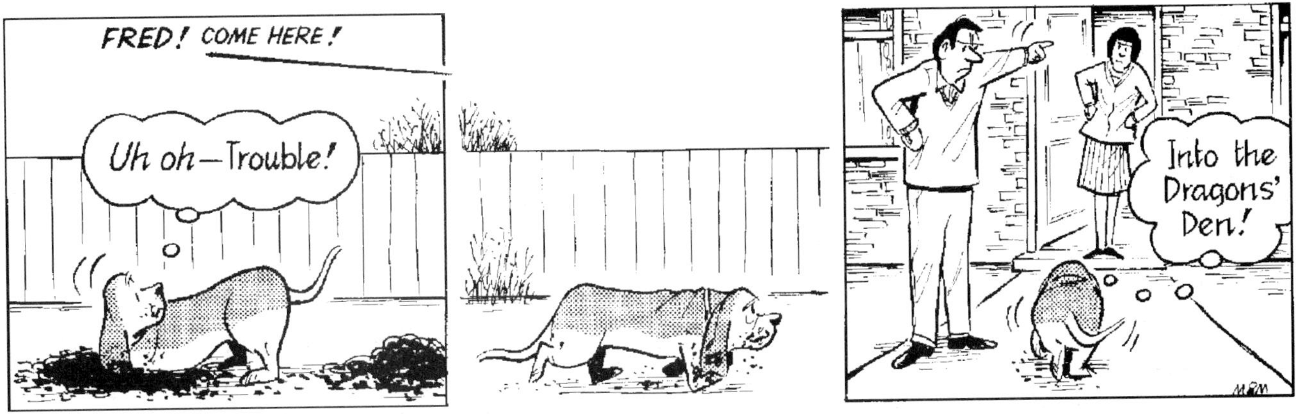
FRED! COME HERE!
Uh oh—Trouble!
Into the Dragons' Den!

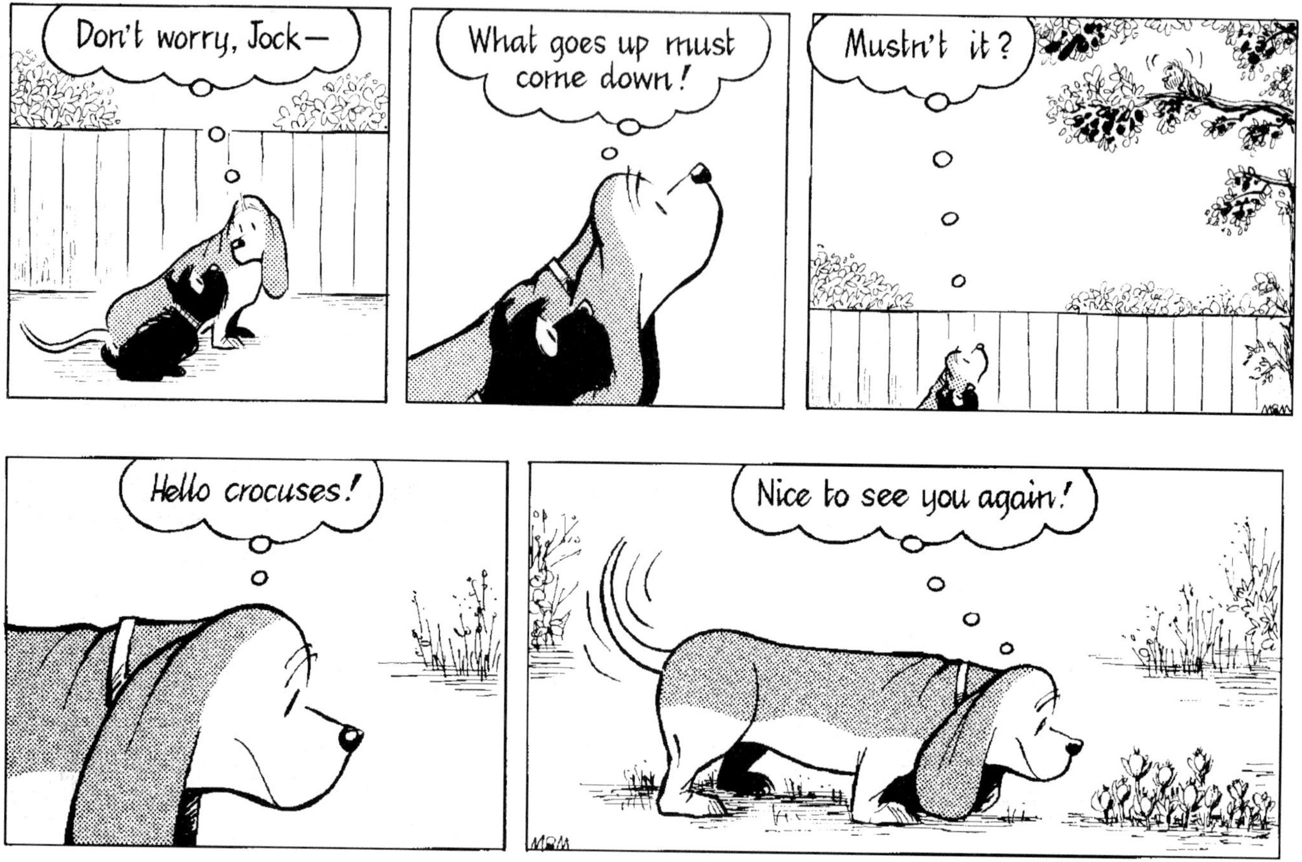
Don't worry, Jock—
What goes up must come down!
Mustn't it?
Hello crocuses!
Nice to see you again!

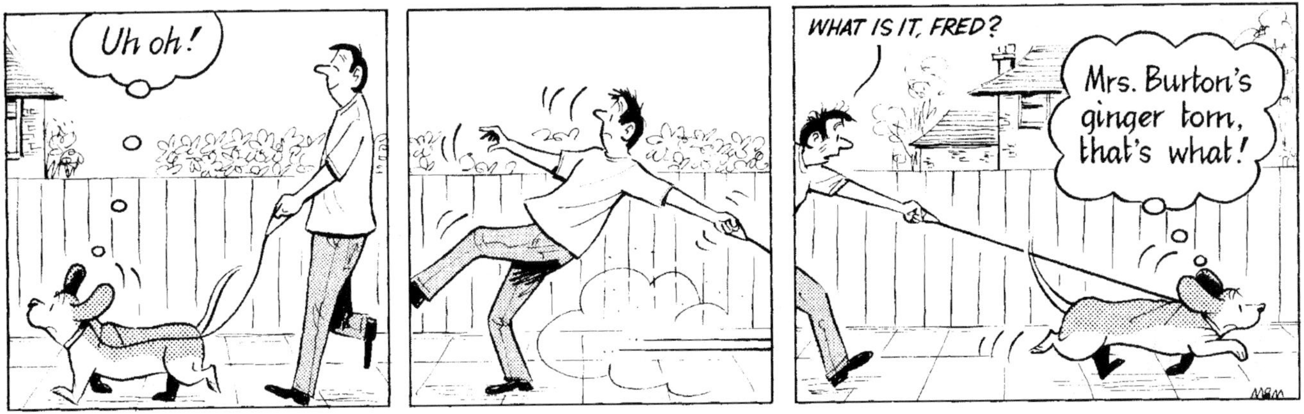
Uh oh!
WHAT IS IT, FRED?
Mrs. Burton's ginger tom, that's what!
MGM

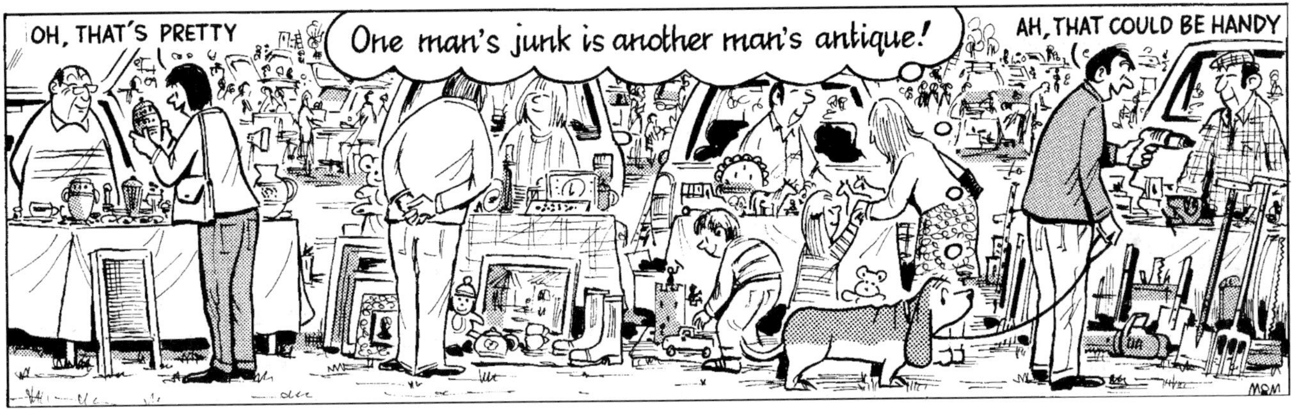
OH, THAT'S PRETTY
One man's junk is another man's antique!
AH, THAT COULD BE HANDY
MGM

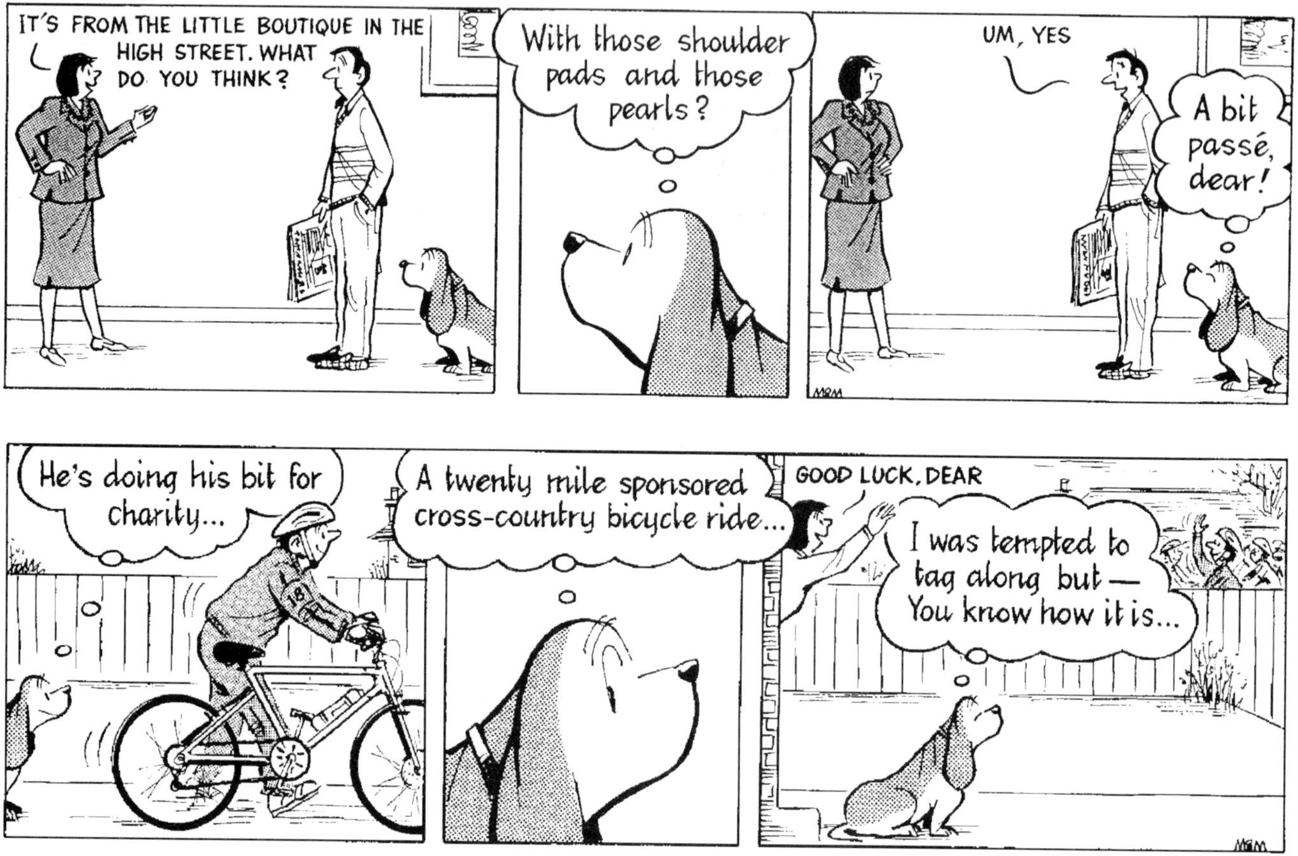
IT'S FROM THE LITTLE BOUTIQUE IN THE HIGH STREET. WHAT DO YOU THINK?
With those shoulder pads and those pearls?
UM, YES
A bit passé, dear!
He's doing his bit for charity...
A twenty mile sponsored cross-country bicycle ride...
GOOD LUCK, DEAR
I was tempted to tag along but — You know how it is...

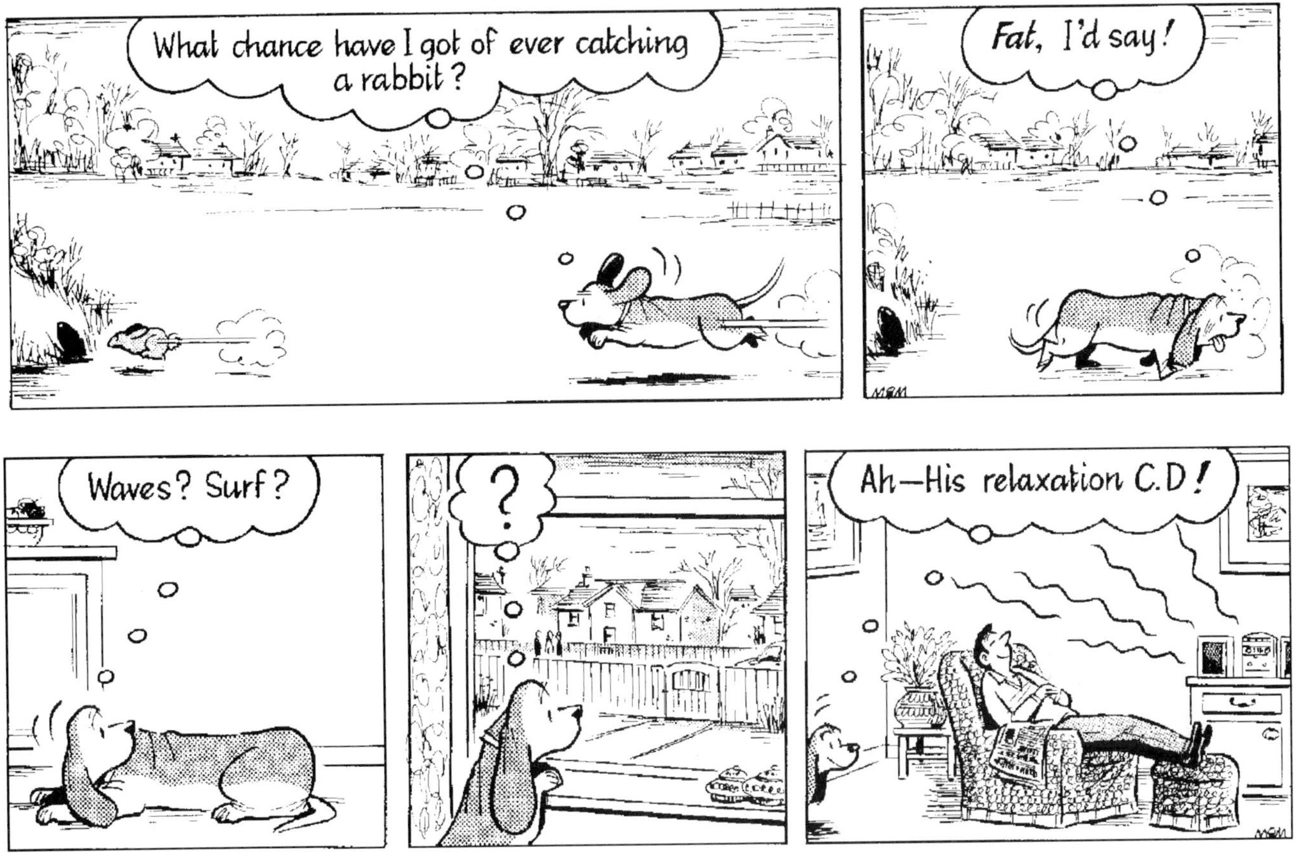
What chance have I got of ever catching a rabbit?
Fat, I'd say!
Waves? Surf?
?
Ah—His relaxation C.D!

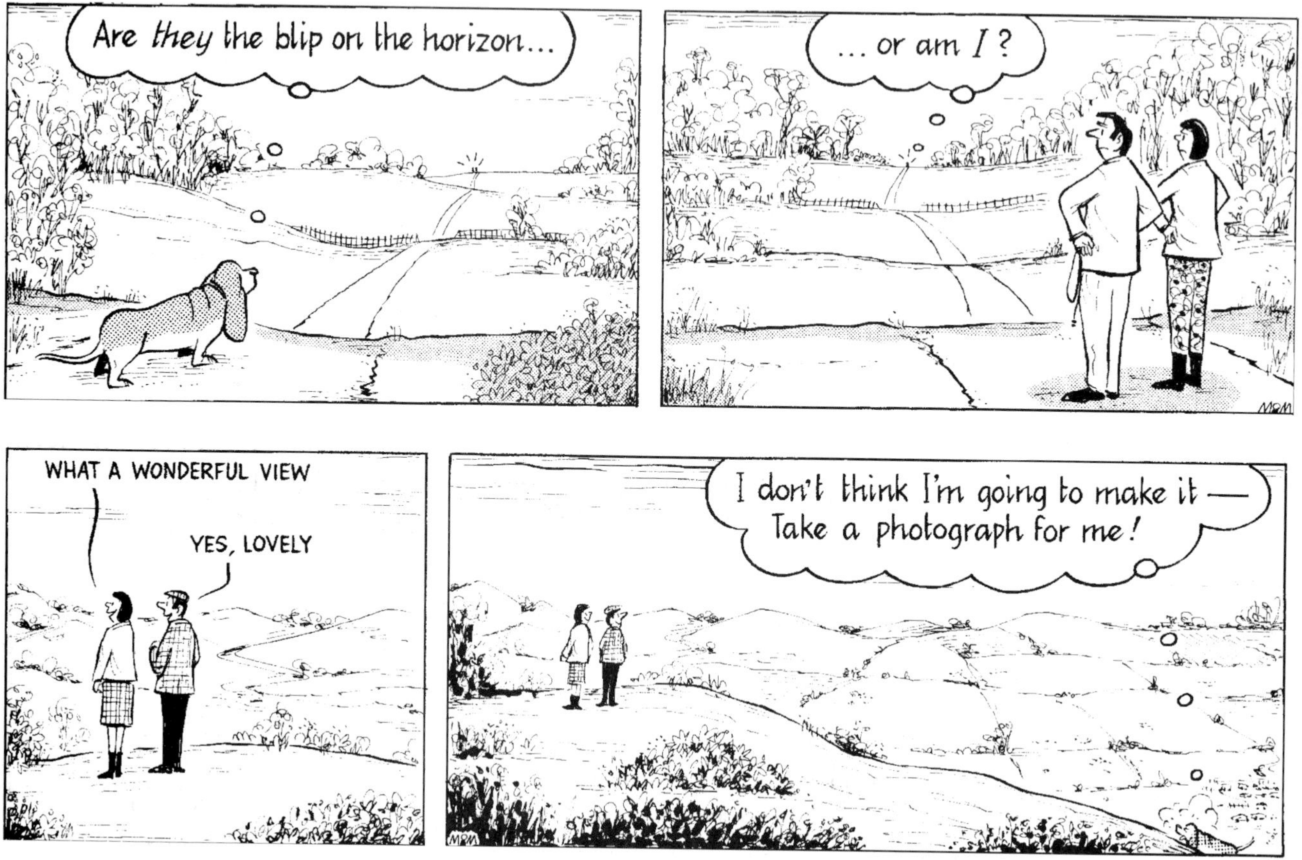
Are they the blip on the horizon...
... or am I ?
WHAT A WONDERFUL VIEW
YES, LOVELY
I don't think I'm going to make it —
Take a photograph for me!

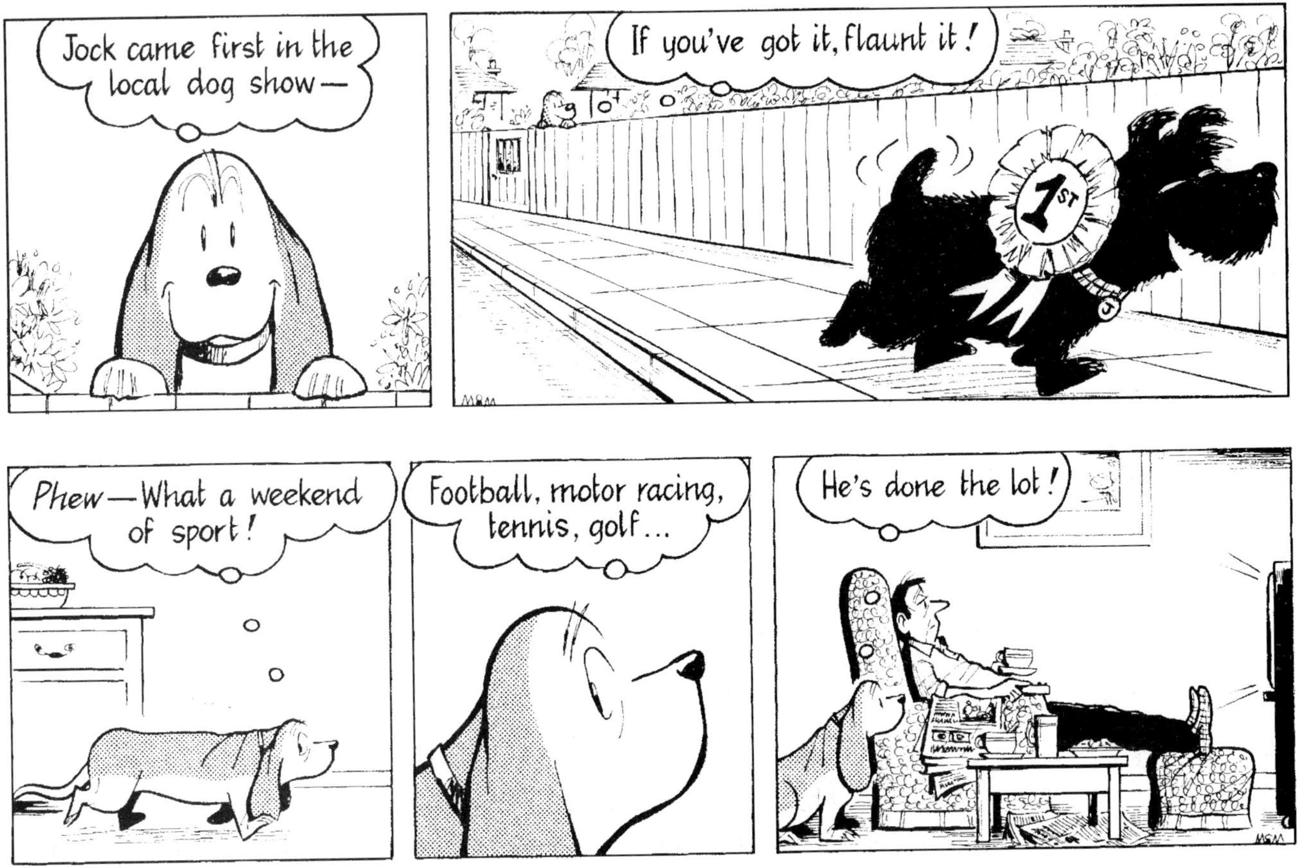
Jock came first in the local dog show—
If you've got it, flaunt it!
1ST
Phew—What a weekend of sport!
Football, motor racing, tennis, golf...
He's done the lot!

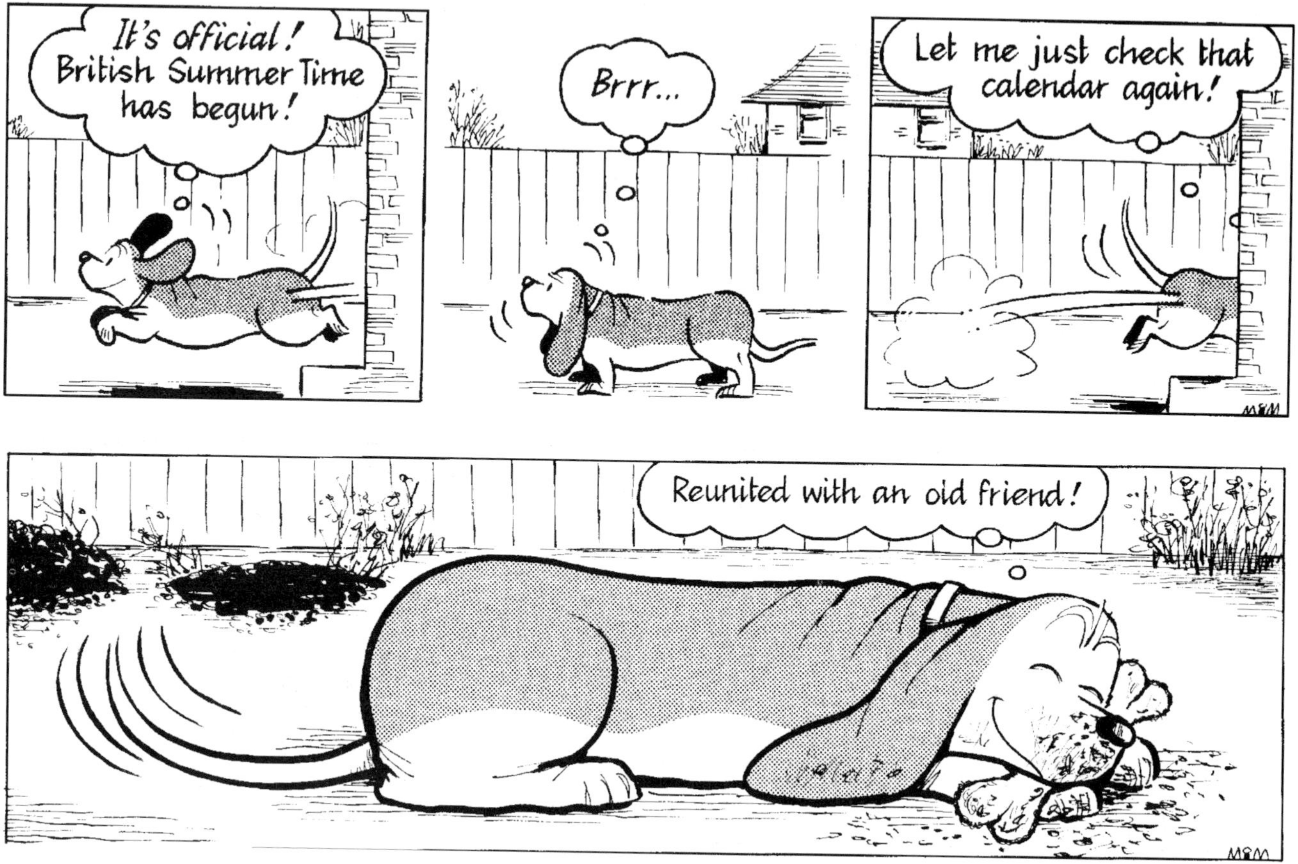
It's official! British Summer Time has begun!
Brrr...
Let me just check that calendar again!
M&M
Reunited with an old friend!
M&M

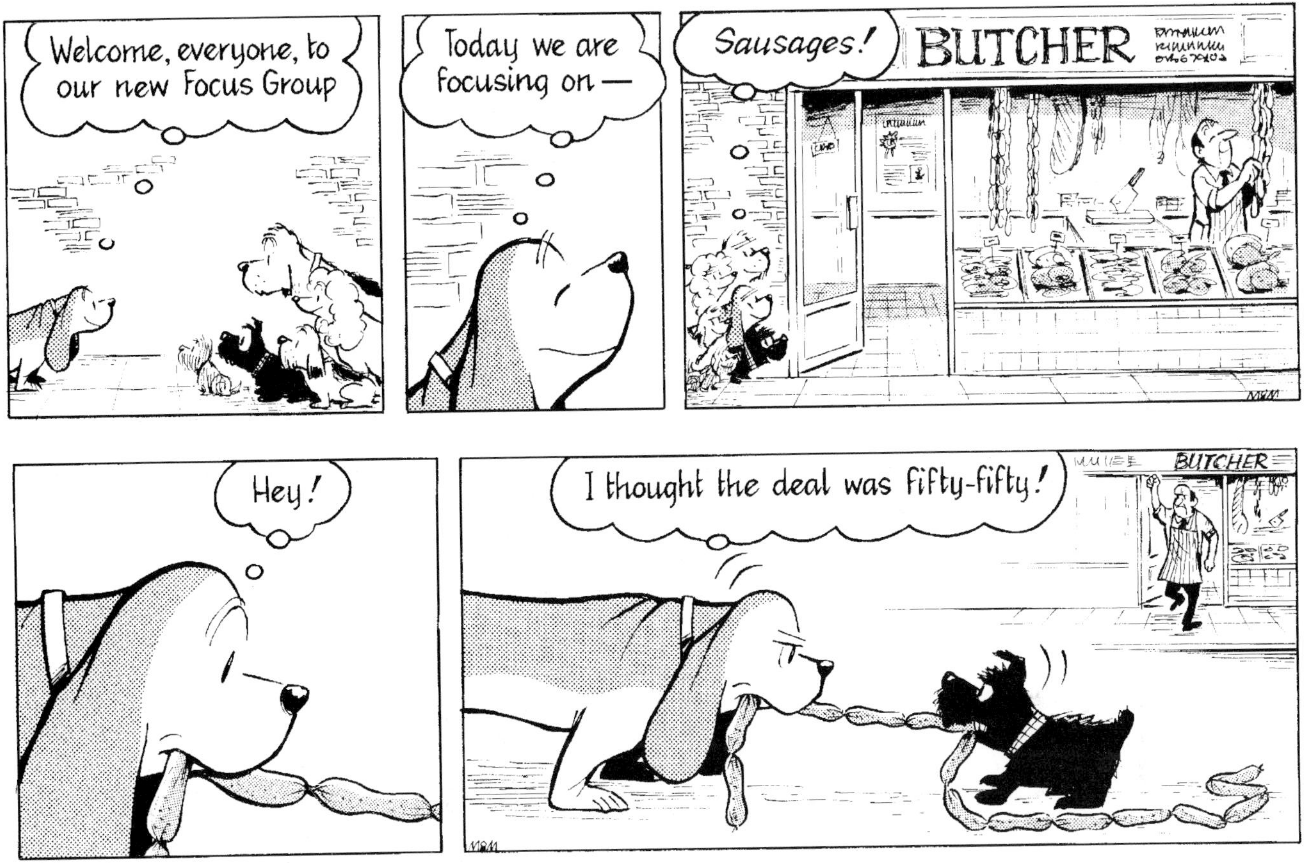
Welcome, everyone, to our new Focus Group
Today we are focusing on —
Sausages!
BUTCHER
Hey!
I thought the deal was fifty-fifty!
BUTCHER

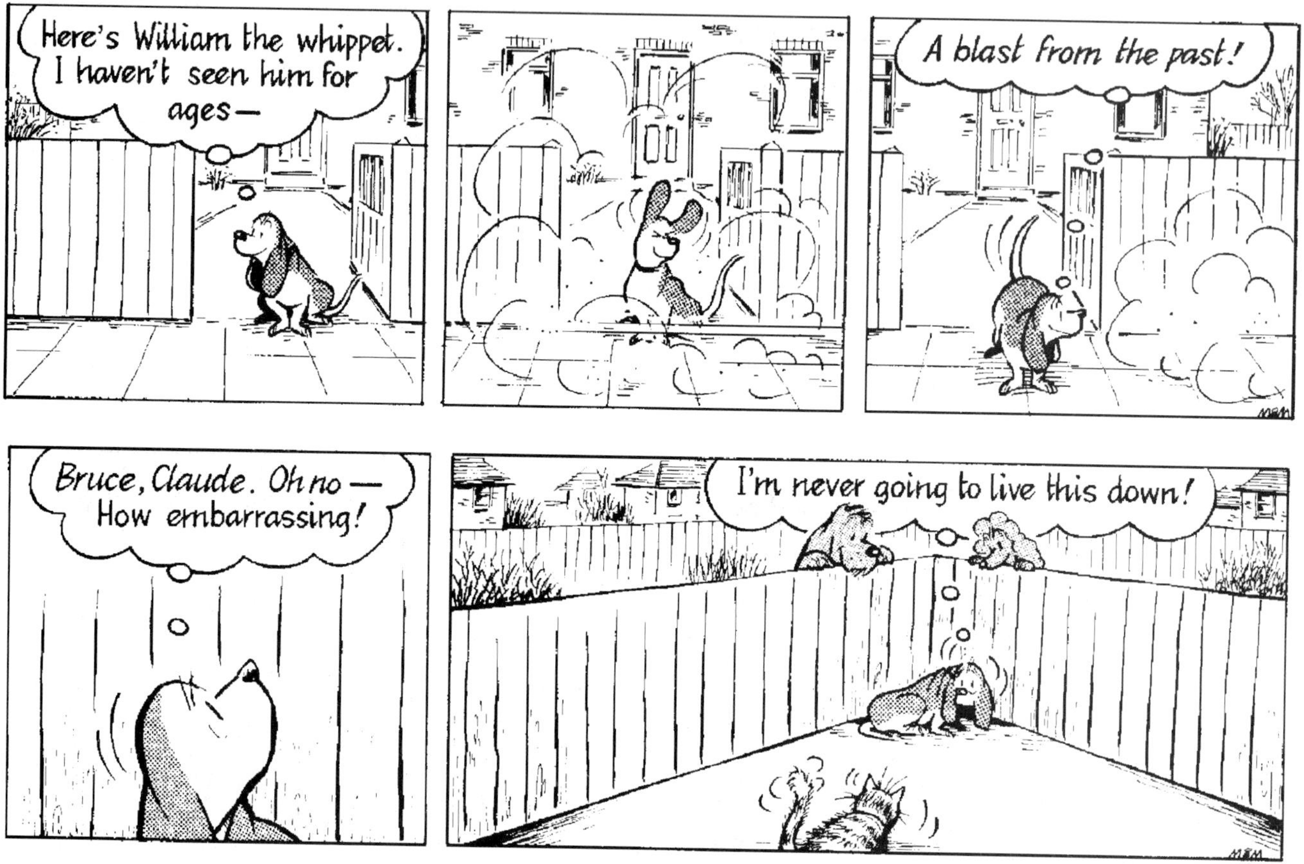
Here's William the whippet. I haven't seen him for ages—
A blast from the past!
Bruce, Claude. Oh no— How embarrassing!
I'm never going to live this down!

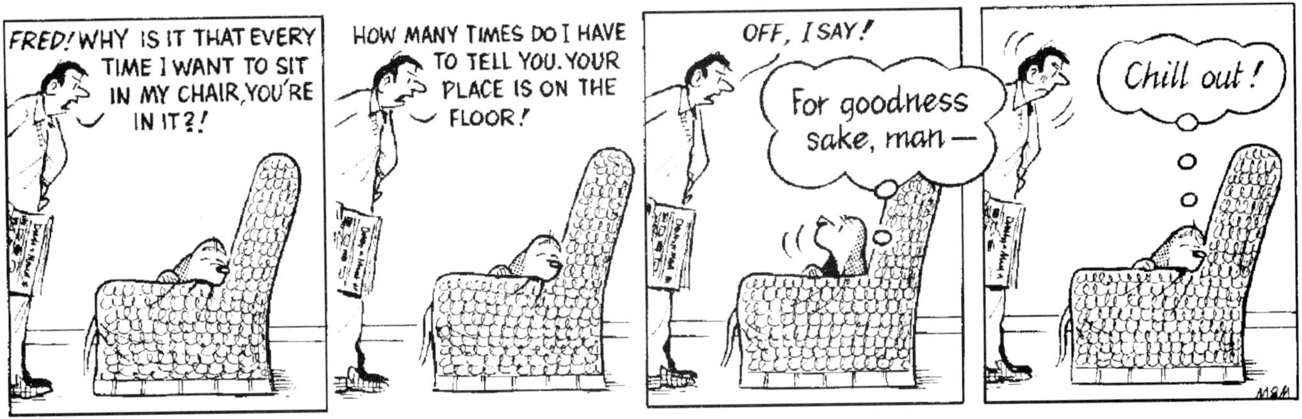
FRED! WHY IS IT THAT EVERY TIME I WANT TO SIT IN MY CHAIR, YOU'RE IN IT?!
HOW MANY TIMES DO I HAVE TO TELL YOU. YOUR PLACE IS ON THE FLOOR!
OFF, I SAY!
For goodness sake, man —
Chill out!

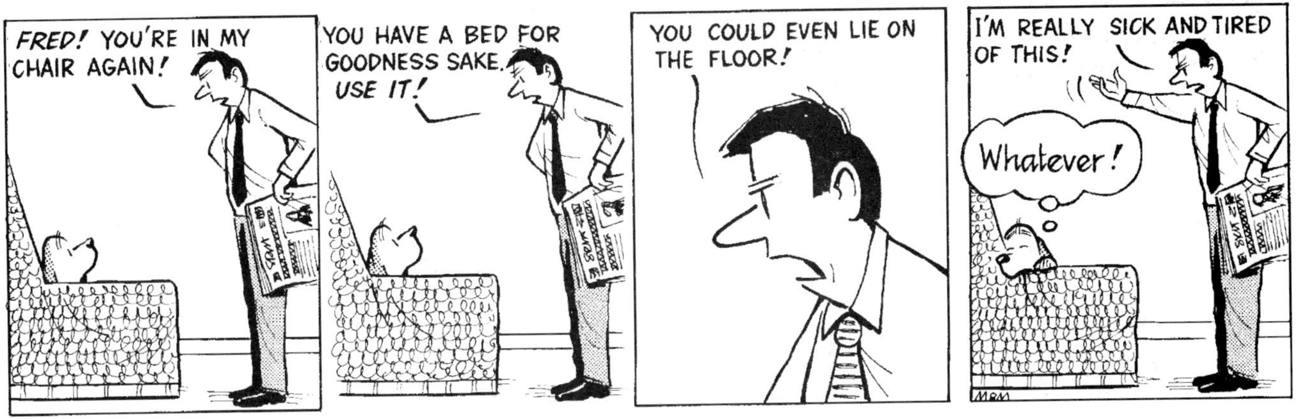
FRED! YOU'RE IN MY CHAIR AGAIN!
YOU HAVE A BED FOR GOODNESS SAKE. USE IT!
YOU COULD EVEN LIE ON THE FLOOR!
I'M REALLY SICK AND TIRED OF THIS!
Whatever!

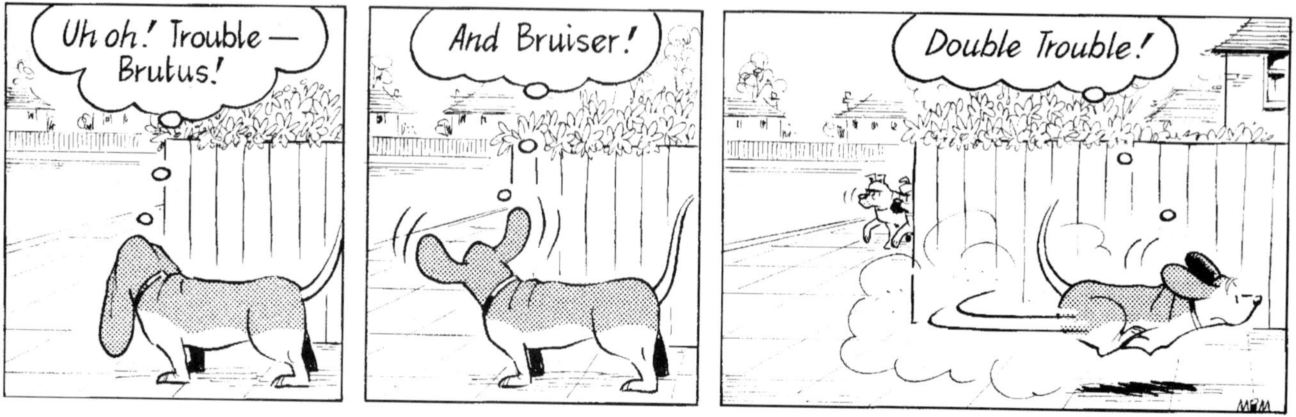
Uh oh! Trouble — Brutus!
And Bruiser!
Double Trouble!
MBM

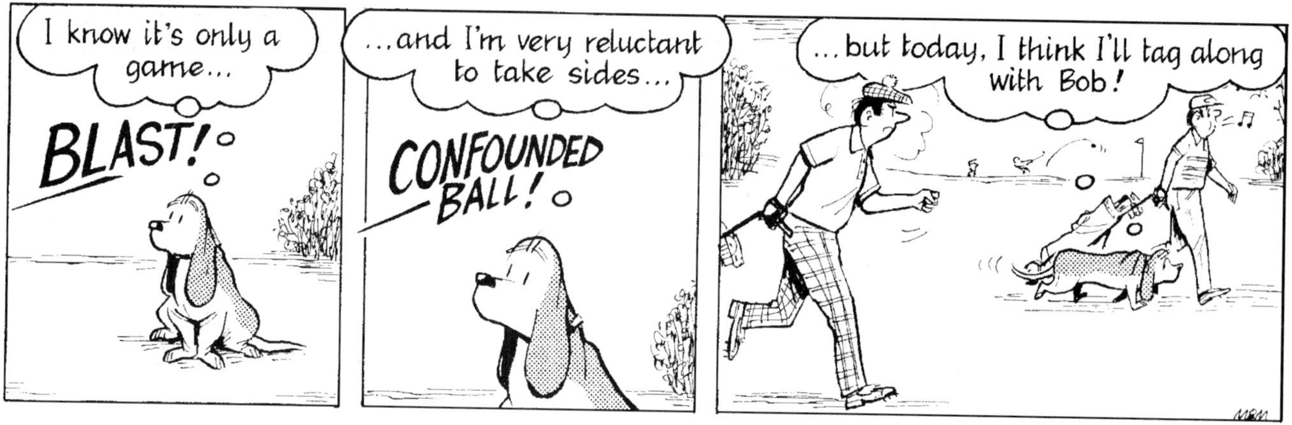
I know it's only a game...
BLAST!
...and I'm very reluctant to take sides...
CONFOUNDED BALL!
...but today, I think I'll tag along with Bob!
MBM

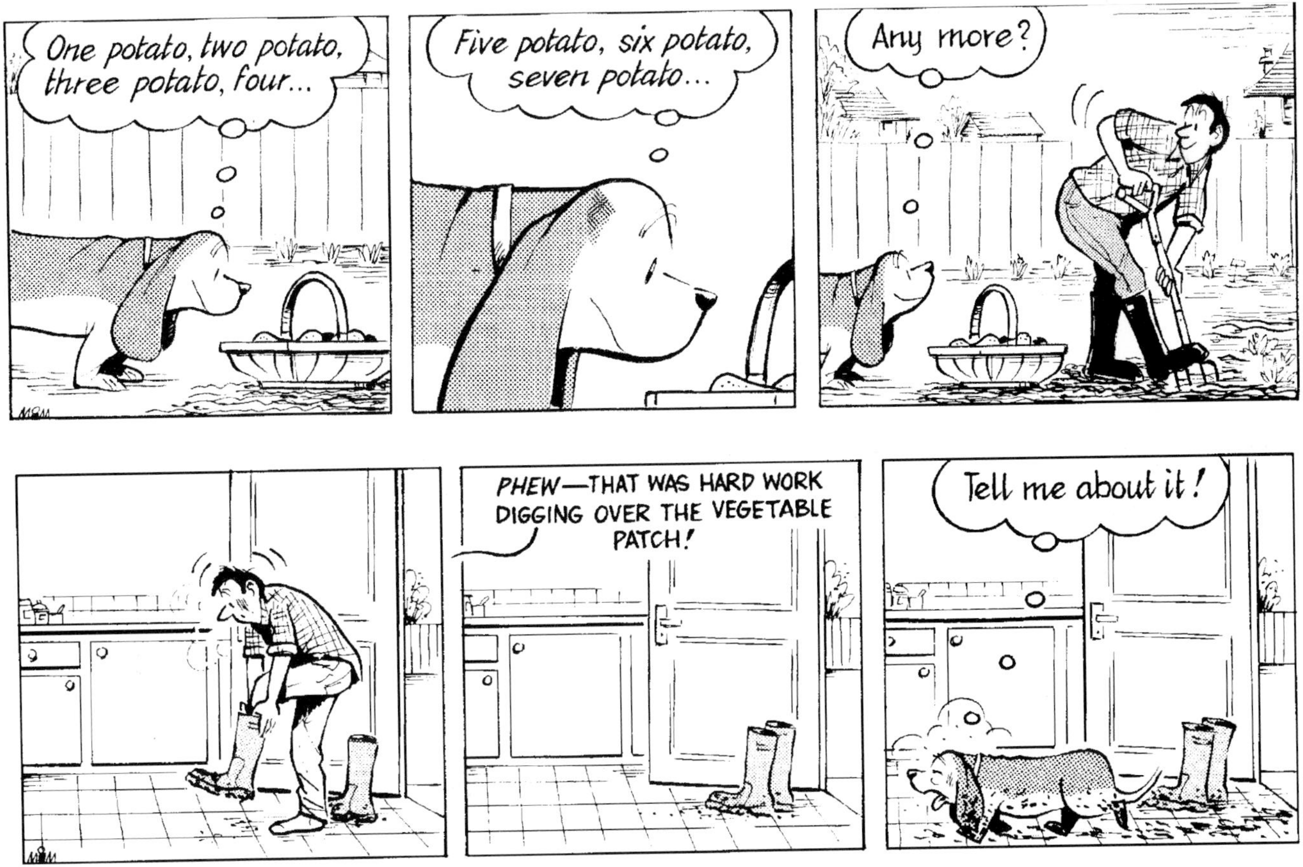

One potato, two potato, three potato, four...
Five potato, six potato, seven potato...
Any more?
PHEW—THAT WAS HARD WORK DIGGING OVER THE VEGETABLE PATCH!
Tell me about it!

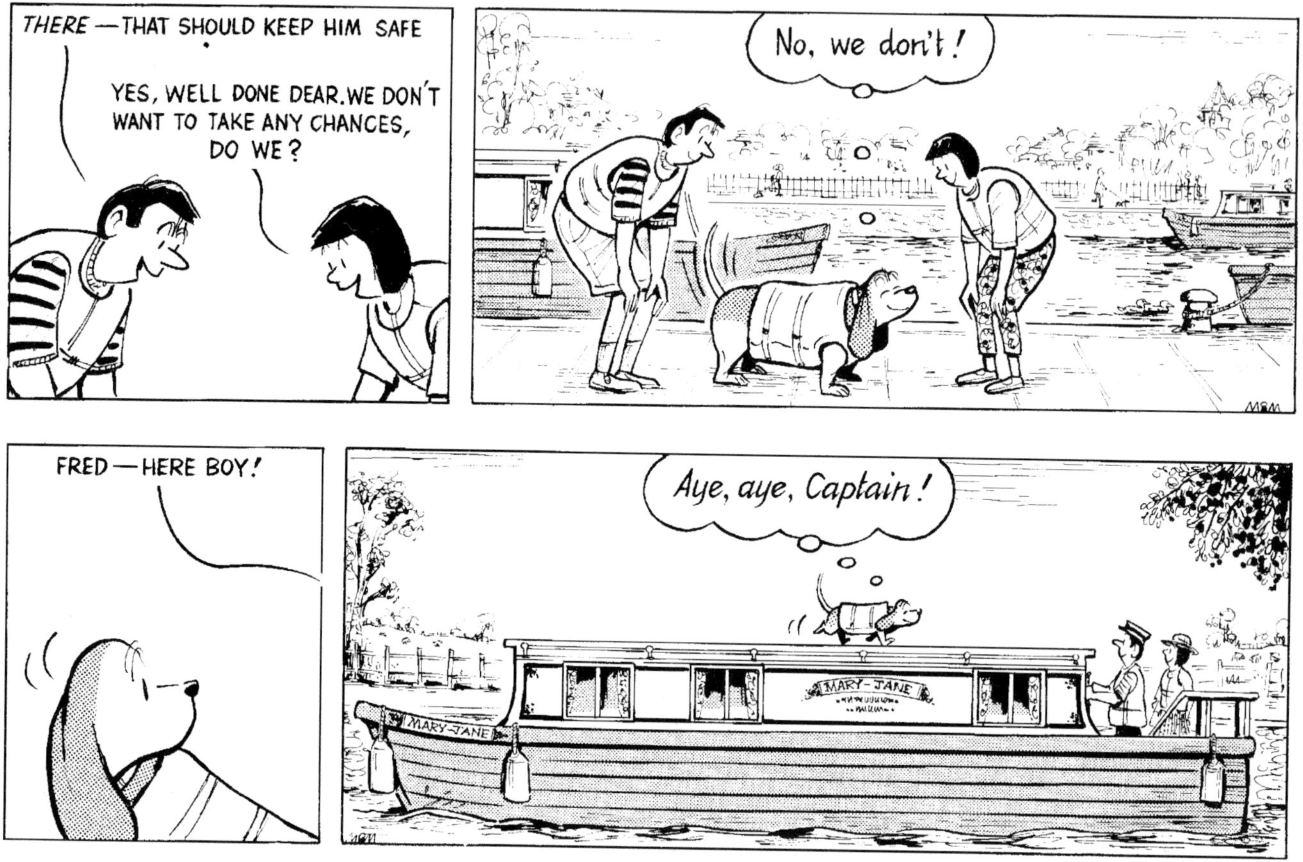
THERE—THAT SHOULD KEEP HIM SAFE.
YES, WELL DONE DEAR. WE DON'T WANT TO TAKE ANY CHANCES, DO WE?
No, we don't!
FRED—HERE BOY!
Aye, aye, Captain!
MARY-JANE
MARY-JANE

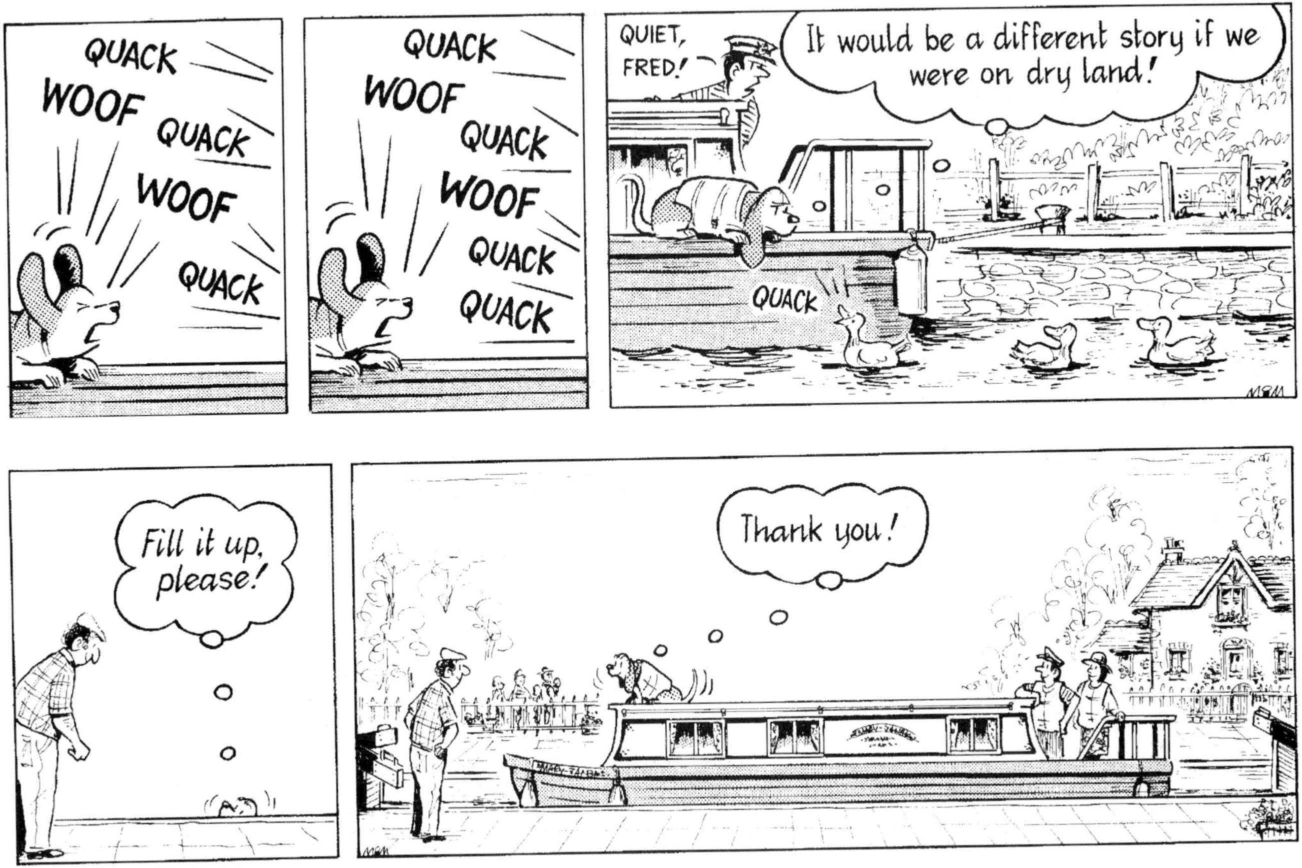
QUACK
WOOF
QUACK
WOOF
QUACK
QUACK
WOOF
QUACK
WOOF
QUACK
QUACK
QUIET, FRED!
It would be a different story if we were on dry land!
QUACK
Fill it up, please!
Thank you!

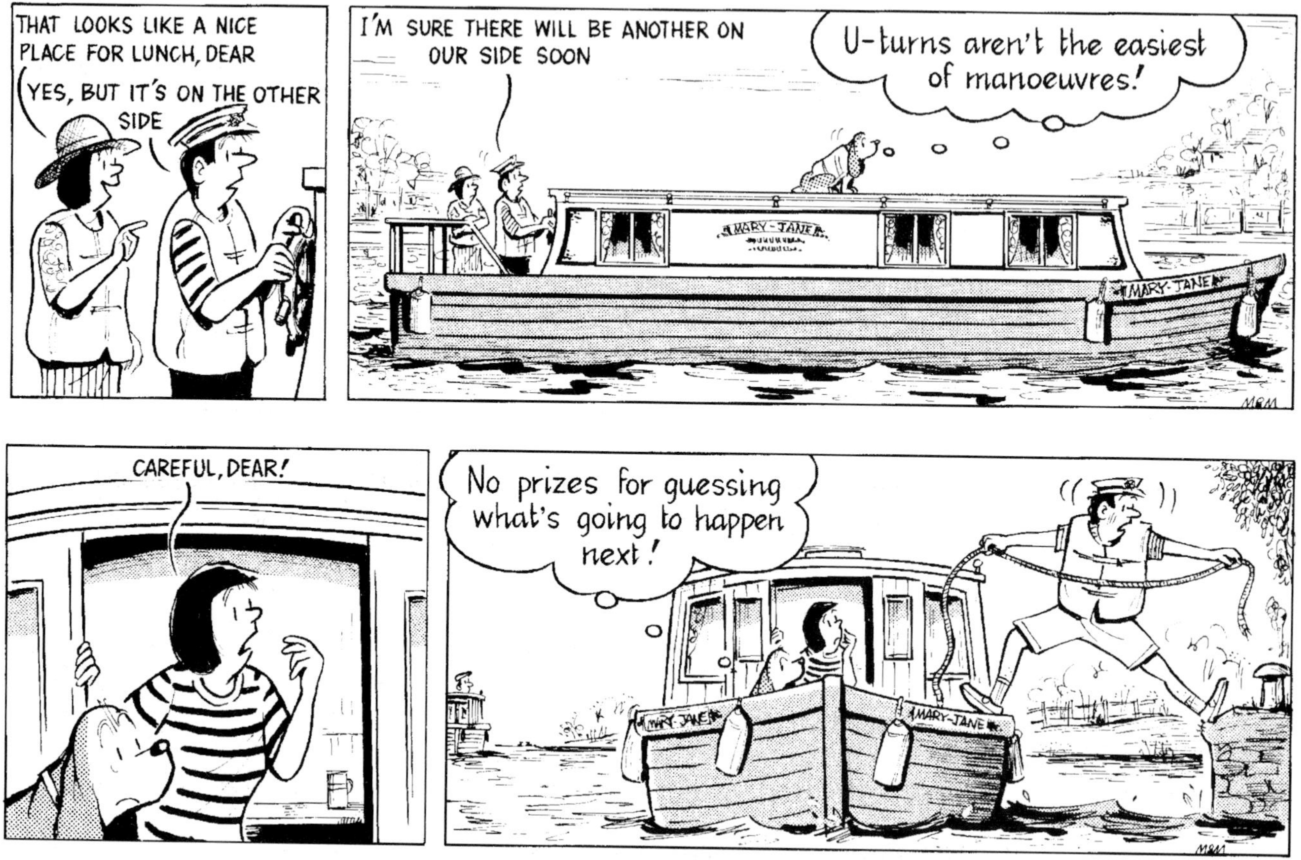
THAT LOOKS LIKE A NICE PLACE FOR LUNCH, DEAR
YES, BUT IT'S ON THE OTHER SIDE
I'M SURE THERE WILL BE ANOTHER ON OUR SIDE SOON
U-turns aren't the easiest of manoeuvres!
MARY-JANE
MARY-JANE
CAREFUL, DEAR!
No prizes for guessing what's going to happen next!
MARY-JANE
MARY-JANE

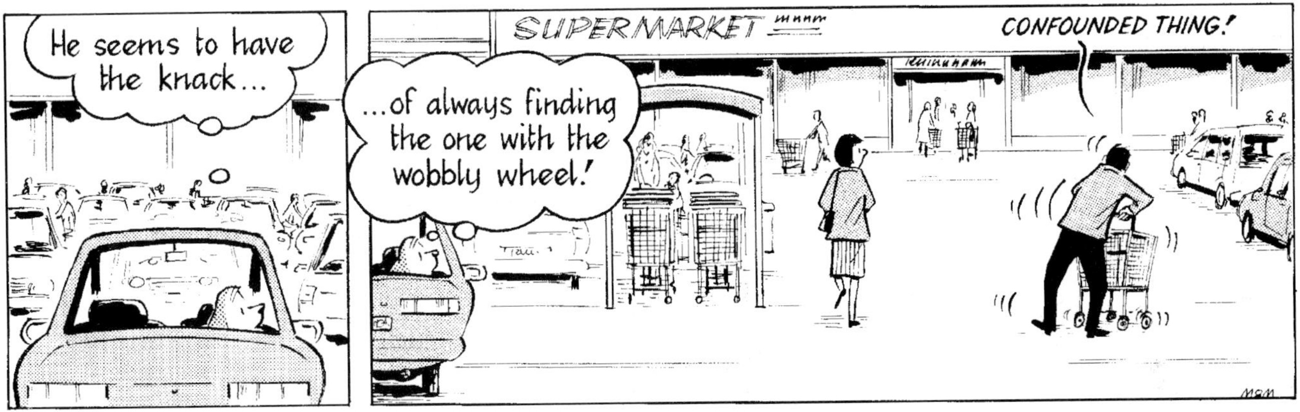
He seems to have the knack...
...of always finding the one with the wobbly wheel!
SUPERMARKET
CONFOUNDED THING!

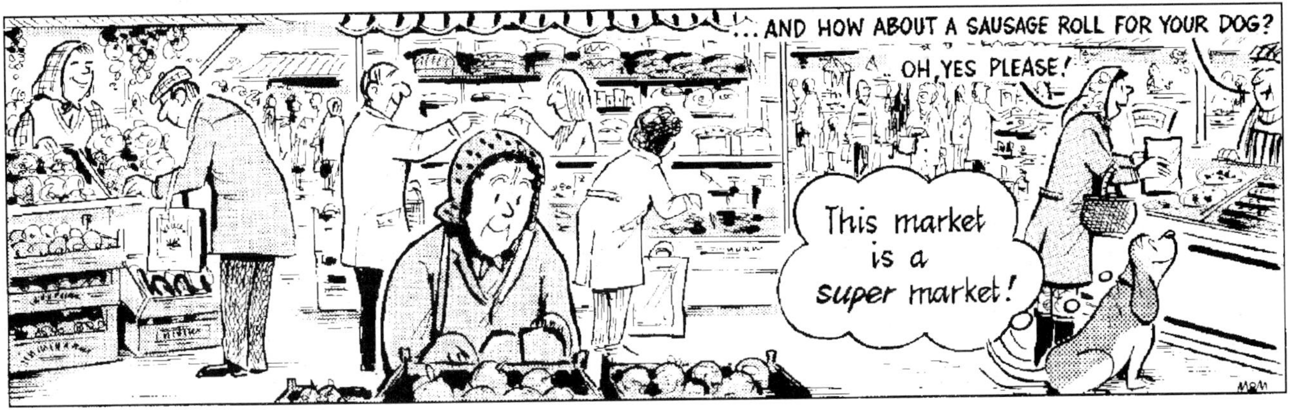
...AND HOW ABOUT A SAUSAGE ROLL FOR YOUR DOG?
.. OH, YES PLEASE!
This market is a super market!

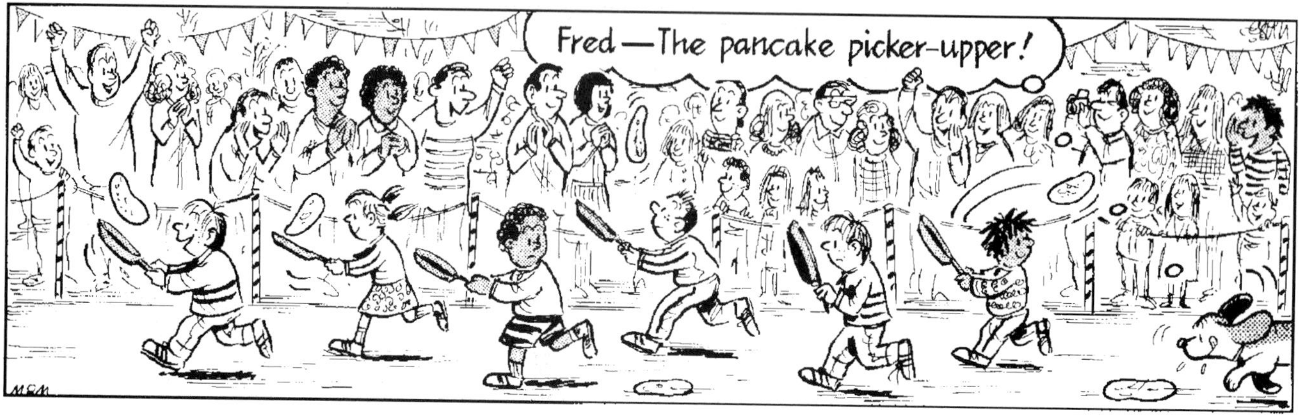
Fred—The pancake picker-upper!

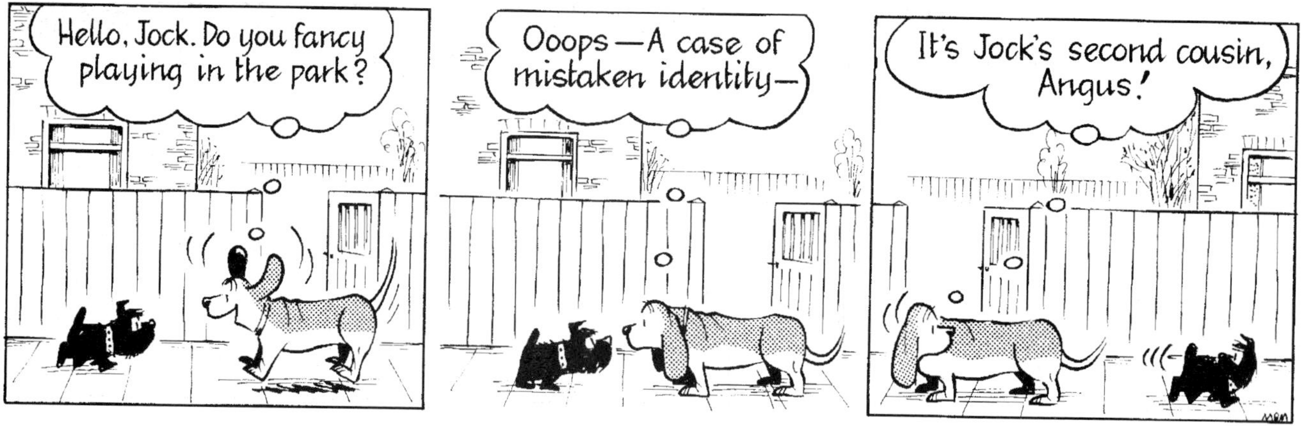
Hello, Jock. Do you fancy playing in the park?
Ooops—A case of mistaken identity—
It's Jock's second cousin, Angus!

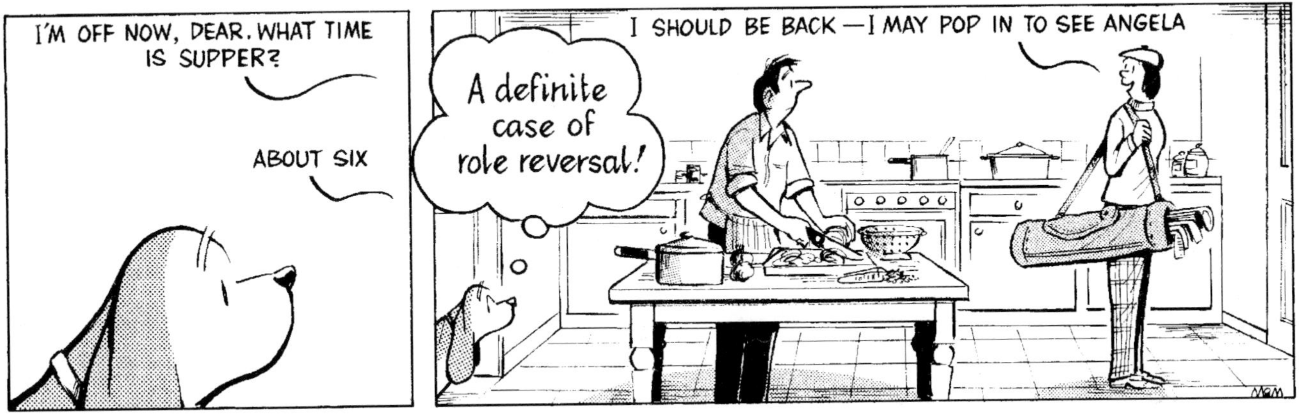
I'M OFF NOW, DEAR. WHAT TIME IS SUPPER?
ABOUT SIX
A definite case of role reversal!
I SHOULD BE BACK — I MAY POP IN TO SEE ANGELA
M&M

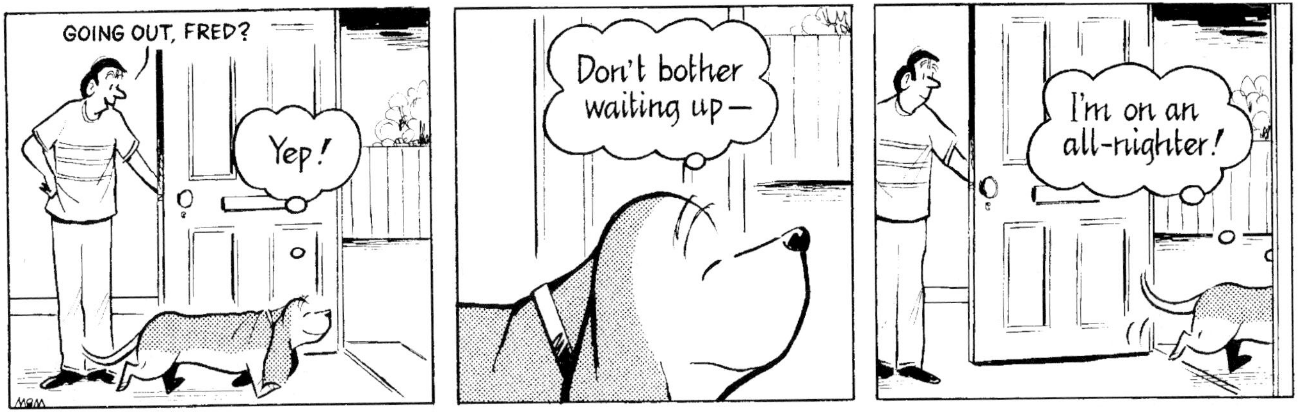
GOING OUT, FRED?
Yep!
Don't bother waiting up —
I'm on an all-nighter!
M&M

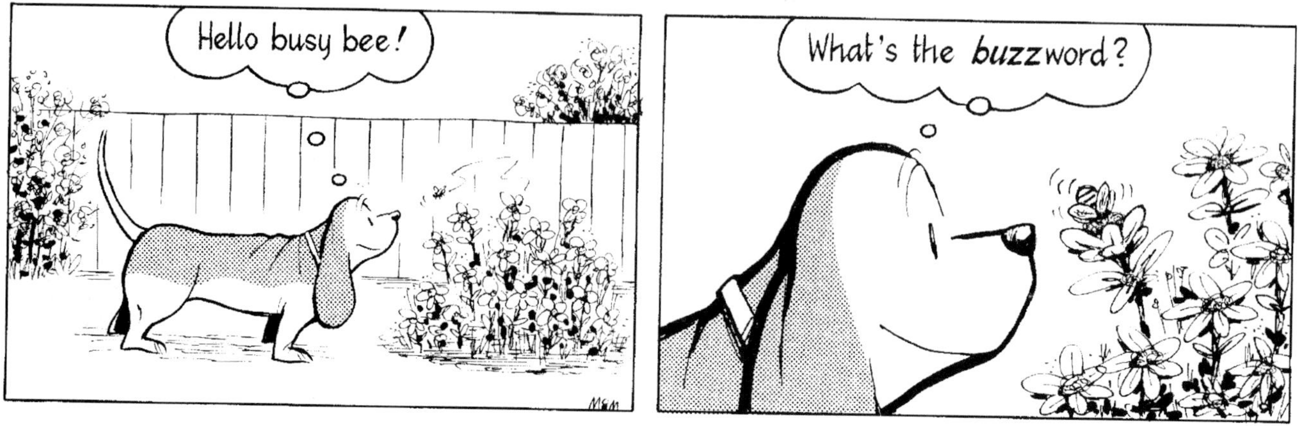
Hello busy bee!
What's the *buzz*word?

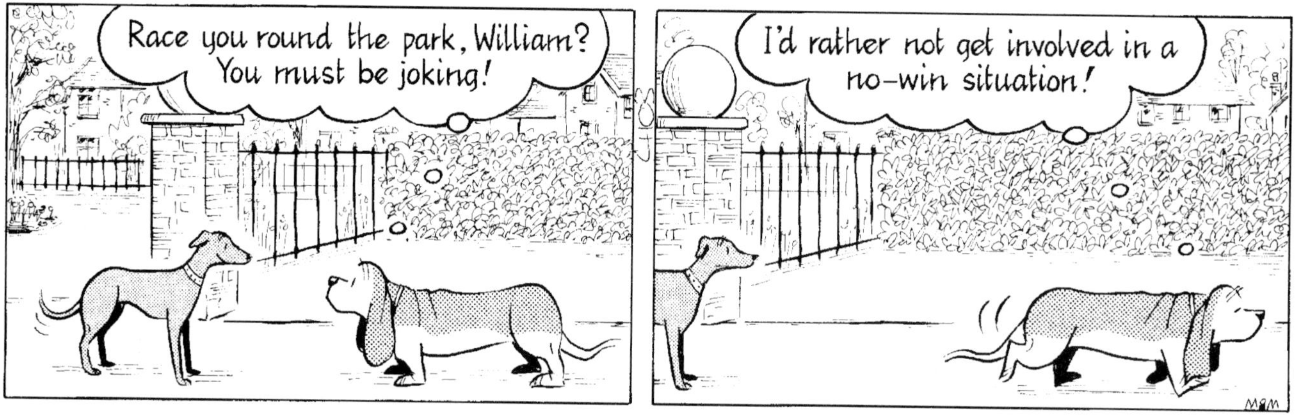
Race you round the park, William? You must be joking!
I'd rather not get involved in a no-win situation!

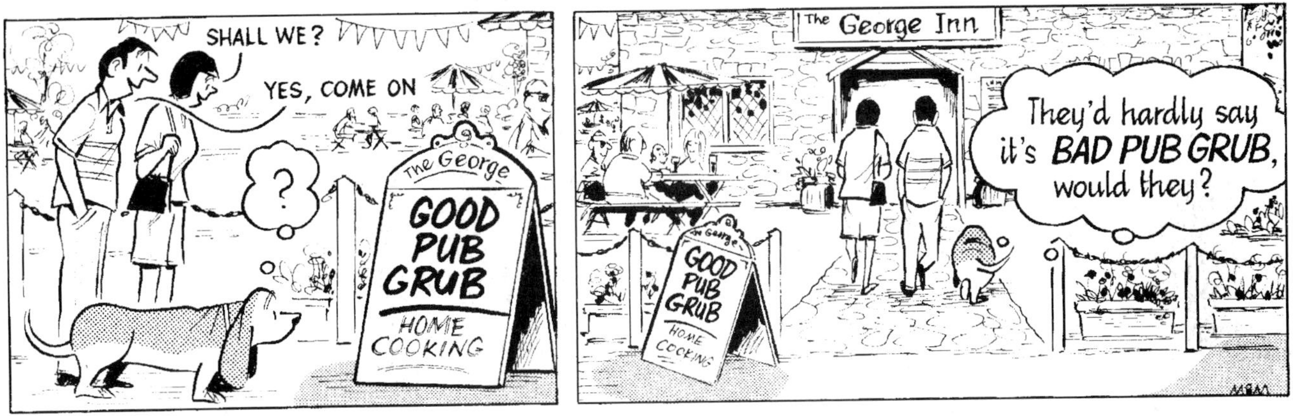
SHALL WE?
YES, COME ON
?
The George
GOOD PUB GRUB
HOME COOKING
The George Inn
They'd hardly say it's **BAD PUB GRUB**, would they?

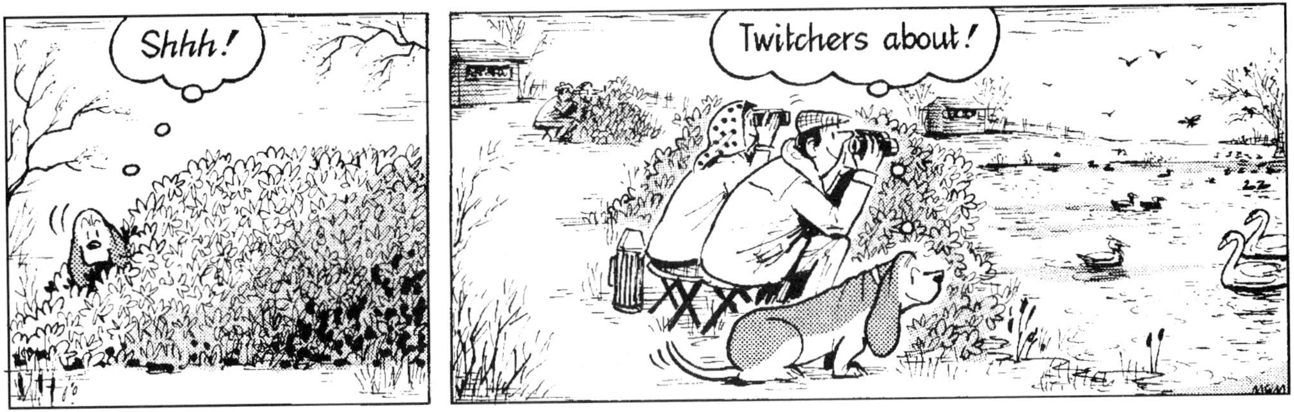
Shhh!
Twitchers about!

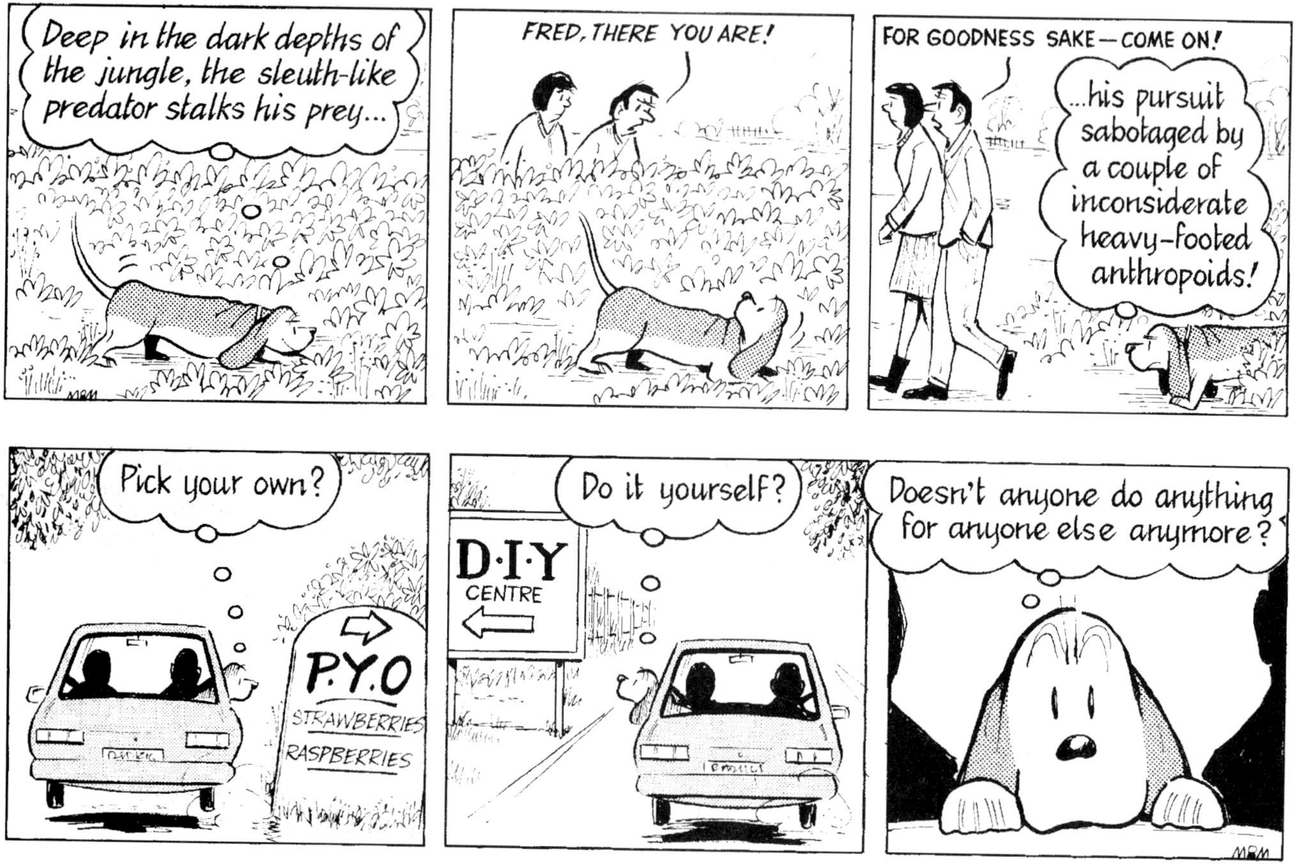
Deep in the dark depths of the jungle, the sleuth-like predator stalks his prey...
FRED, THERE YOU ARE!
FOR GOODNESS SAKE—COME ON!
...his pursuit sabotaged by a couple of inconsiderate heavy-footed anthropoids!
Pick your own?
P.Y.O
STRAWBERRIES
RASPBERRIES
Do it yourself?
D·I·Y
CENTRE
Doesn't anyone do anything for anyone else anymore?

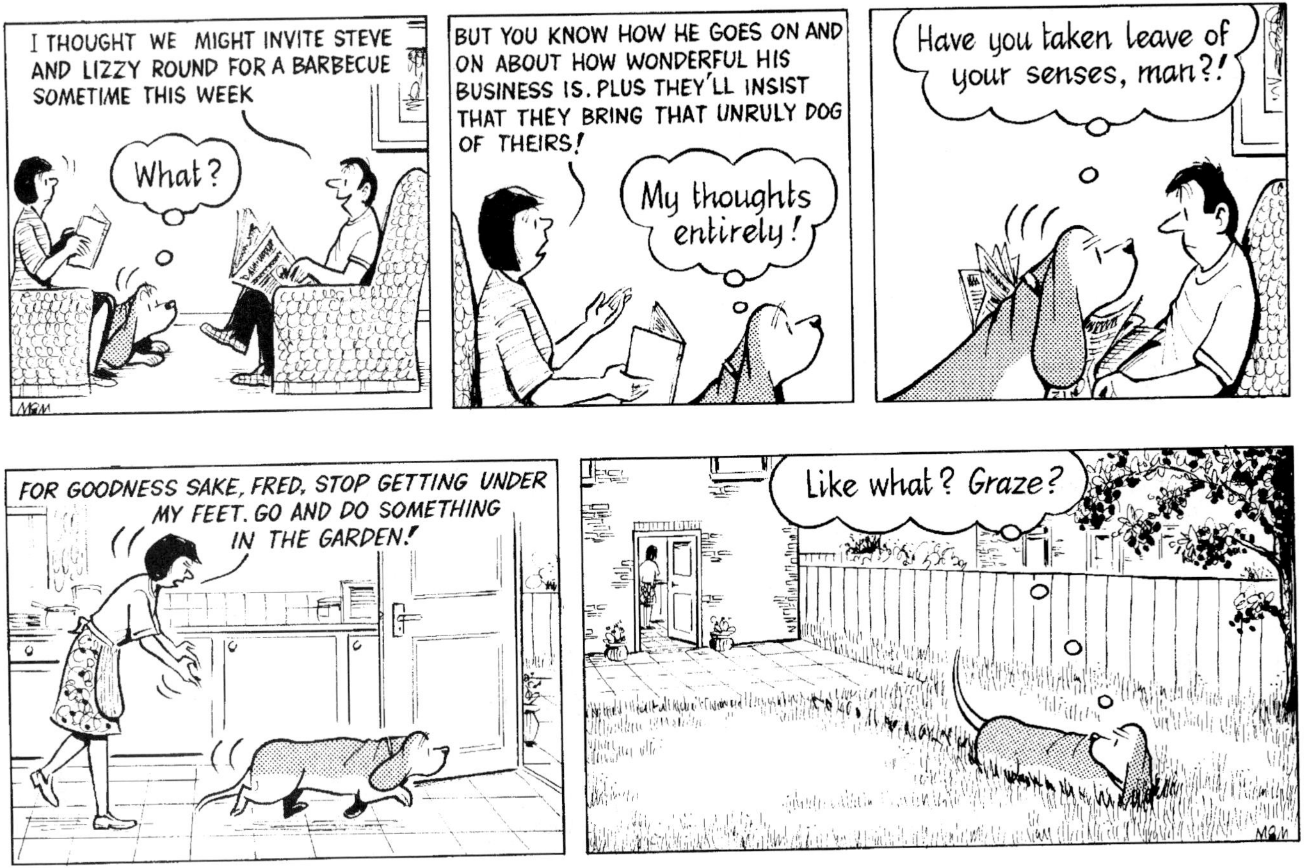
I THOUGHT WE MIGHT INVITE STEVE AND LIZZY ROUND FOR A BARBECUE SOMETIME THIS WEEK
What?
BUT YOU KNOW HOW HE GOES ON AND ON ABOUT HOW WONDERFUL HIS BUSINESS IS. PLUS THEY'LL INSIST THAT THEY BRING THAT UNRULY DOG OF THEIRS!
My thoughts entirely!
Have you taken leave of your senses, man?!
FOR GOODNESS SAKE, FRED, STOP GETTING UNDER MY FEET. GO AND DO SOMETHING IN THE GARDEN!
Like what? Graze?

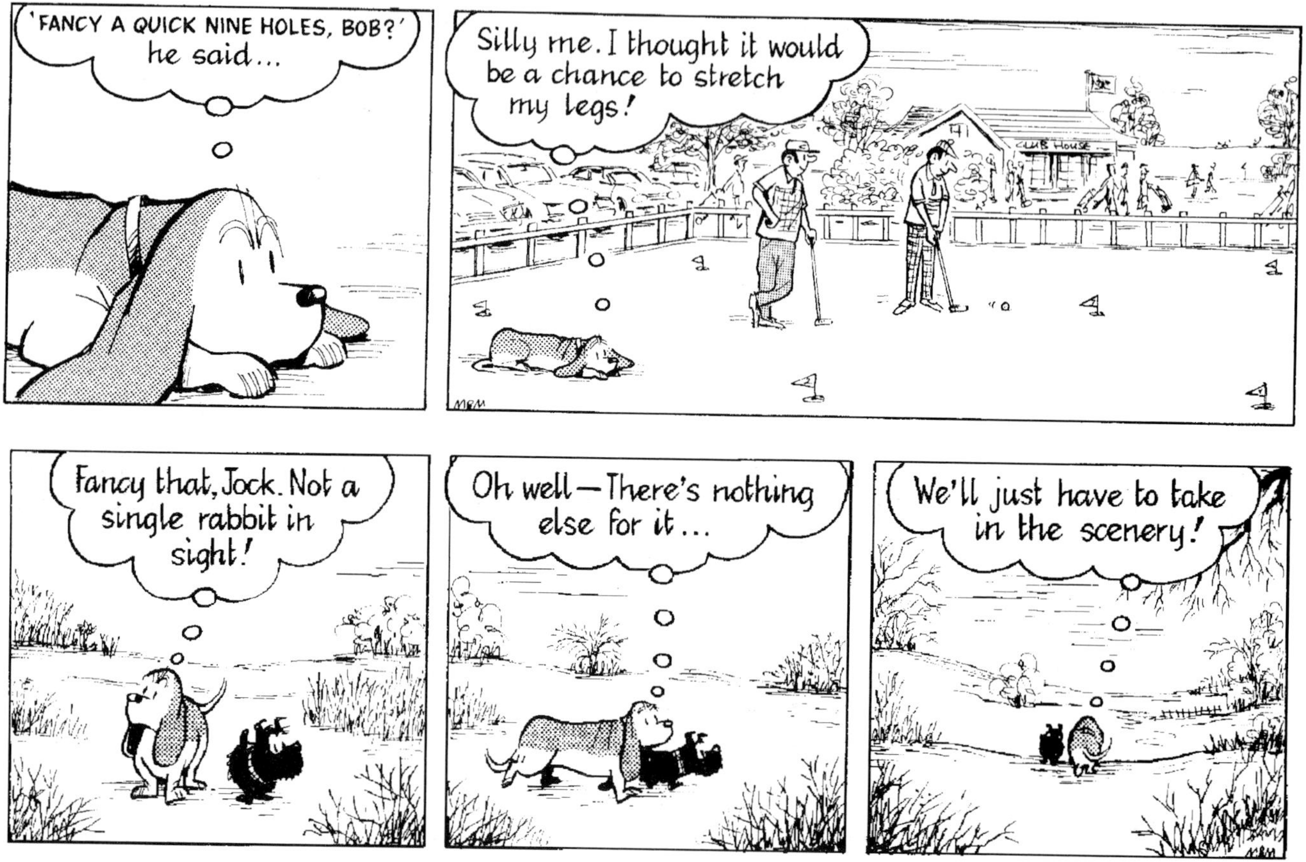
'FANCY A QUICK NINE HOLES, BOB?' he said...
Silly me. I thought it would be a chance to stretch my legs!
CLUB HOUSE
Fancy that, Jock. Not a single rabbit in sight!
Oh well—There's nothing else for it...
We'll just have to take in the scenery!

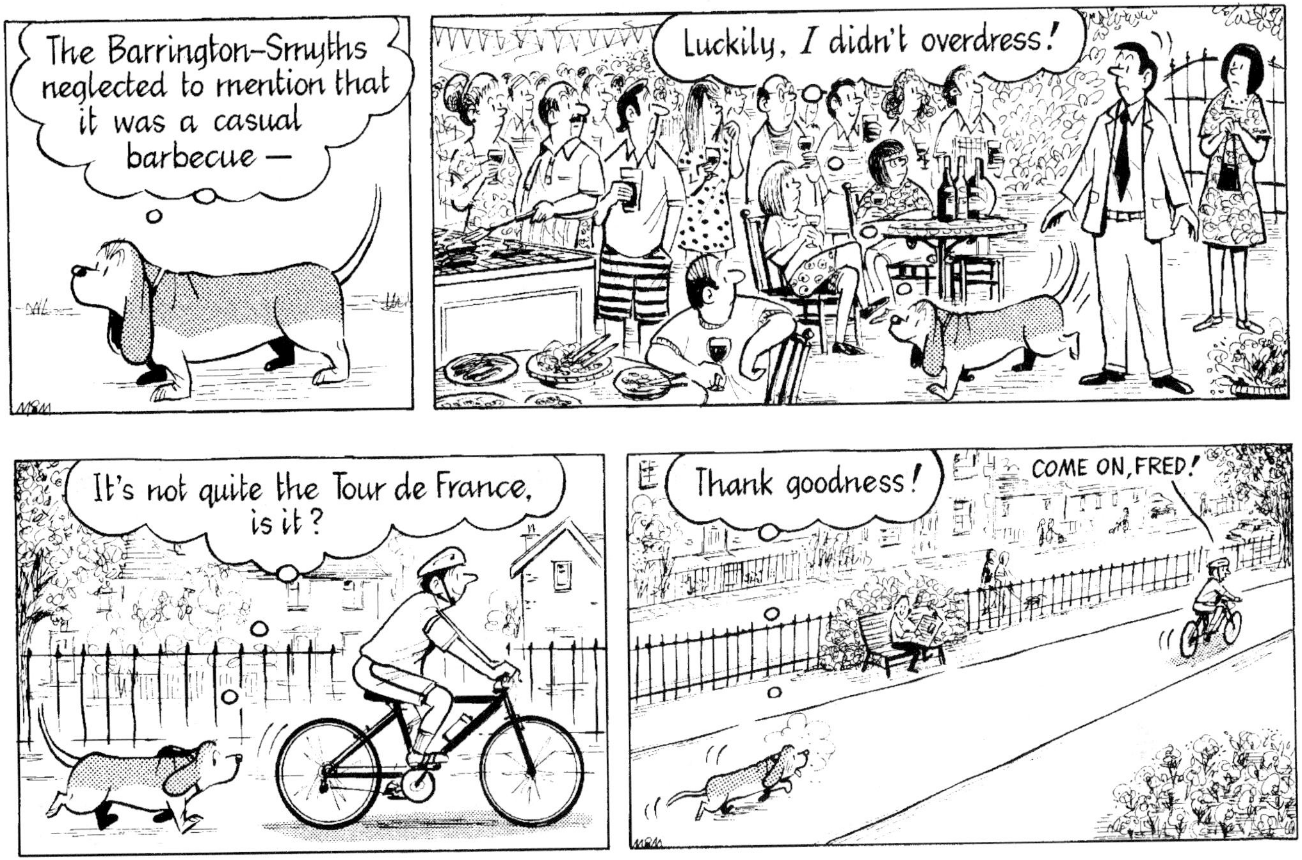
The Barrington-Smyths neglected to mention that it was a casual barbecue –
Luckily, *I* didn't overdress!
It's not quite the Tour de France, is it?
Thank goodness!
COME ON, FRED!

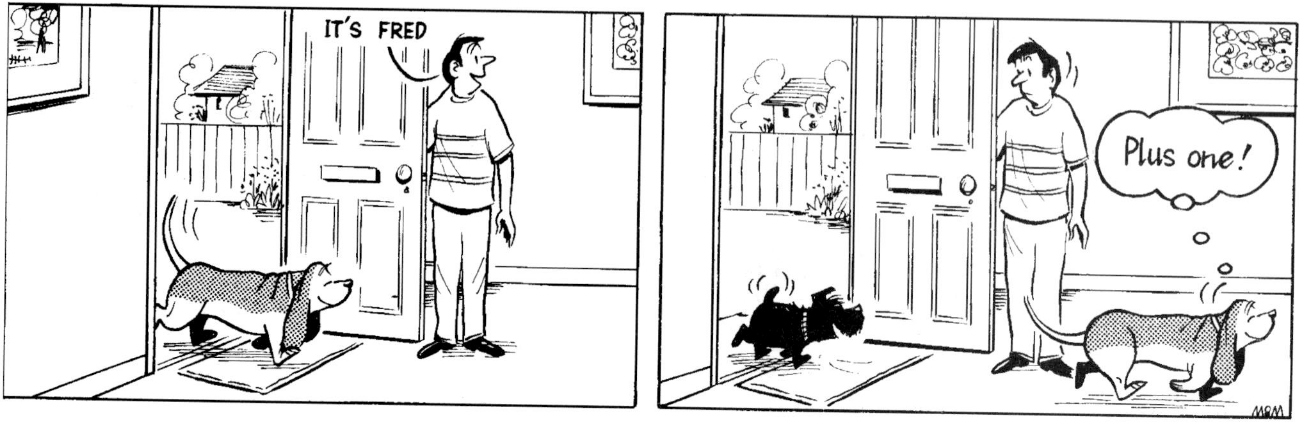
IT'S FRED
Plus one!

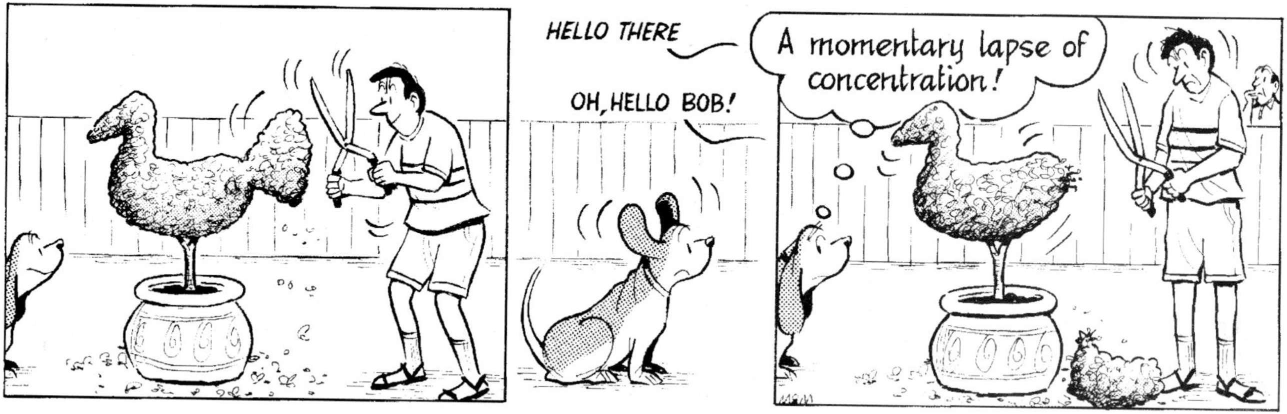
HELLO THERE
OH, HELLO BOB!
A momentary lapse of concentration!

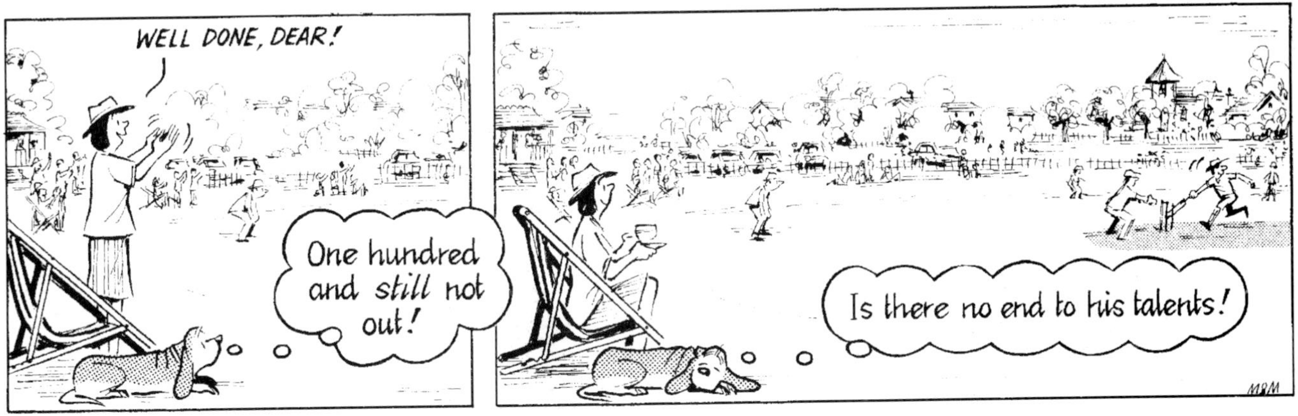
WELL DONE, DEAR!
One hundred and *still* not out!
Is there no end to his talents!

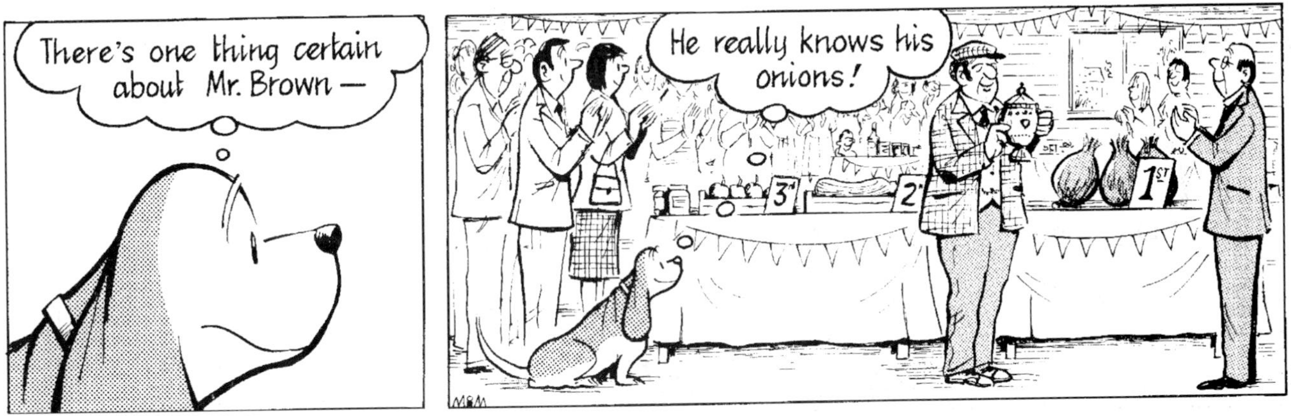
There's one thing certain about Mr. Brown –
He really knows his onions!

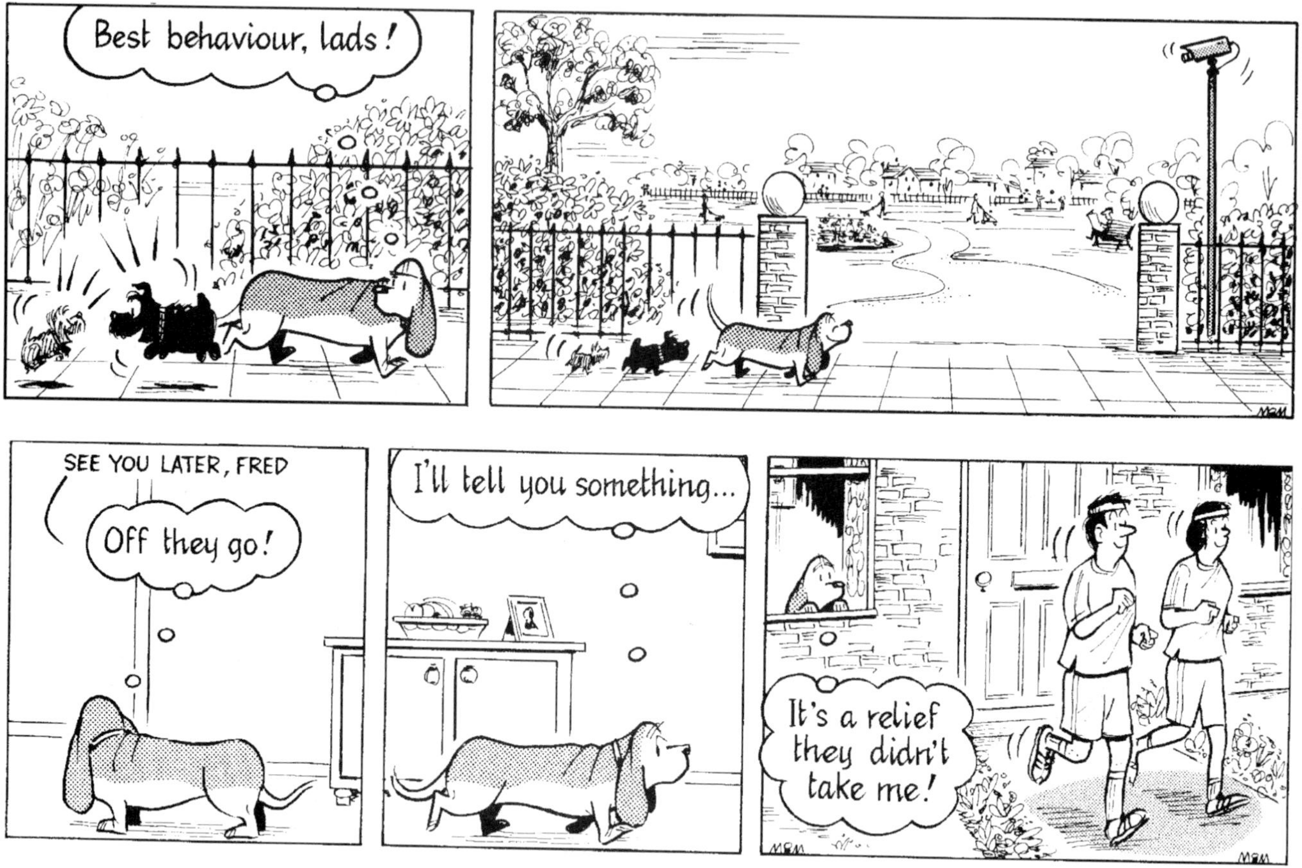
Best behaviour, lads!
SEE YOU LATER, FRED
Off they go!
I'll tell you something...
It's a relief they didn't take me!

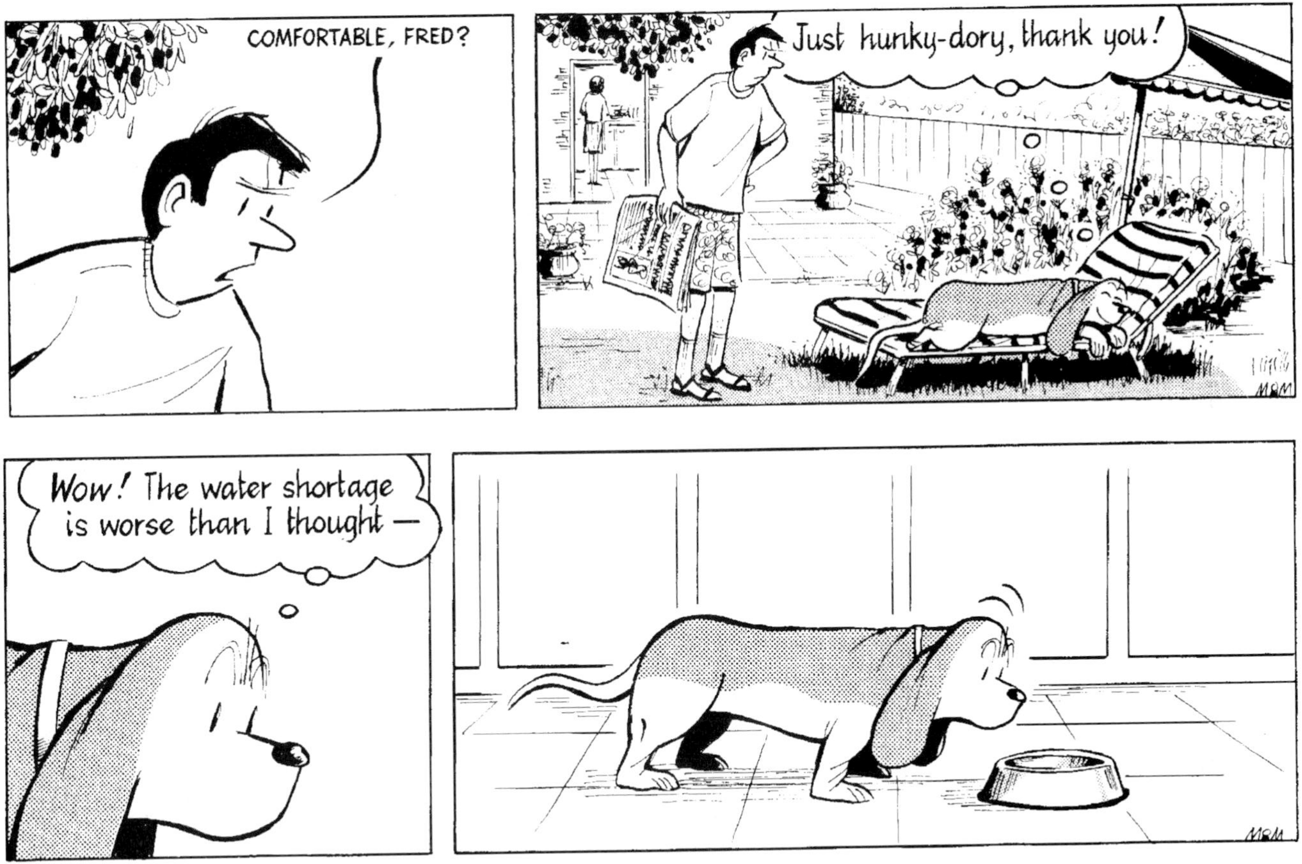
COMFORTABLE, FRED?
Just hunky-dory, thank you!
Wow! The water shortage is worse than I thought —

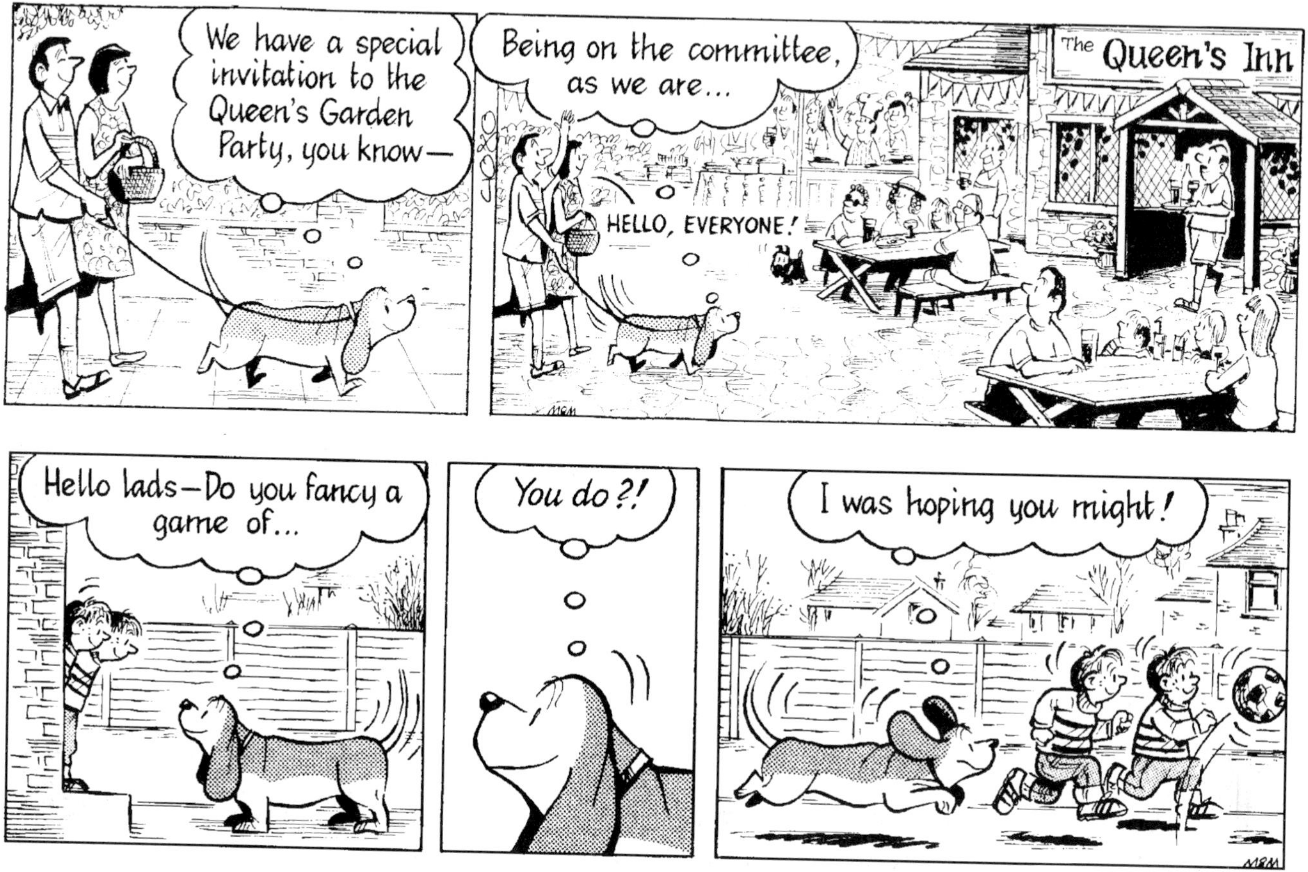
We have a special invitation to the Queen's Garden Party, you know—
Being on the committee, as we are...
The Queen's Inn
HELLO, EVERYONE!
Hello lads—Do you fancy a game of...
You do?!
I was hoping you might!
MBM

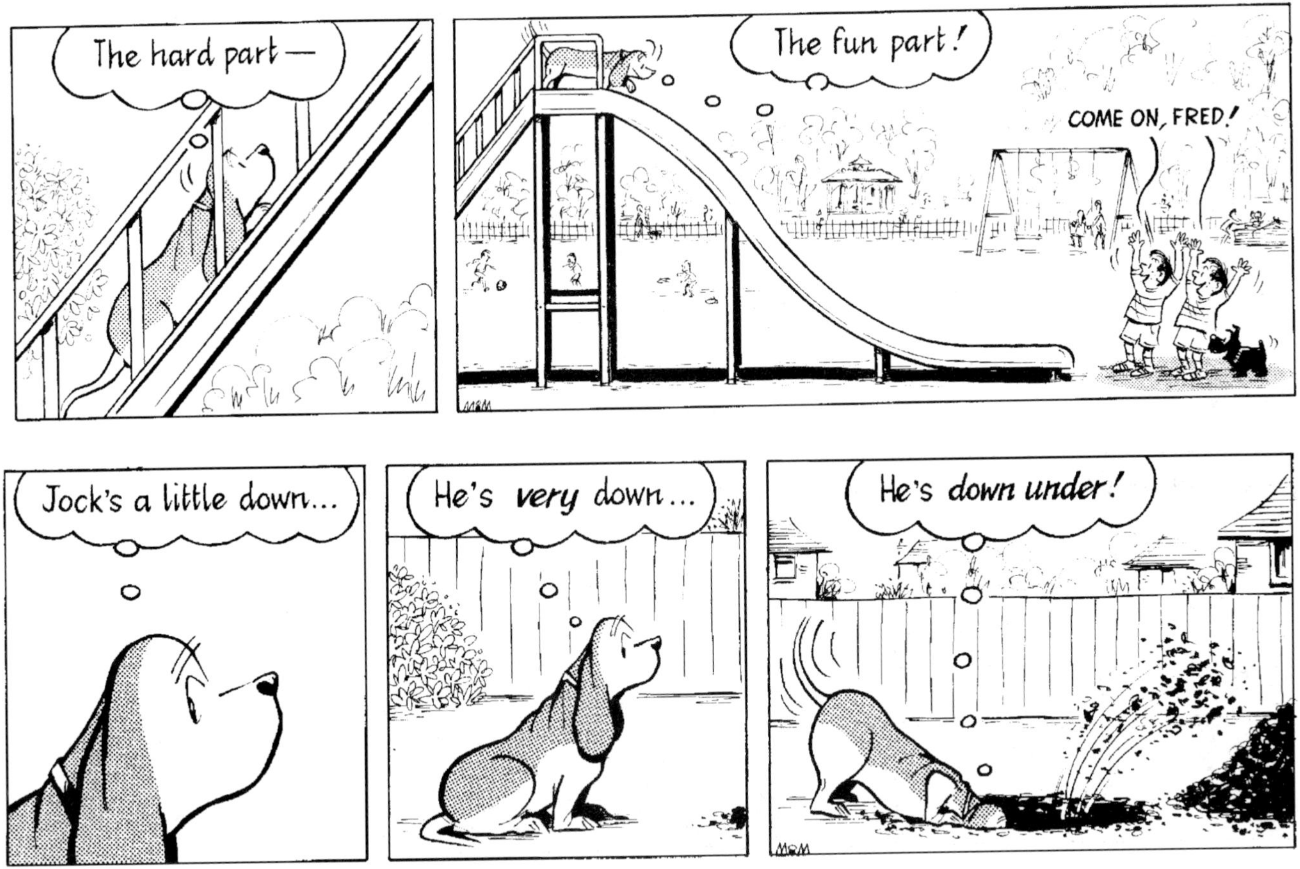
The hard part —
The fun part!
COME ON, FRED!
Jock's a little down...
He's very down...
He's down under!

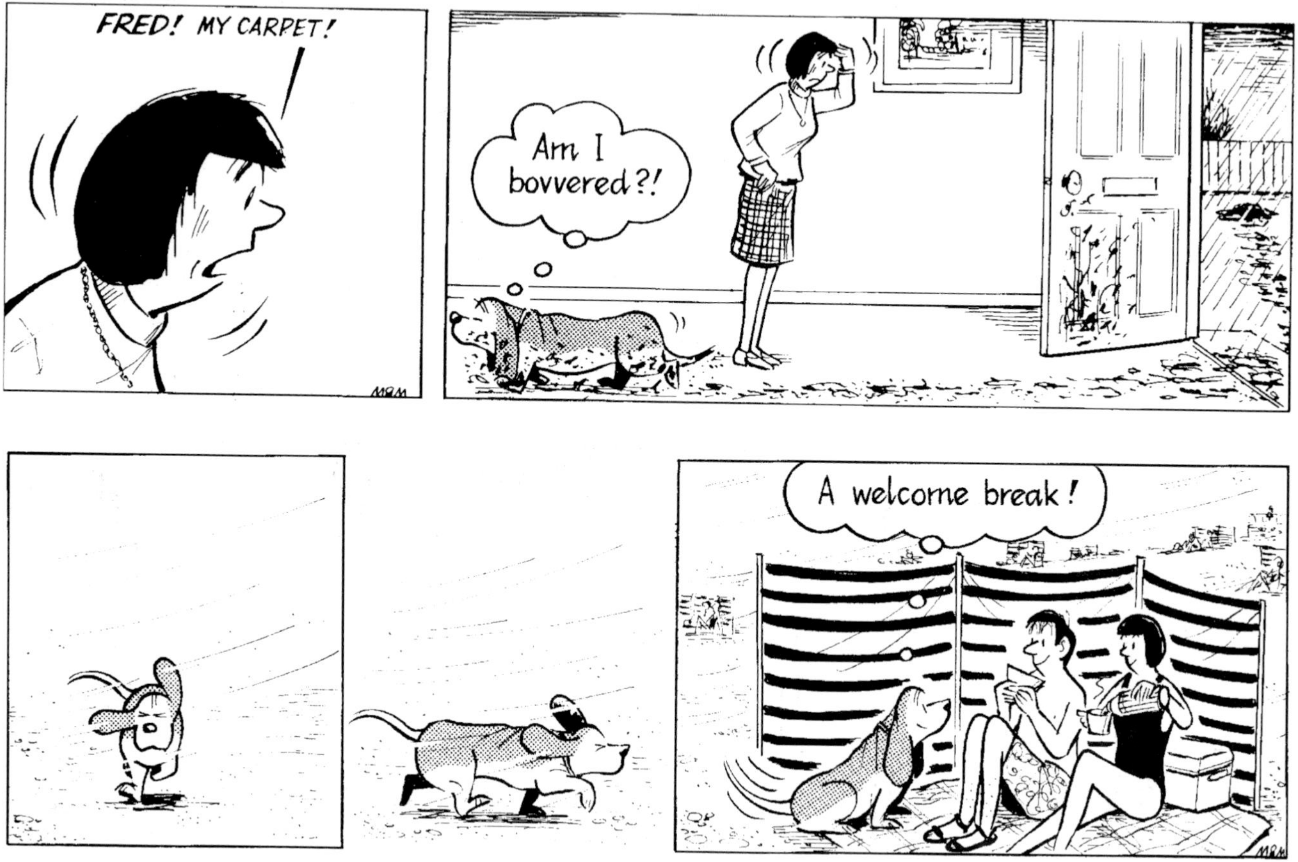

FRED! MY CARPET!
Am I bovvered?!
A welcome break!

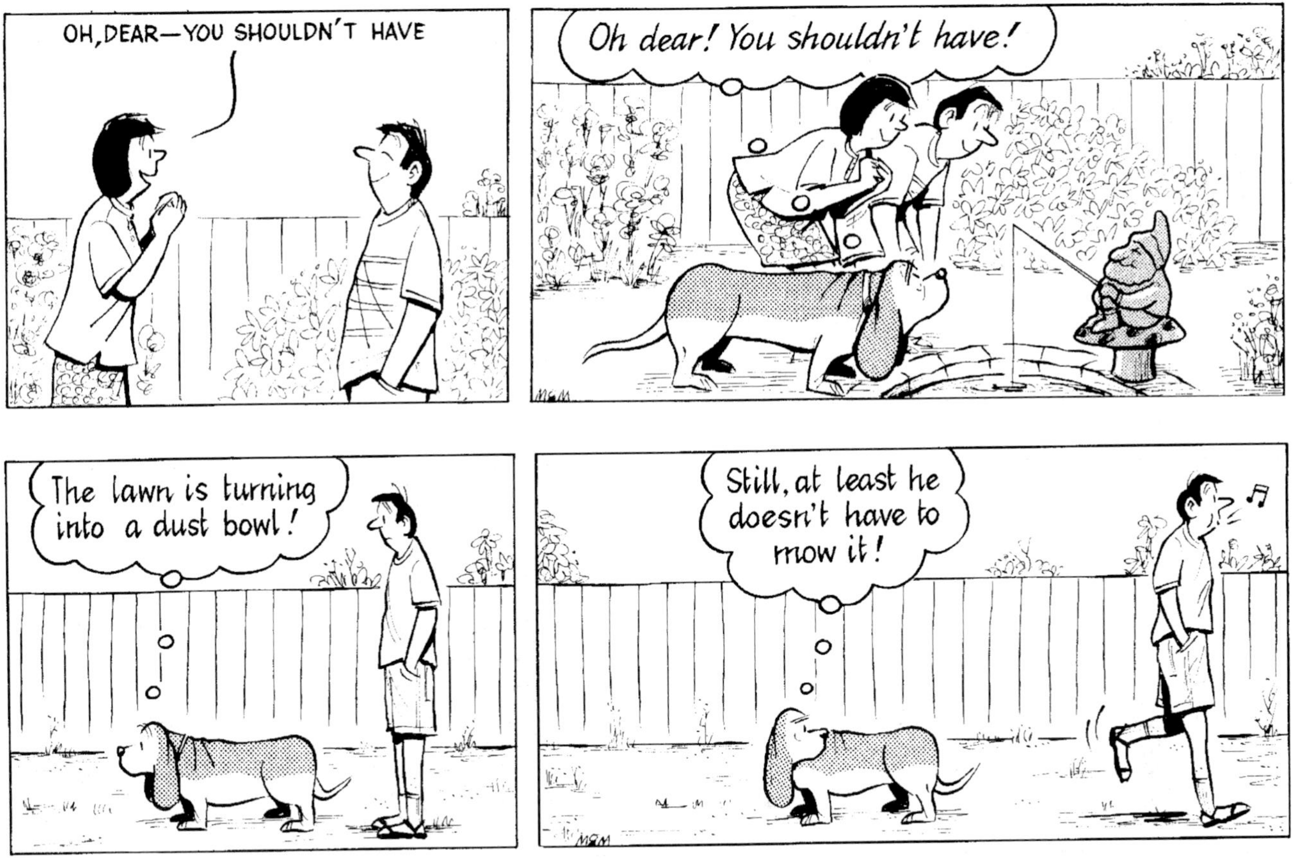
OH, DEAR—YOU SHOULDN'T HAVE
Oh dear! You shouldn't have!
MGM
The lawn is turning into a dust bowl!
Still, at least he doesn't have to mow it!
MGM

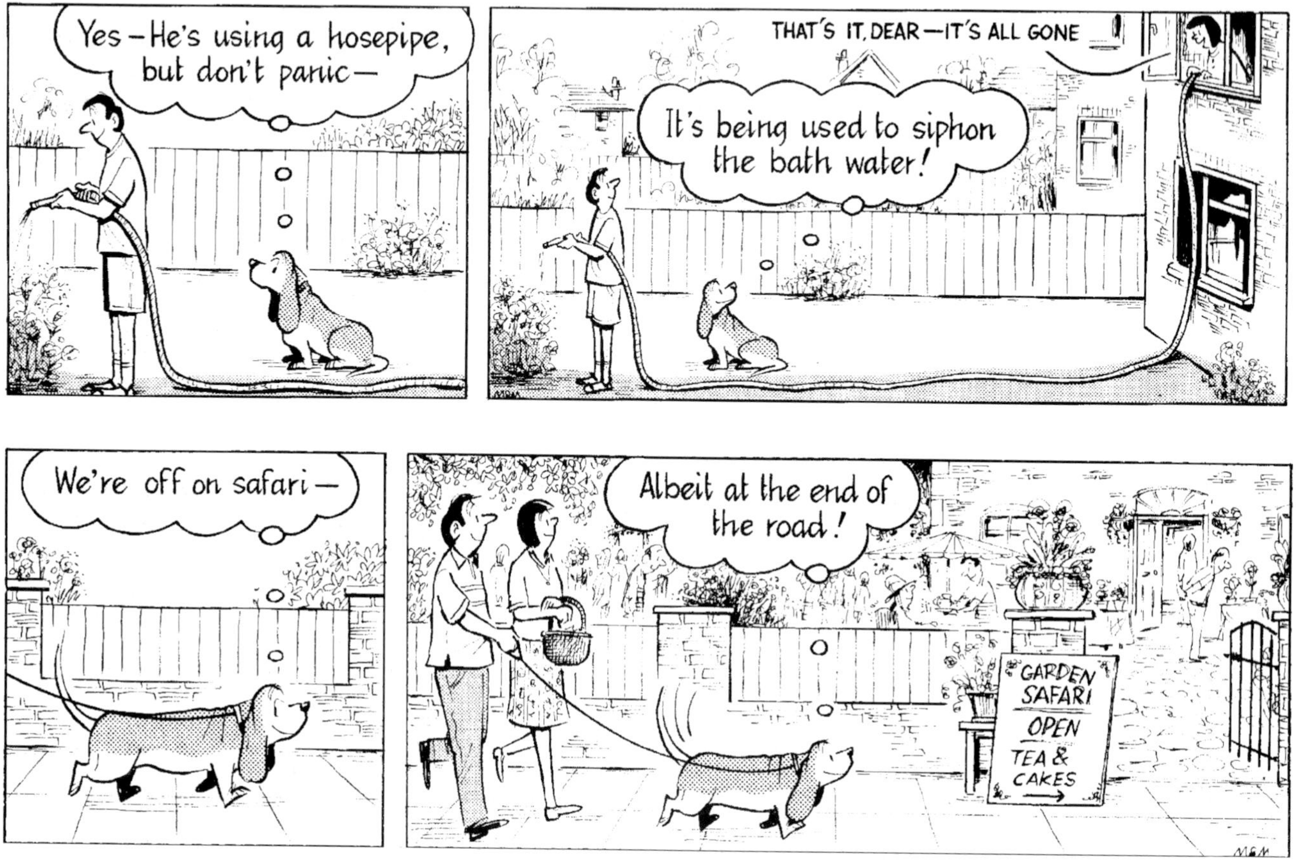

Yes—He's using a hosepipe, but don't panic—
THAT'S IT, DEAR—IT'S ALL GONE
It's being used to siphon the bath water!
We're off on safari—
Albeit at the end of the road!
GARDEN SAFARI
OPEN
TEA & CAKES
MGM

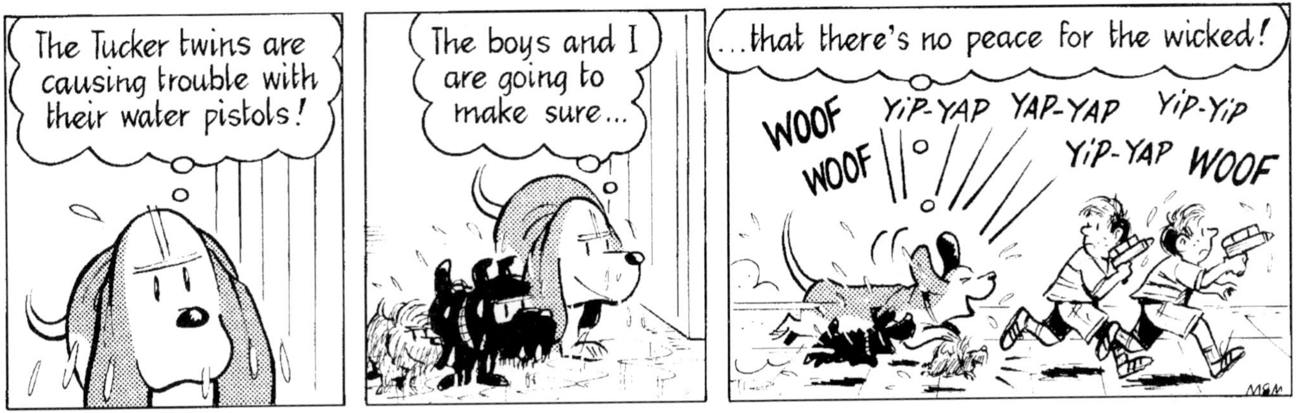
The Tucker twins are causing trouble with their water pistols!
The boys and I are going to make sure...
...that there's no peace for the wicked!
WOOF
WOOF
YIP-YAP
YAP-YAP
YIP-YIP
YIP-YAP
WOOF
MGM

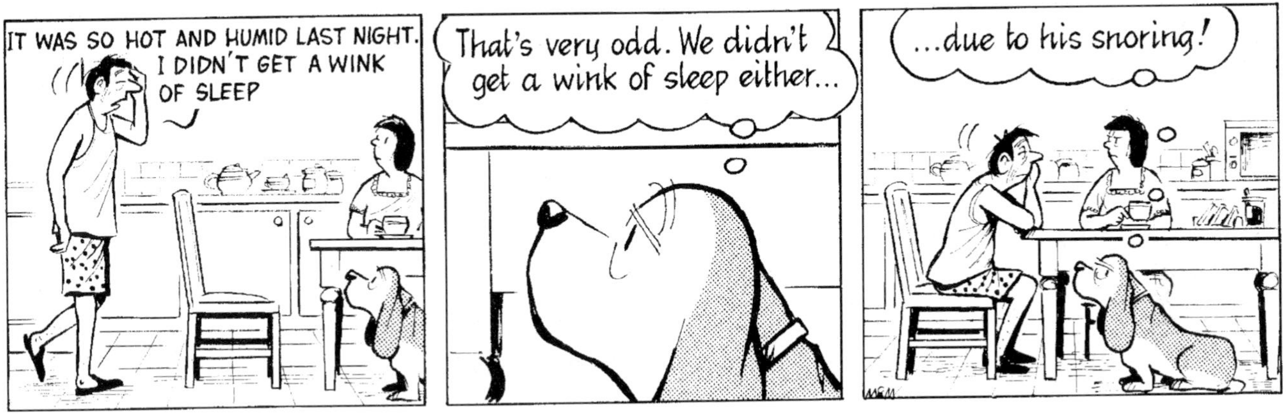
IT WAS SO HOT AND HUMID LAST NIGHT. I DIDN'T GET A WINK OF SLEEP
That's very odd. We didn't get a wink of sleep either...
...due to his snoring!
MGM

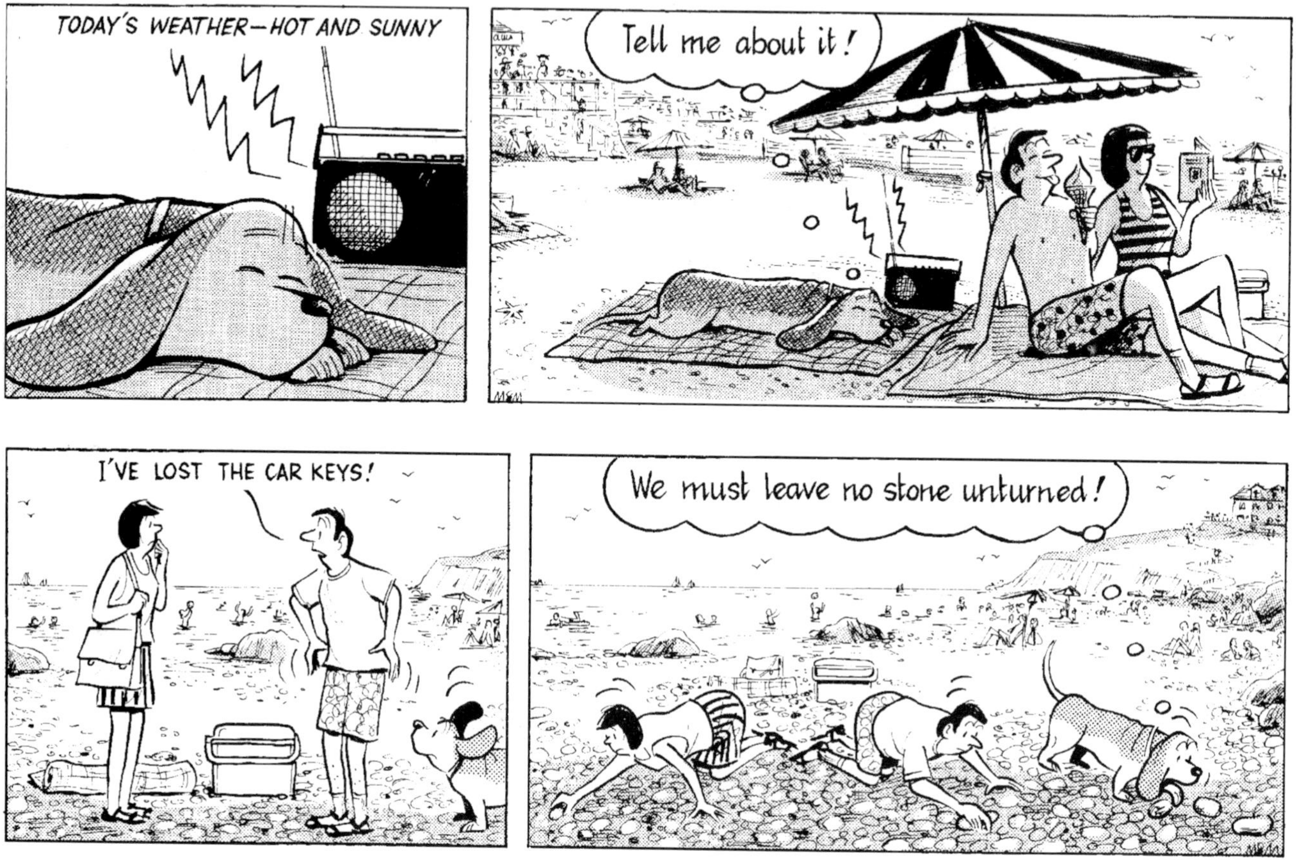
TODAY'S WEATHER—HOT AND SUNNY
Tell me about it!
I'VE LOST THE CAR KEYS!
We must leave no stone unturned!

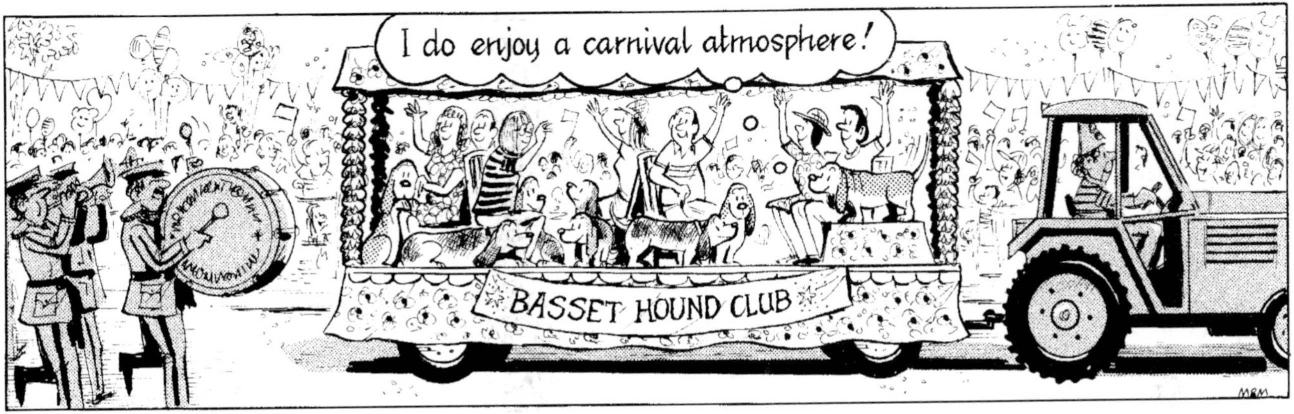
I do enjoy a carnival atmosphere!
BASSET HOUND CLUB

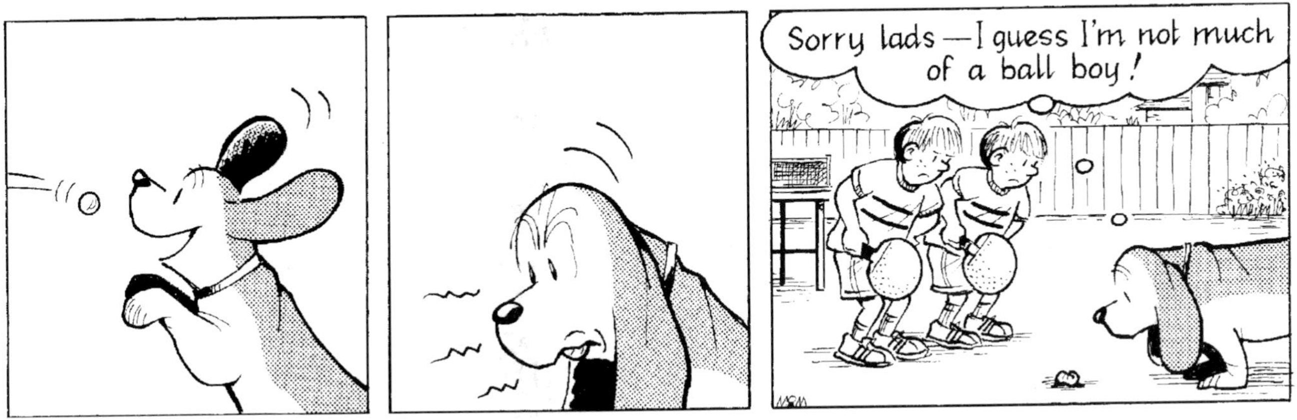
Sorry lads—I guess I'm not much of a ball boy!

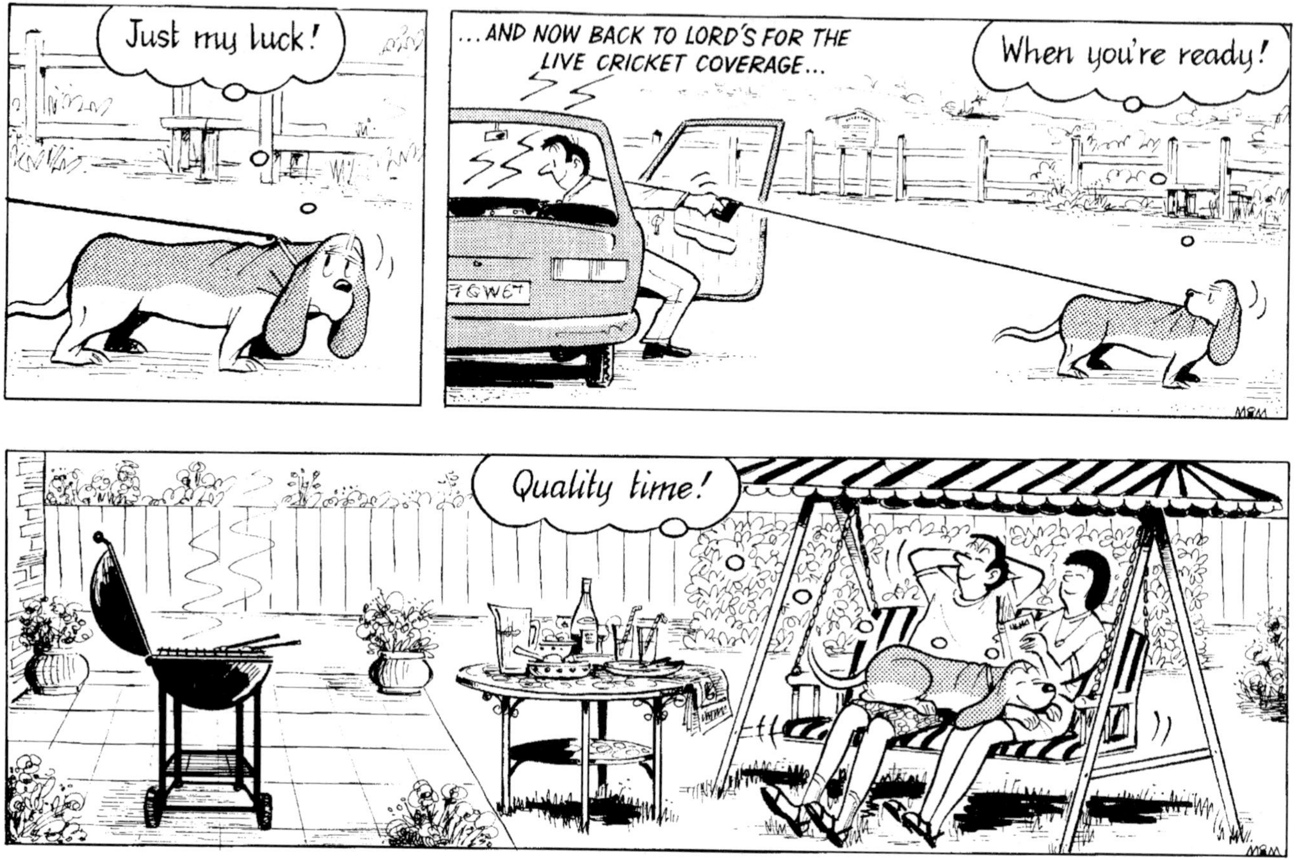
Just my luck!
...AND NOW BACK TO LORD'S FOR THE LIVE CRICKET COVERAGE...
When you're ready!
Quality time!

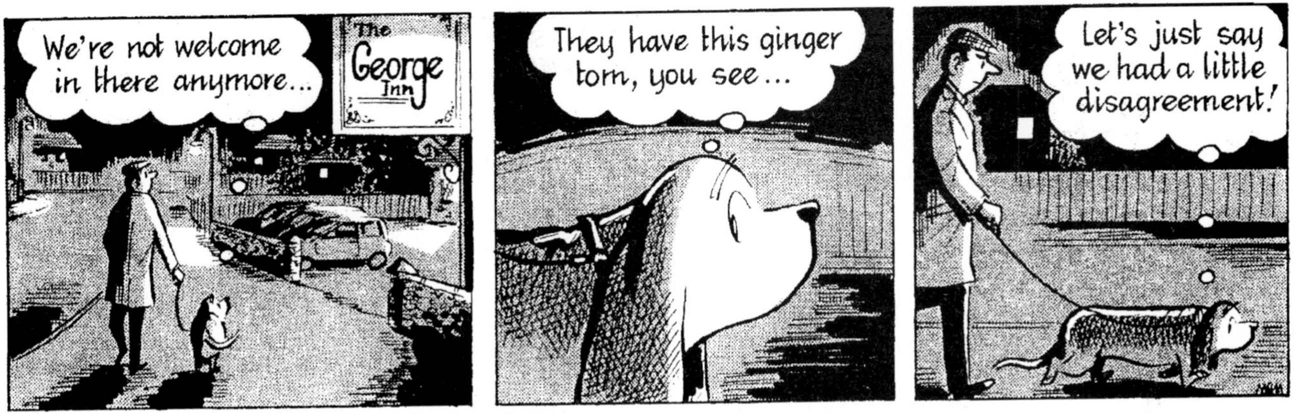
We're not welcome in there anymore...
The George Inn
They have this ginger tom, you see...
Let's just say we had a little disagreement!

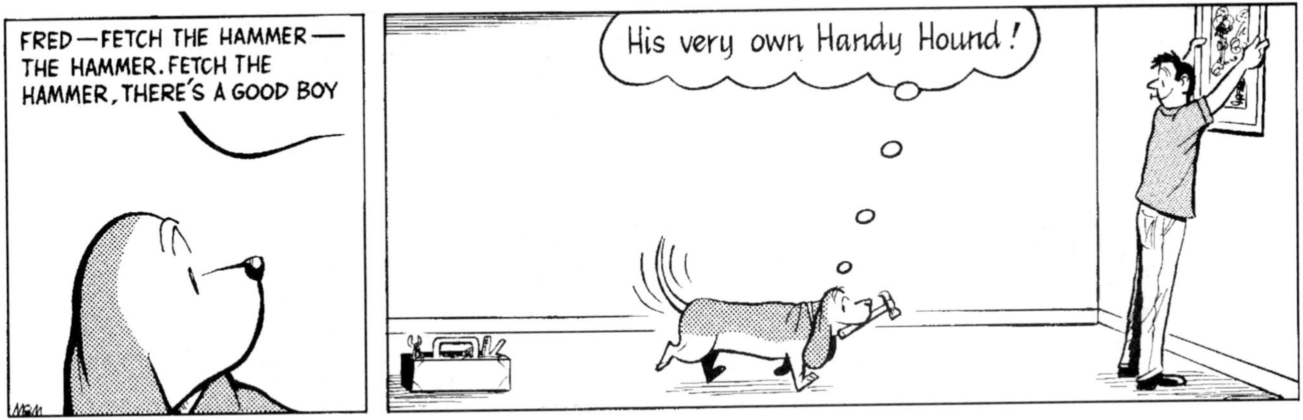
FRED—FETCH THE HAMMER— THE HAMMER. FETCH THE HAMMER, THERE'S A GOOD BOY
His very own Handy Hound!

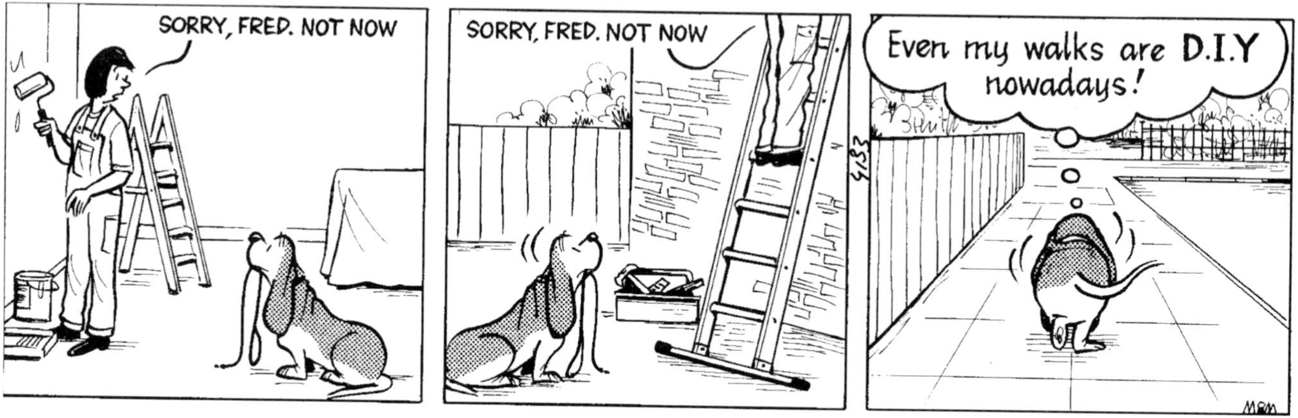
SORRY, FRED. NOT NOW
SORRY, FRED. NOT NOW
Even my walks are D.I.Y nowadays!

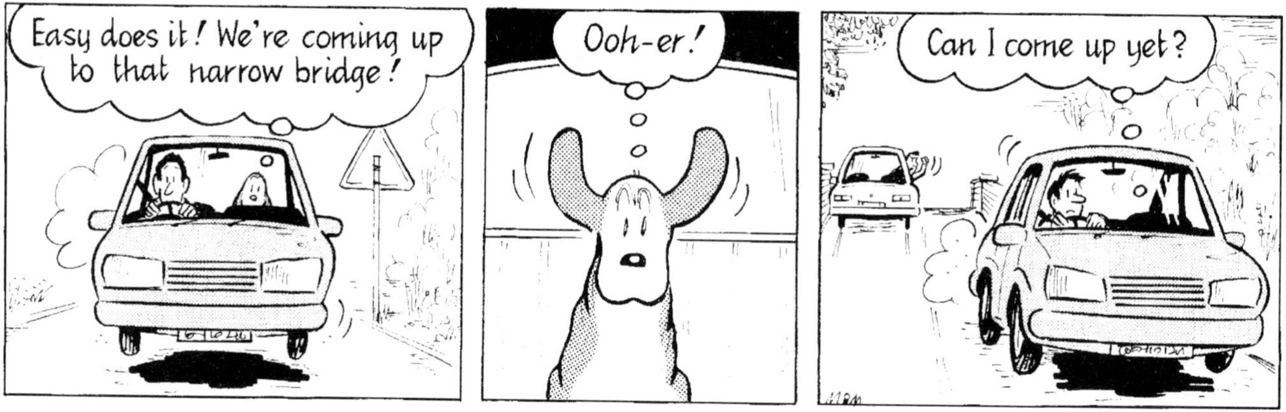
Easy does it! We're coming up to that narrow bridge!
Ooh-er!
Can I come up yet?

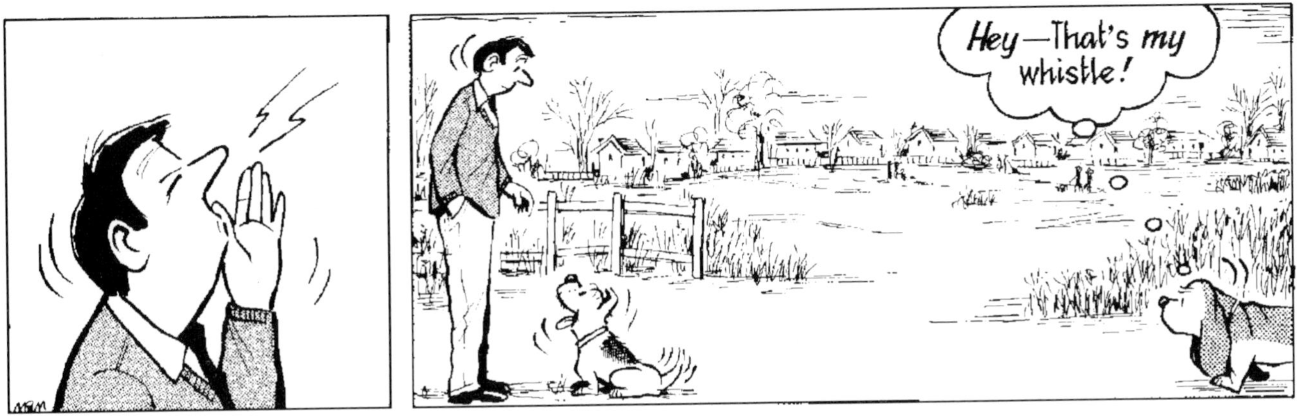
Hey—That's my whistle!

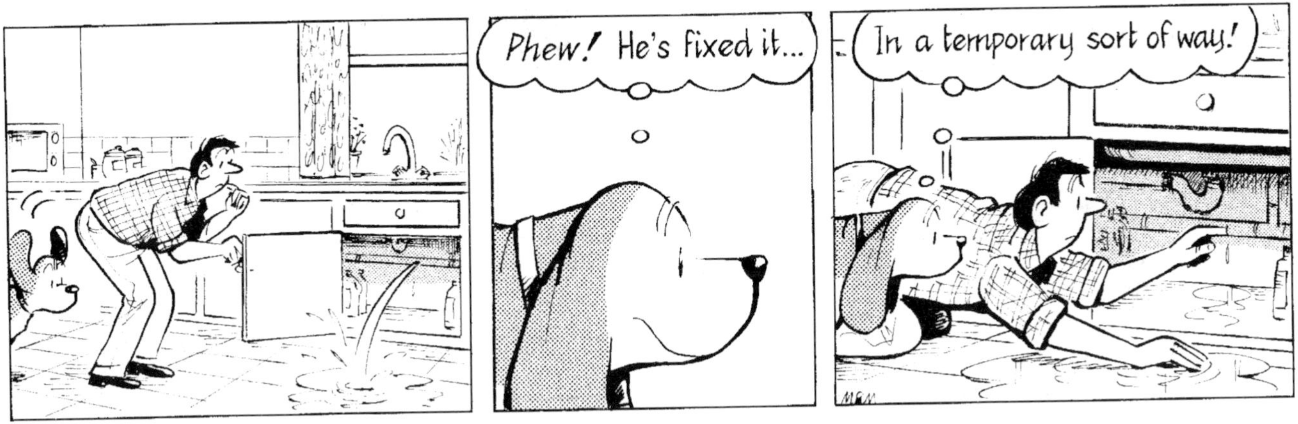
Phew! He's fixed it...
In a temporary sort of way!

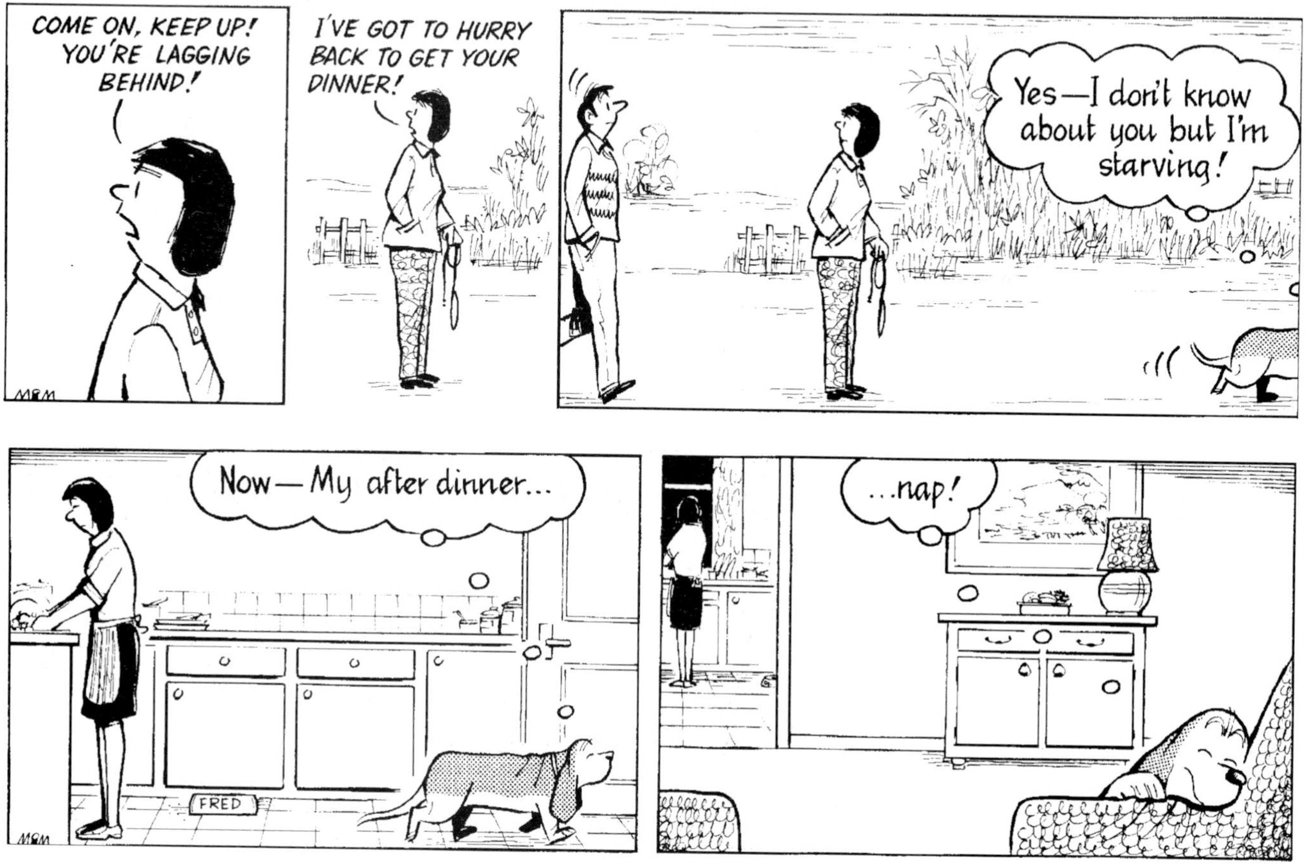
COME ON, KEEP UP! YOU'RE LAGGING BEHIND!
I'VE GOT TO HURRY BACK TO GET YOUR DINNER!
Yes—I don't know about you but I'm starving!
Now—My after dinner...
FRED
...nap!
MGM
MGM

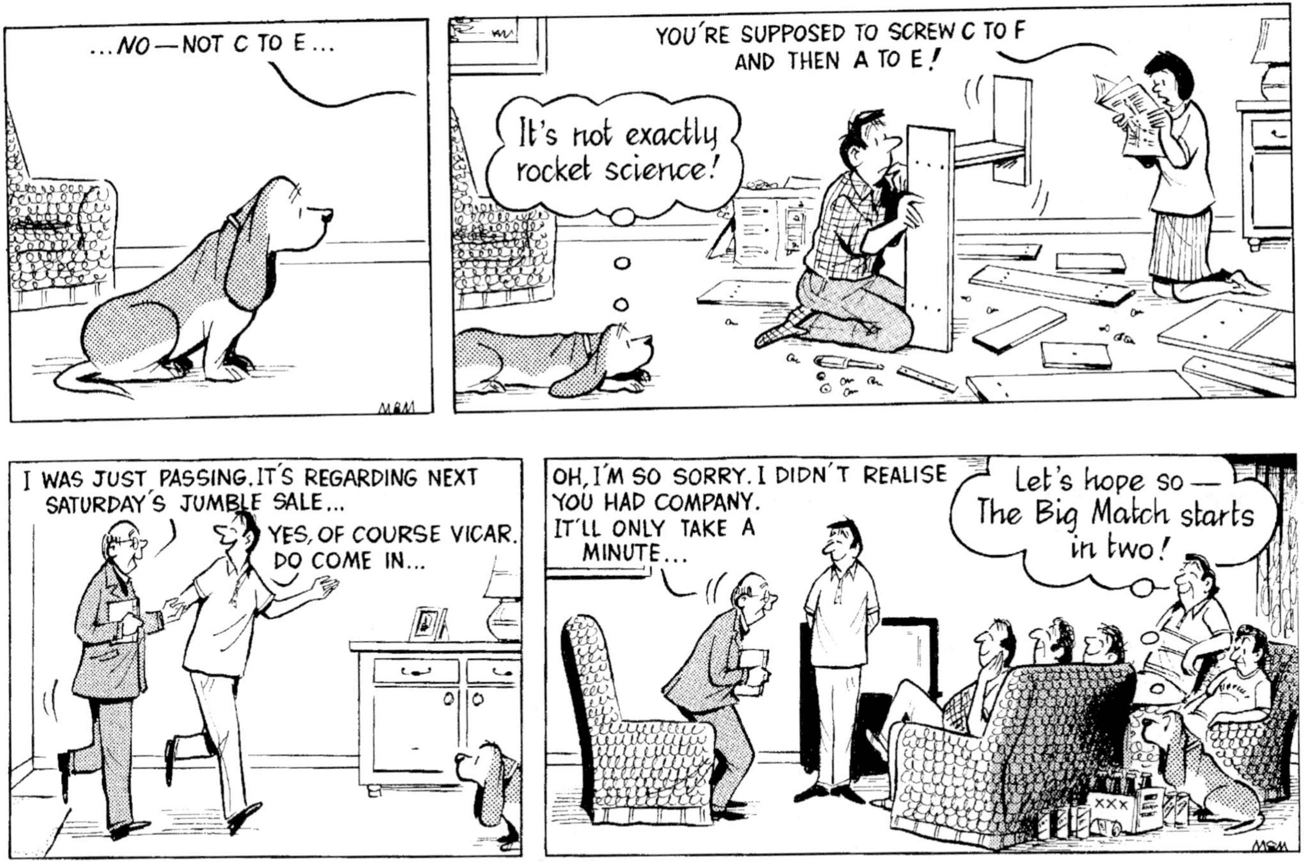
...NO—NOT C TO E...
YOU'RE SUPPOSED TO SCREW C TO F AND THEN A TO E!
It's not exactly rocket science!
MBM
I WAS JUST PASSING. IT'S REGARDING NEXT SATURDAY'S JUMBLE SALE...
YES, OF COURSE VICAR. DO COME IN...
OH, I'M SO SORRY. I DIDN'T REALISE YOU HAD COMPANY. IT'LL ONLY TAKE A MINUTE...
Let's hope so — The Big Match starts in two!
XXX
MBM

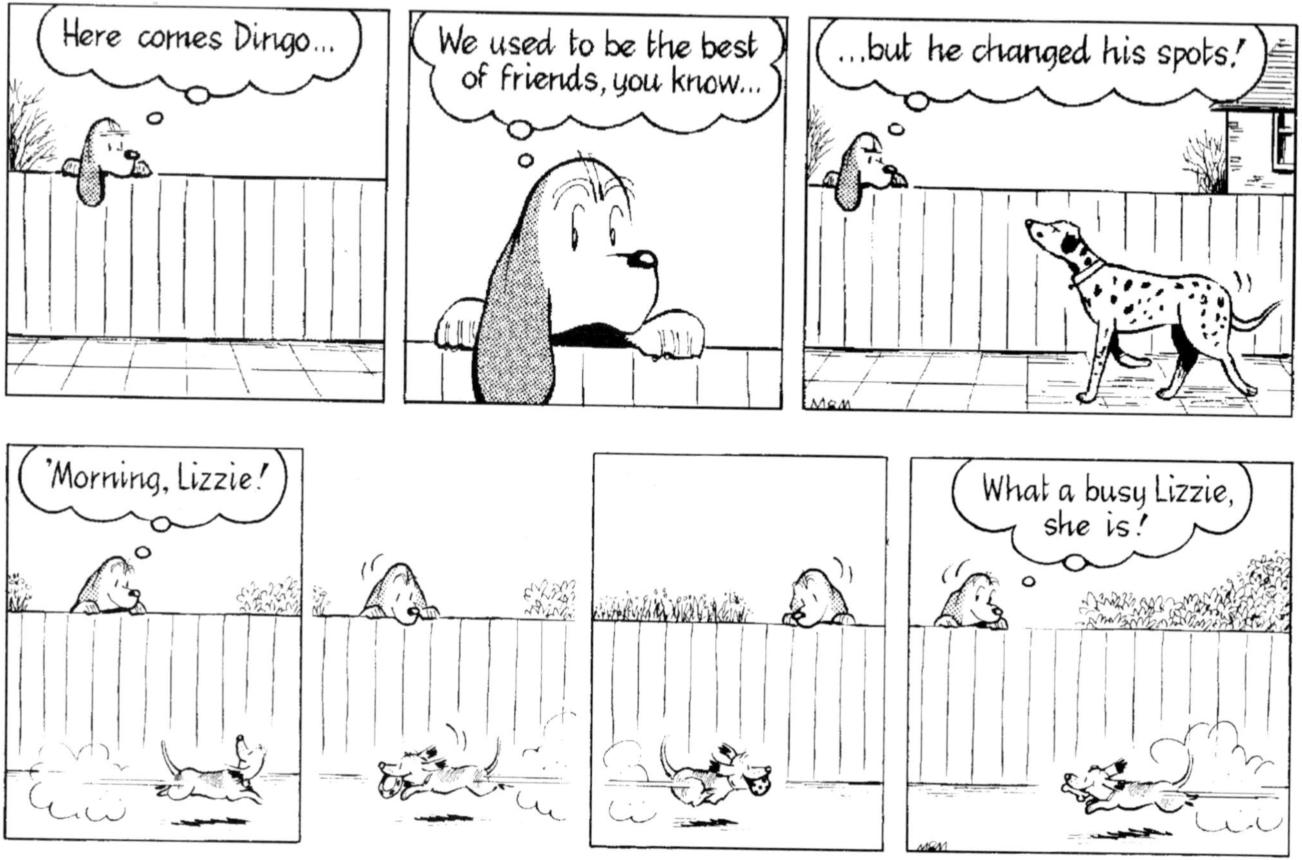
Here comes Dingo...
We used to be the best of friends, you know...
...but he changed his spots!
'Morning, Lizzie!
What a busy Lizzie, she is!

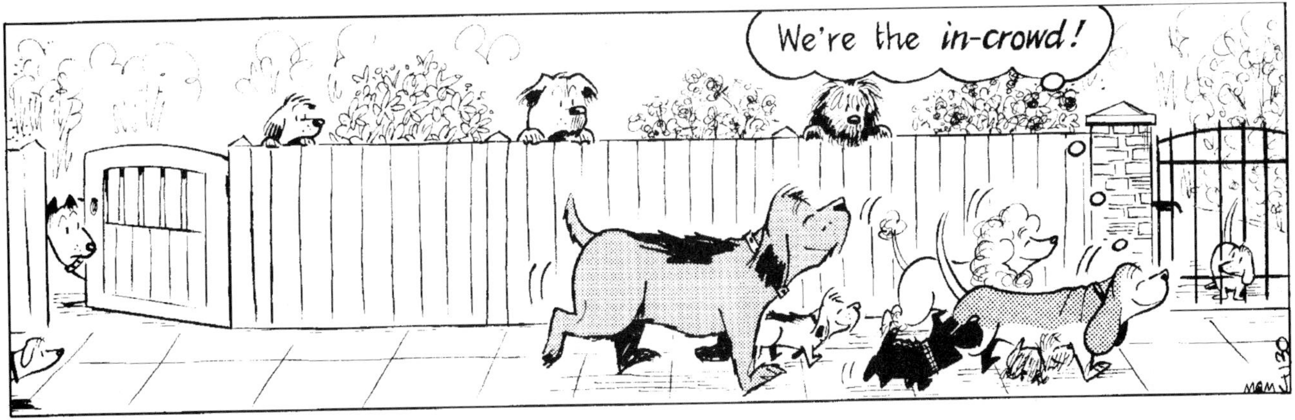
We're the *in-crowd!*
MGM

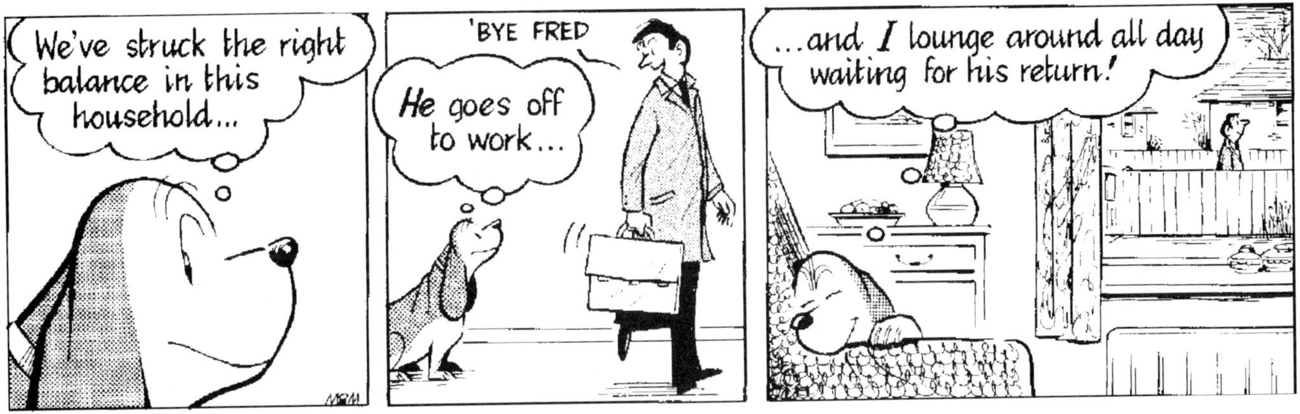
We've struck the right balance in this household...
MGM
'BYE FRED
He goes off to work...
...and *I* lounge around all day waiting for his return!

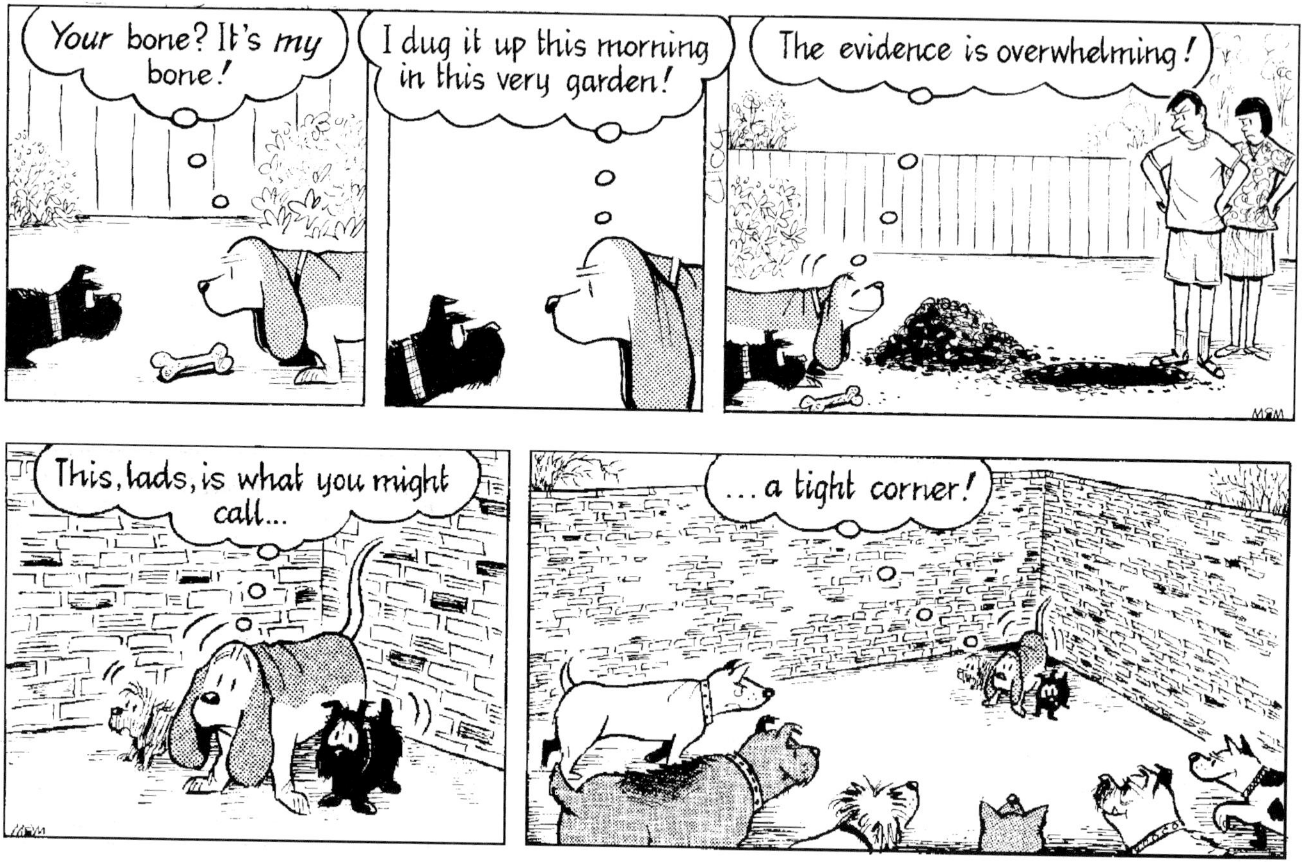

Your bone? It's *my* bone!
I dug it up this morning in this very garden!
The evidence is overwhelming!
MGM
This, lads, is what you might call...
... a tight corner!

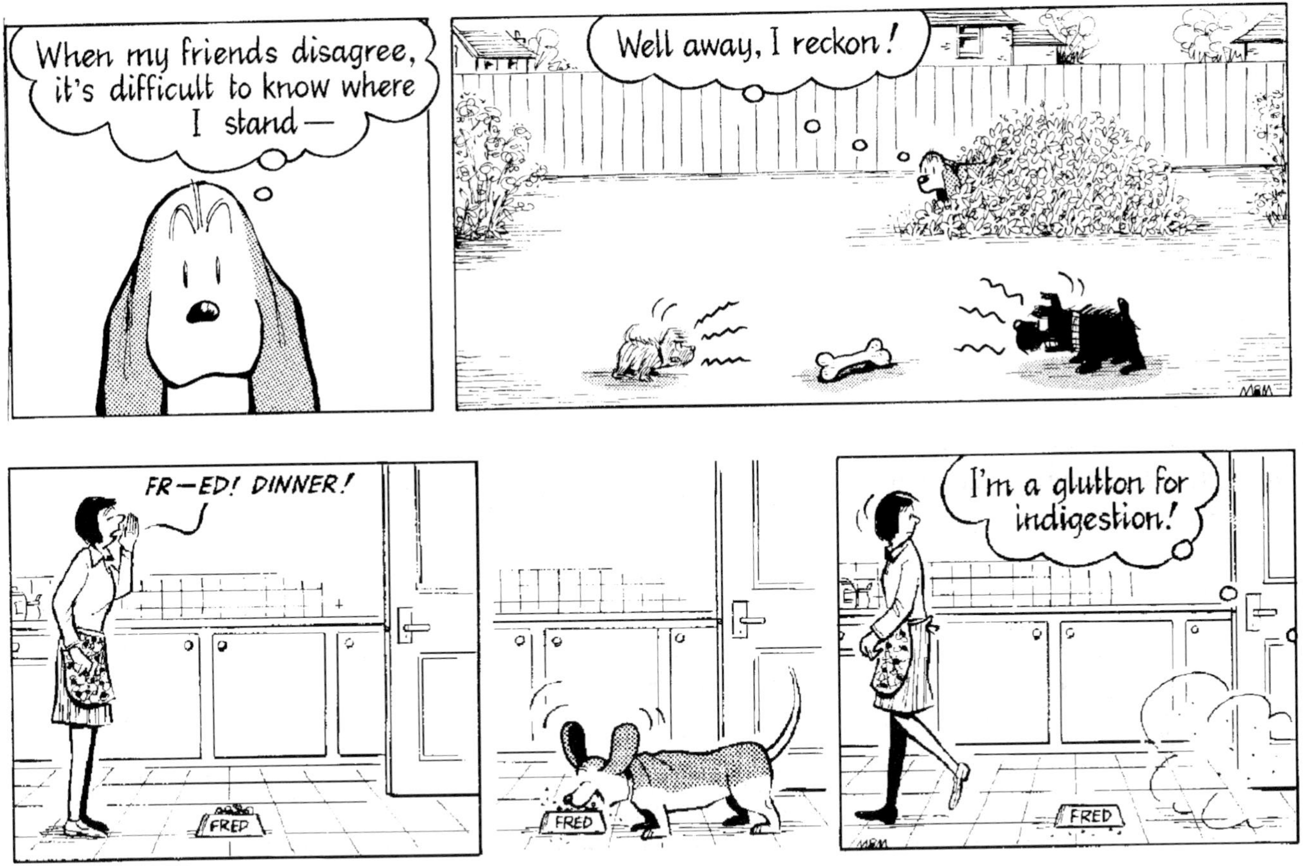
When my friends disagree, it's difficult to know where I stand—
Well away, I reckon!
MBM
FR—ED! DINNER!
FRED
FRED
I'm a glutton for indigestion!
FRED
MBM

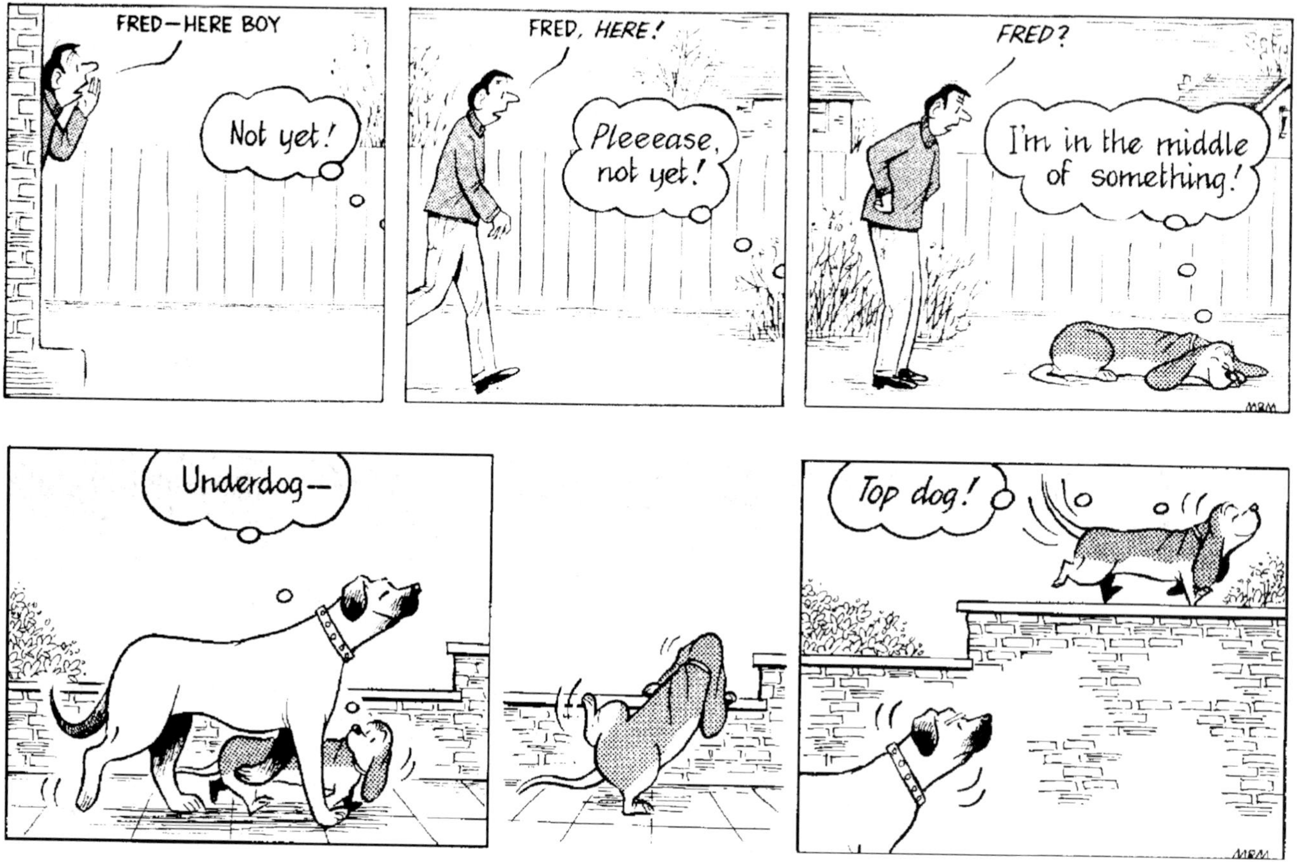
FRED—HERE BOY
Not yet!
FRED, HERE!
Pleeease, not yet!
FRED?
I'm in the middle of something!
MBM
Underdog—
Top dog!
MBM

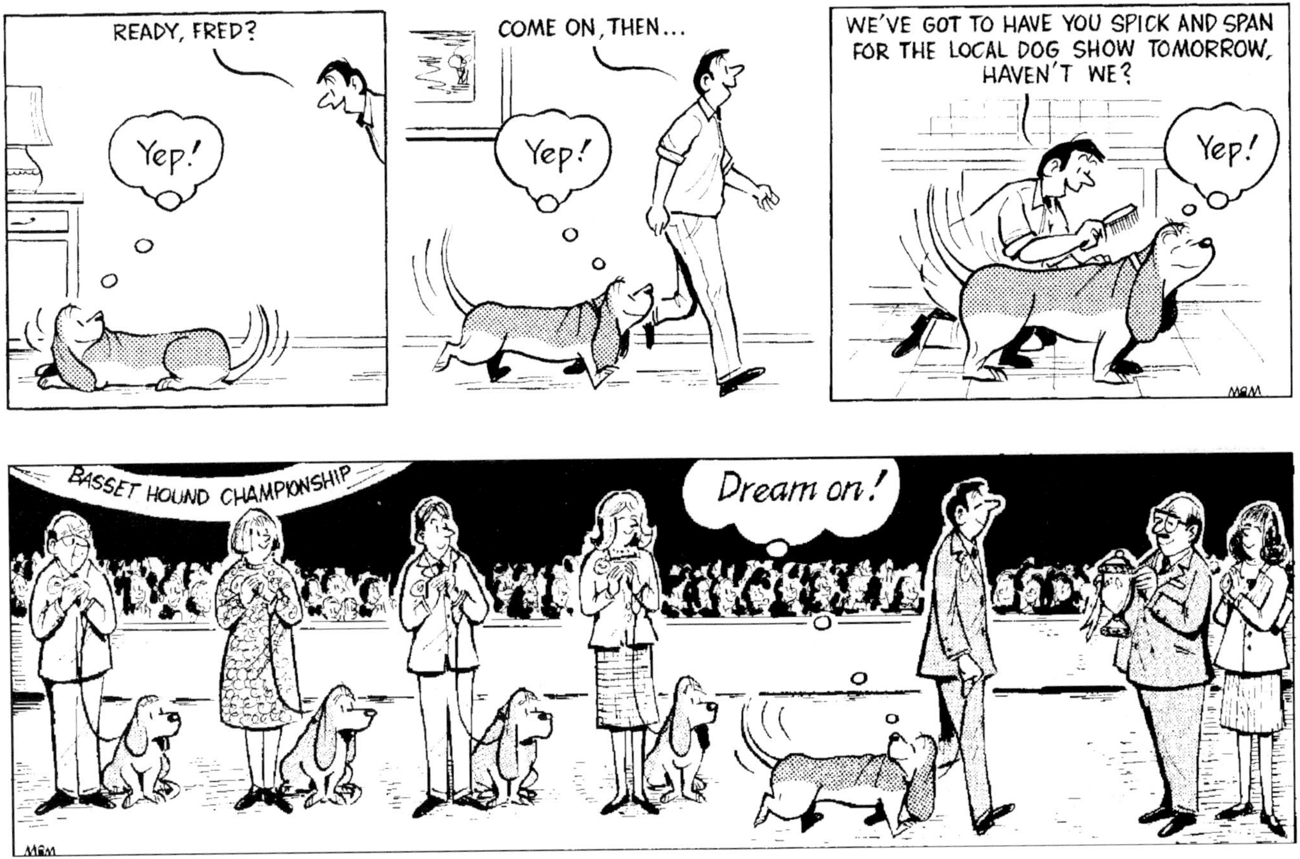
READY, FRED?
Yep!
COME ON, THEN...
Yep!
WE'VE GOT TO HAVE YOU SPICK AND SPAN FOR THE LOCAL DOG SHOW TOMORROW, HAVEN'T WE?
Yep!
MGM
BASSET HOUND CHAMPIONSHIP
Dream on!
MGM

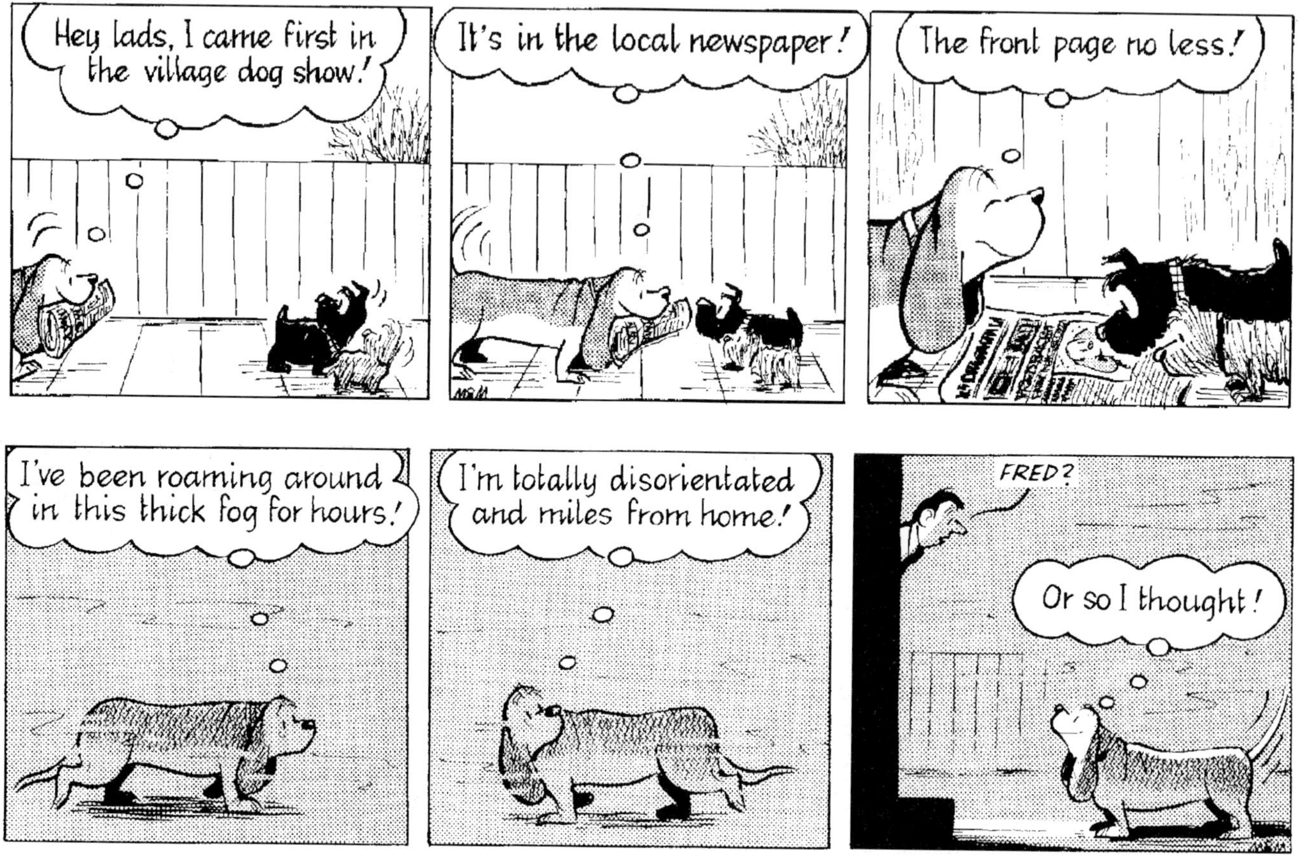
Hey lads, I came first in the village dog show!
It's in the local newspaper!
The front page no less!
I've been roaming around in this thick fog for hours!
I'm totally disorientated and miles from home!
FRED?
Or so I thought!

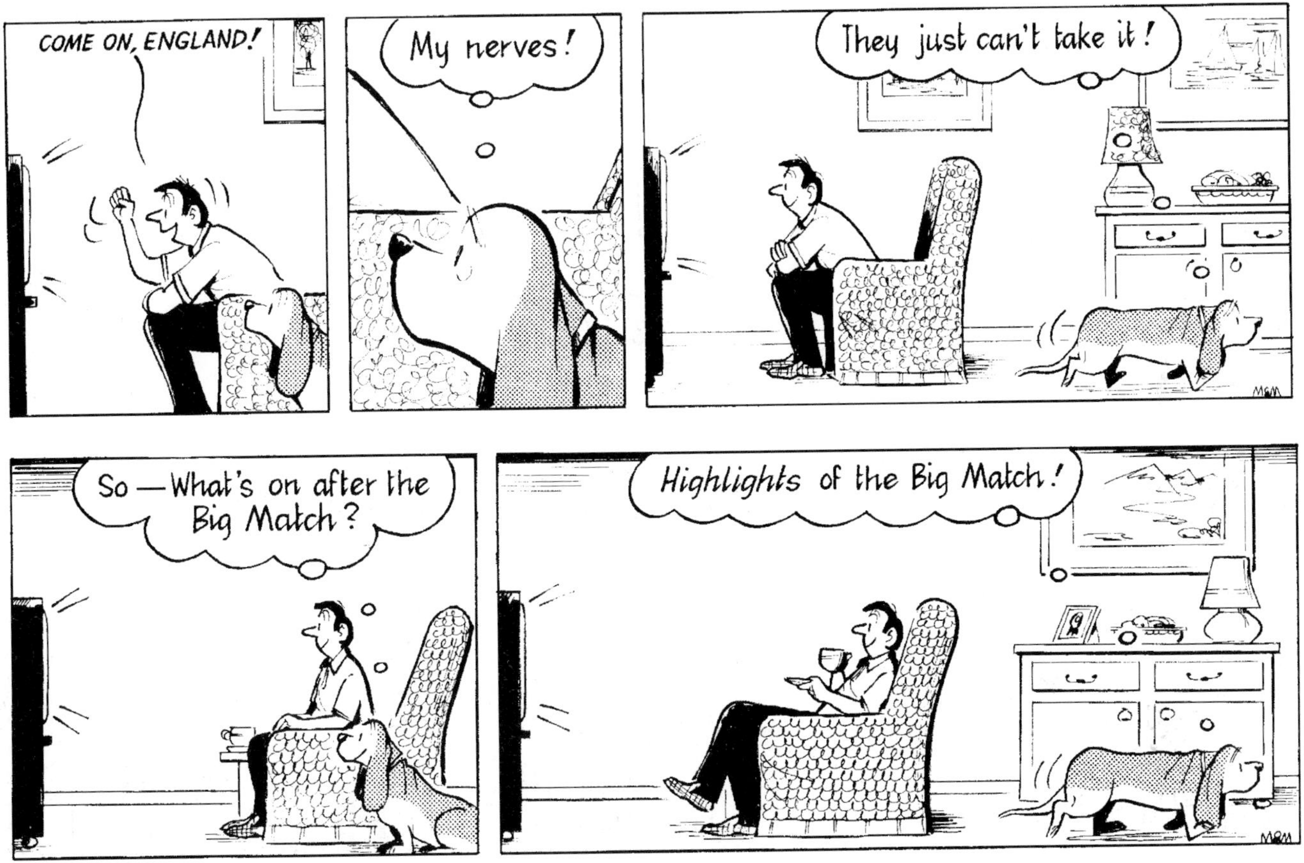
COME ON, ENGLAND!
My nerves!
They just can't take it!
So — What's on after the Big Match?
Highlights of the Big Match!
MGM
MGM

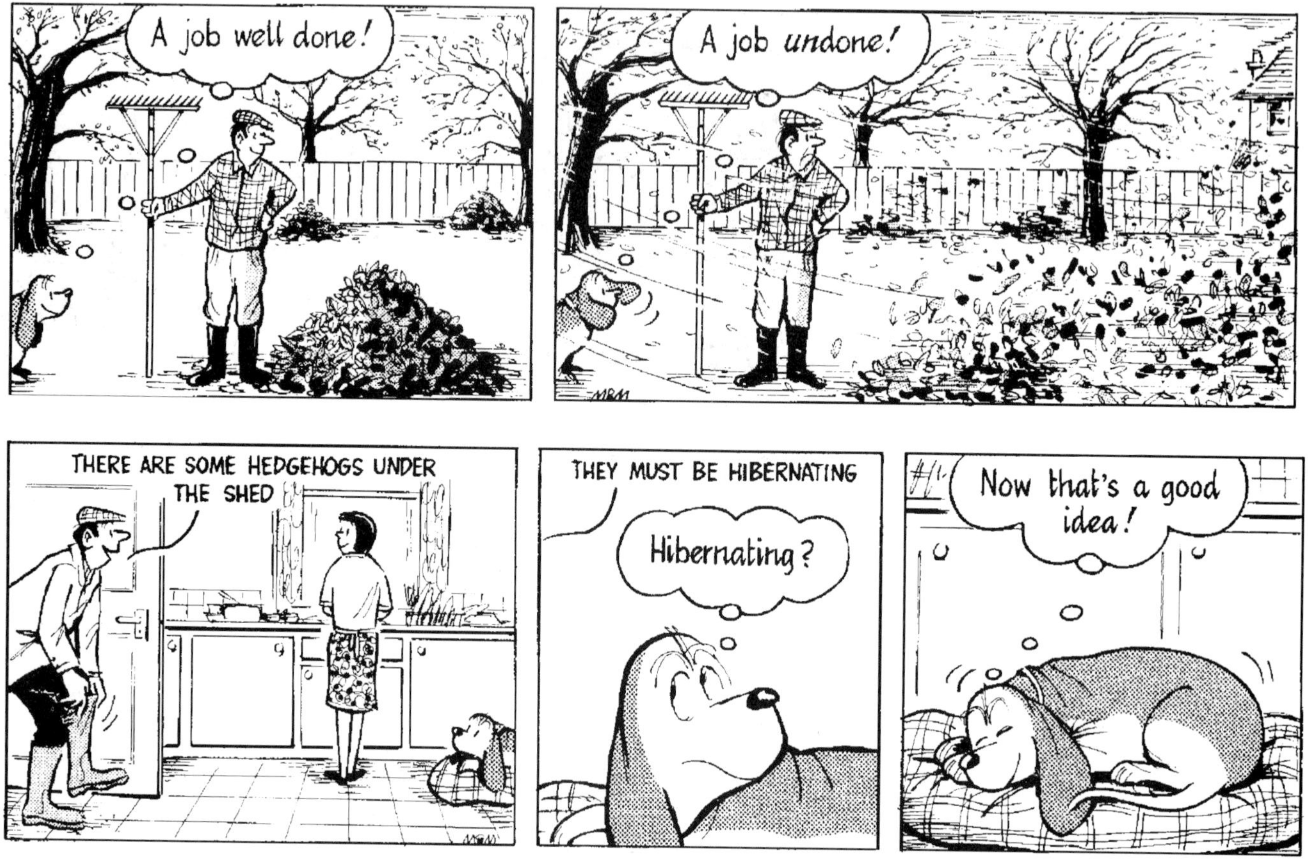
A job well done!
A job undone!
THERE ARE SOME HEDGEHOGS UNDER THE SHED
THEY MUST BE HIBERNATING
Hibernating?
Now that's a good idea!

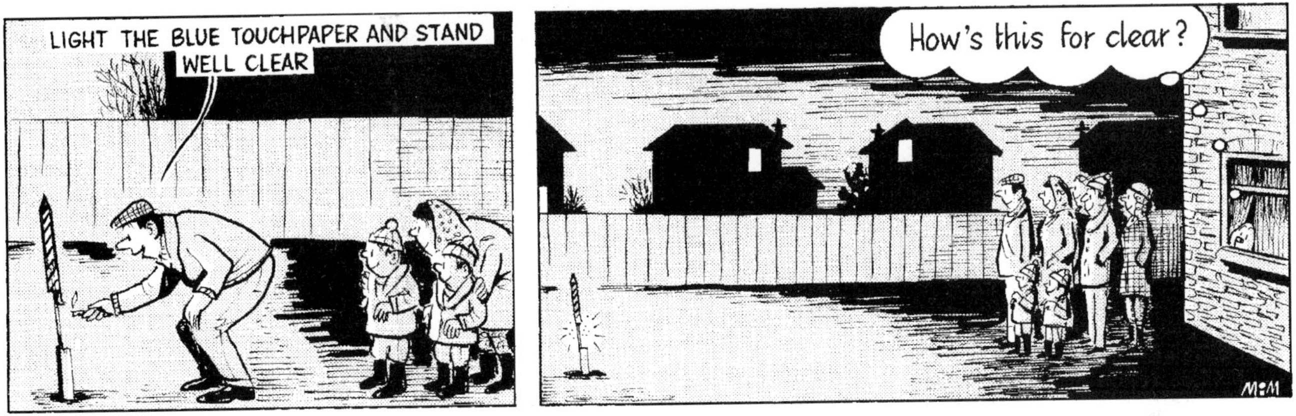
LIGHT THE BLUE TOUCHPAPER AND STAND WELL CLEAR
How's this for clear?

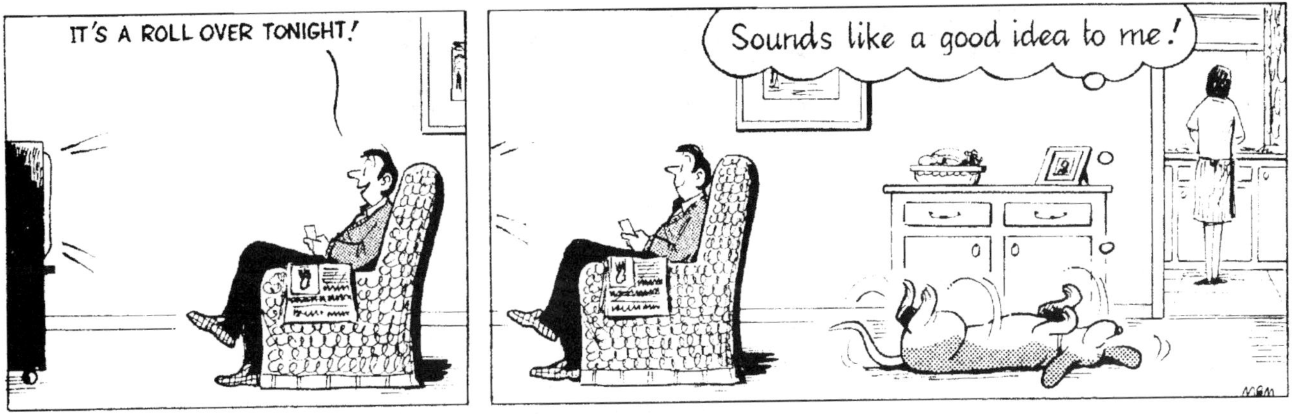
IT'S A ROLL OVER TONIGHT!
Sounds like a good idea to me!

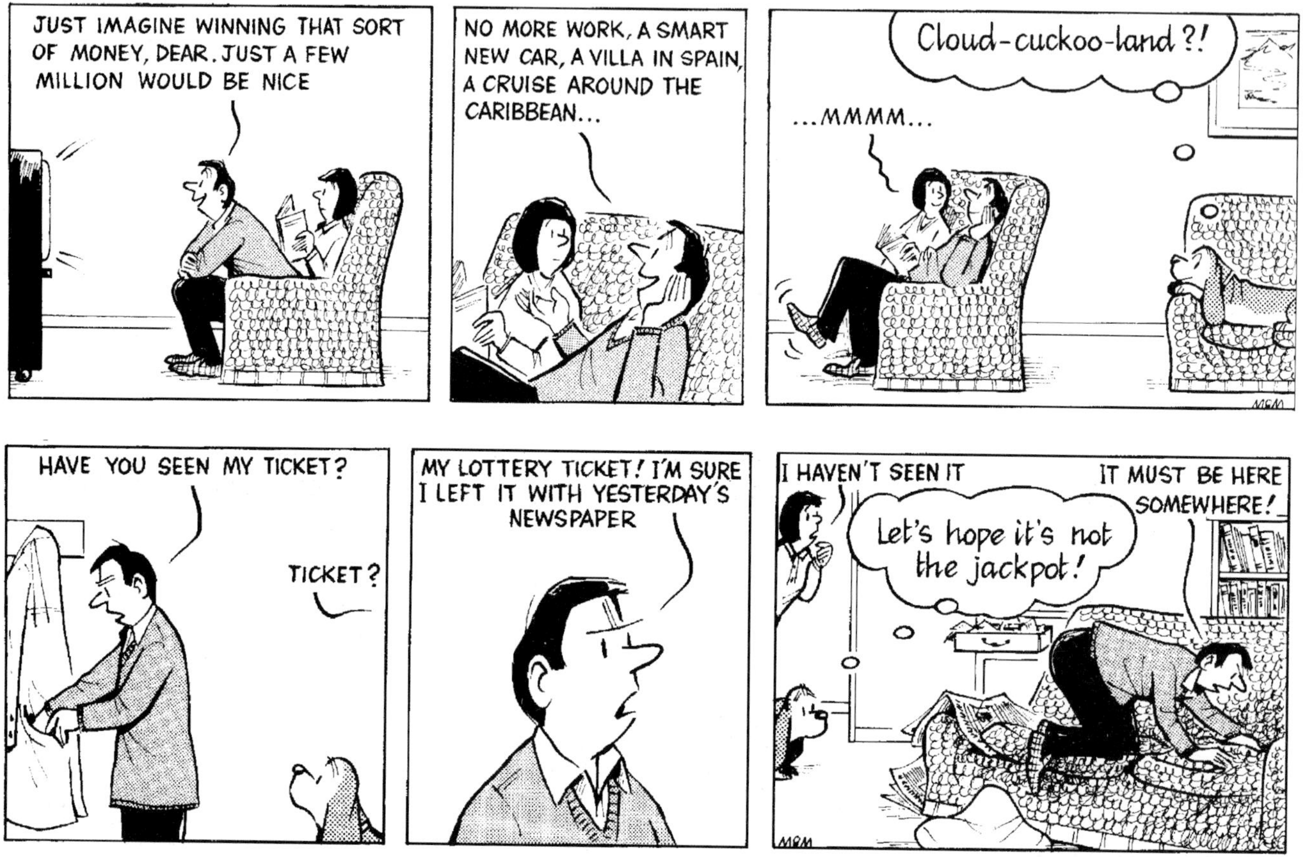
JUST IMAGINE WINNING THAT SORT OF MONEY, DEAR. JUST A FEW MILLION WOULD BE NICE
NO MORE WORK, A SMART NEW CAR, A VILLA IN SPAIN, A CRUISE AROUND THE CARIBBEAN...
Cloud-cuckoo-land?!
...MMMM...
MGM
HAVE YOU SEEN MY TICKET?
TICKET?
MY LOTTERY TICKET! I'M SURE I LEFT IT WITH YESTERDAY'S NEWSPAPER
I HAVEN'T SEEN IT
IT MUST BE HERE SOMEWHERE!
Let's hope it's not the jackpot!
MGM

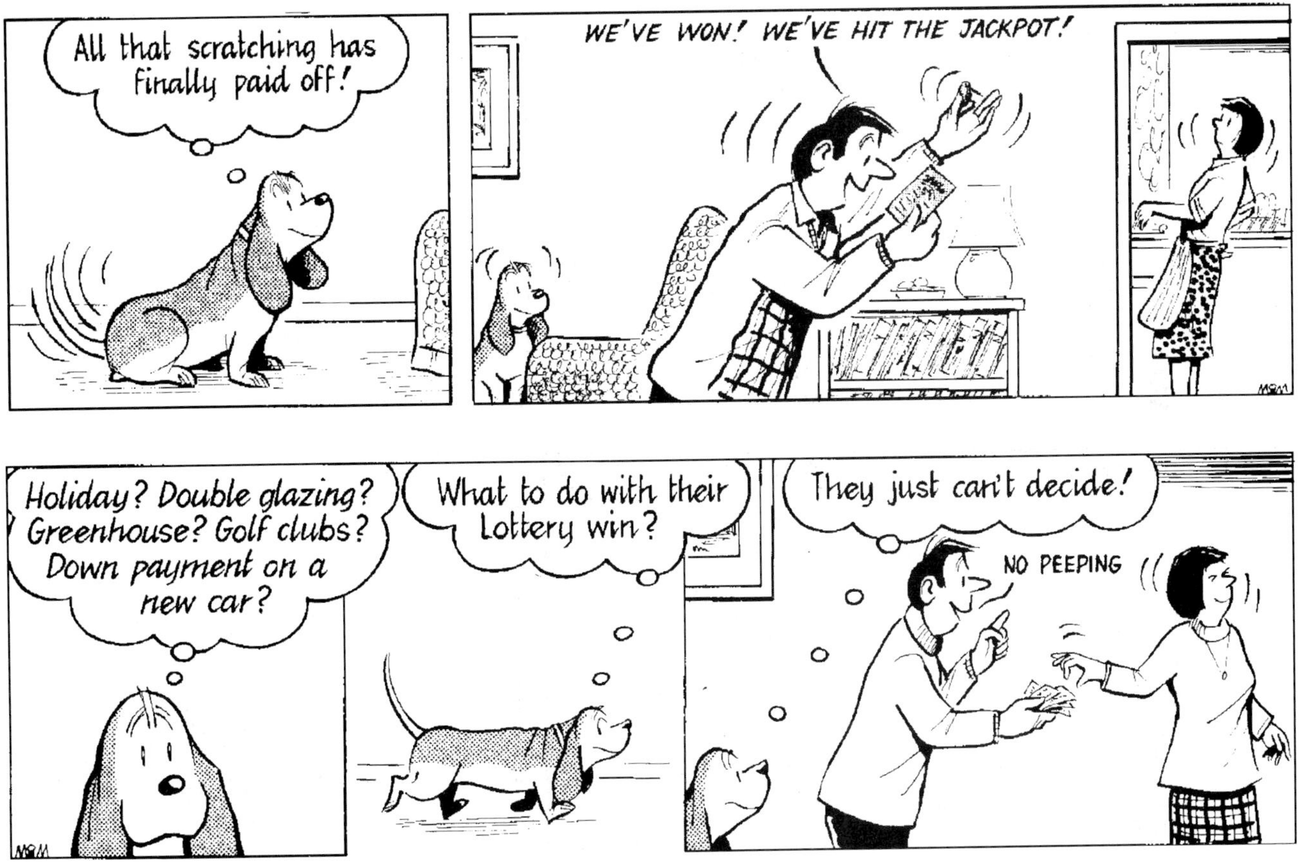

All that scratching has finally paid off!
WE'VE WON! WE'VE HIT THE JACKPOT!
MGM
Holiday? Double glazing? Greenhouse? Golf clubs? Down payment on a new car?
MGM
What to do with their Lottery win?
They just can't decide!
NO PEEPING

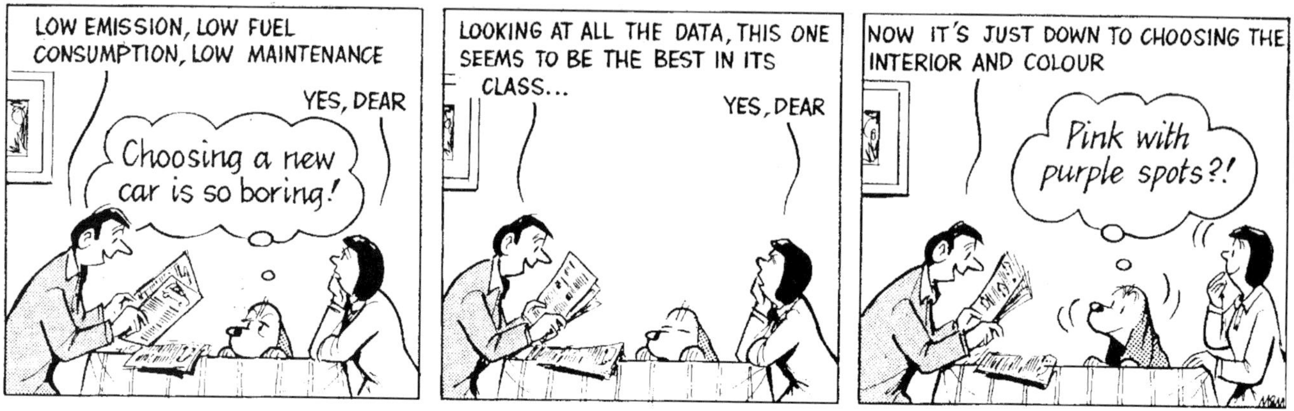
LOW EMISSION, LOW FUEL CONSUMPTION, LOW MAINTENANCE
YES, DEAR
Choosing a new car is so boring!
LOOKING AT ALL THE DATA, THIS ONE SEEMS TO BE THE BEST IN ITS CLASS...
YES, DEAR
NOW IT'S JUST DOWN TO CHOOSING THE INTERIOR AND COLOUR
Pink with purple spots?!
MRM

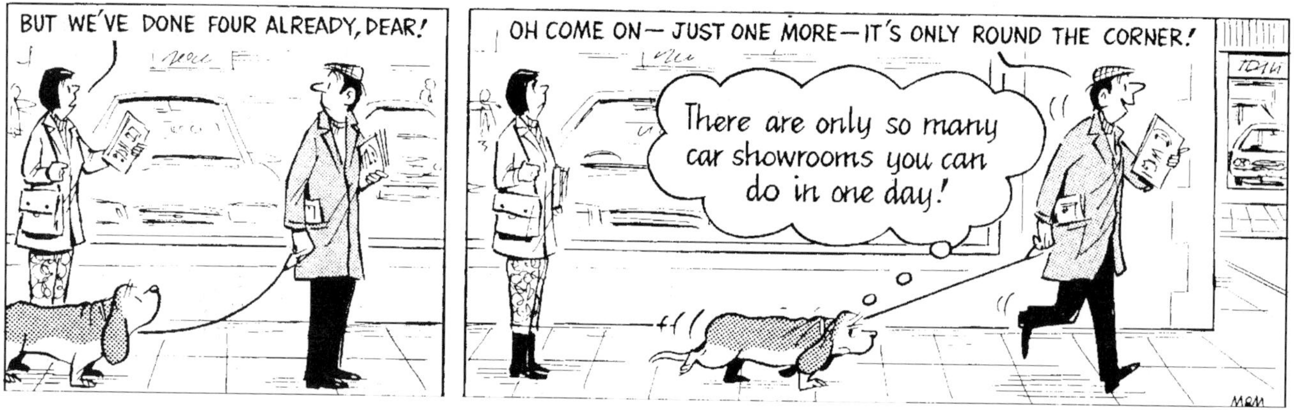
BUT WE'VE DONE FOUR ALREADY, DEAR!
OH COME ON— JUST ONE MORE—IT'S ONLY ROUND THE CORNER!
There are only so many car showrooms you can do in one day!
MRM

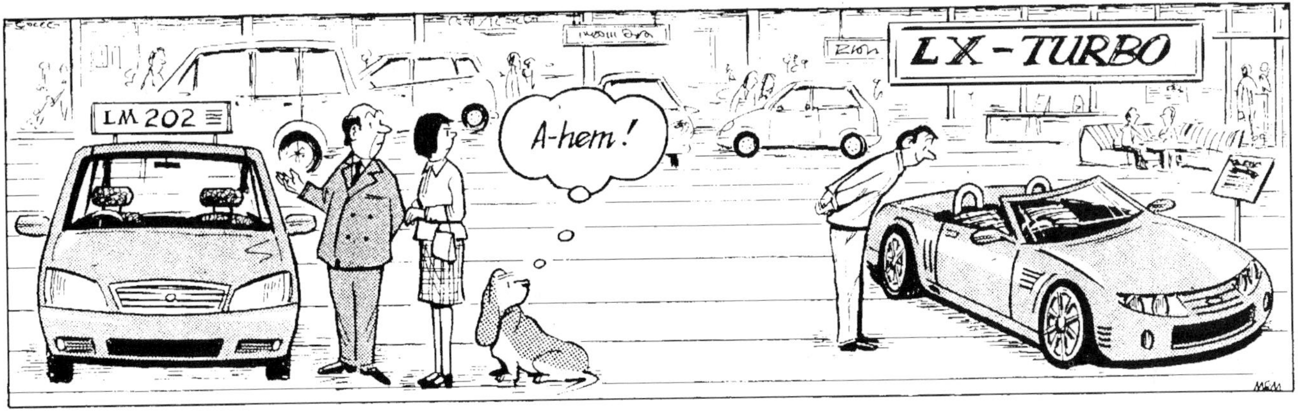
LM 202
LX-TURBO
A-hem!

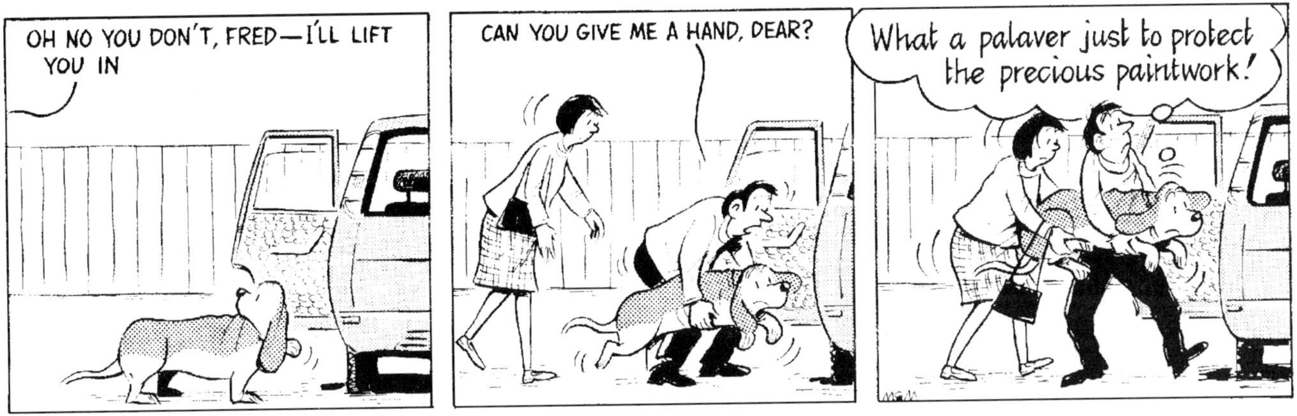
OH NO YOU DON'T, FRED—I'LL LIFT YOU IN
CAN YOU GIVE ME A HAND, DEAR?
What a palaver just to protect the precious paintwork!

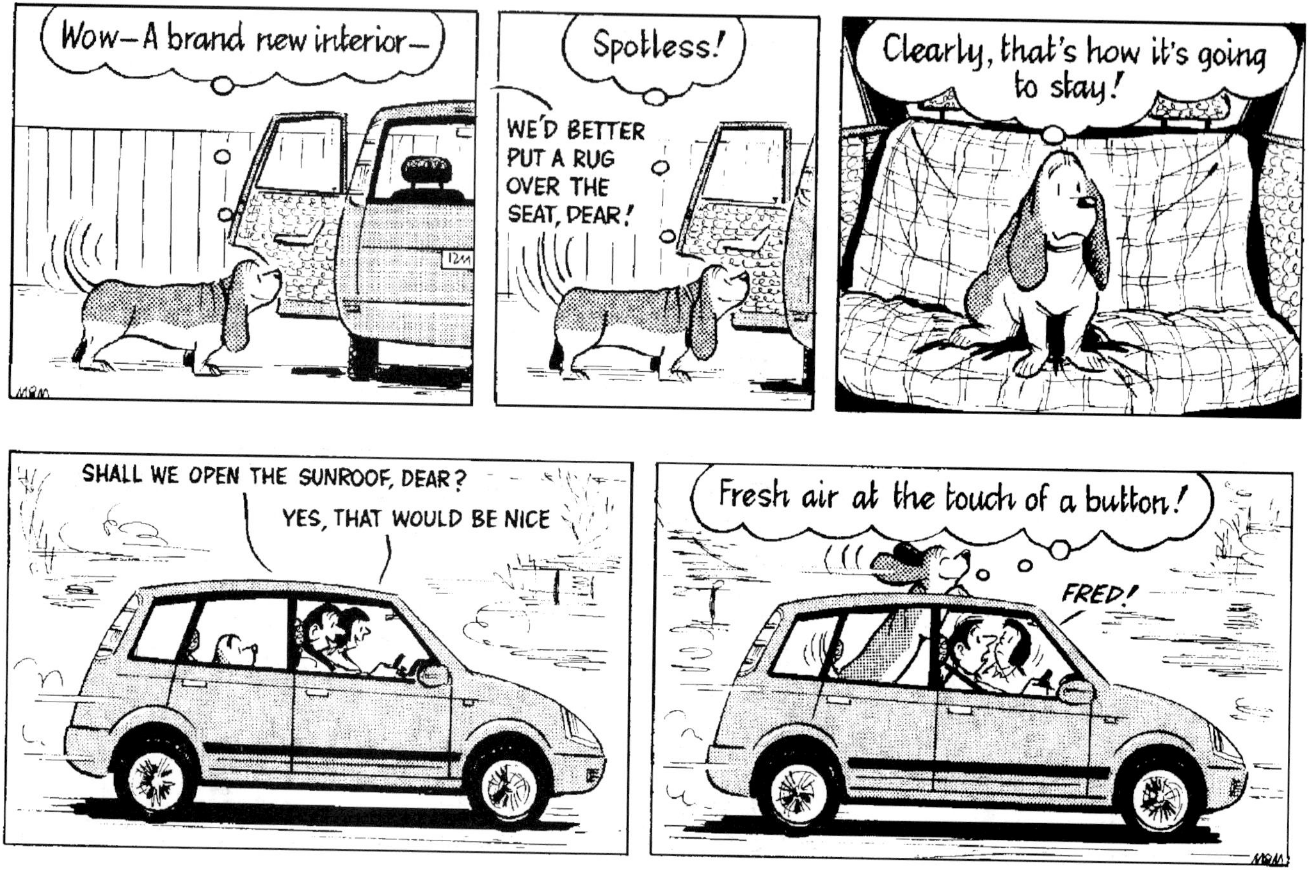
Wow—A brand new interior—
Spotless!
WE'D BETTER PUT A RUG OVER THE SEAT, DEAR!
Clearly, that's how it's going to stay!
SHALL WE OPEN THE SUNROOF, DEAR?
YES, THAT WOULD BE NICE
Fresh air at the touch of a button!
FRED!

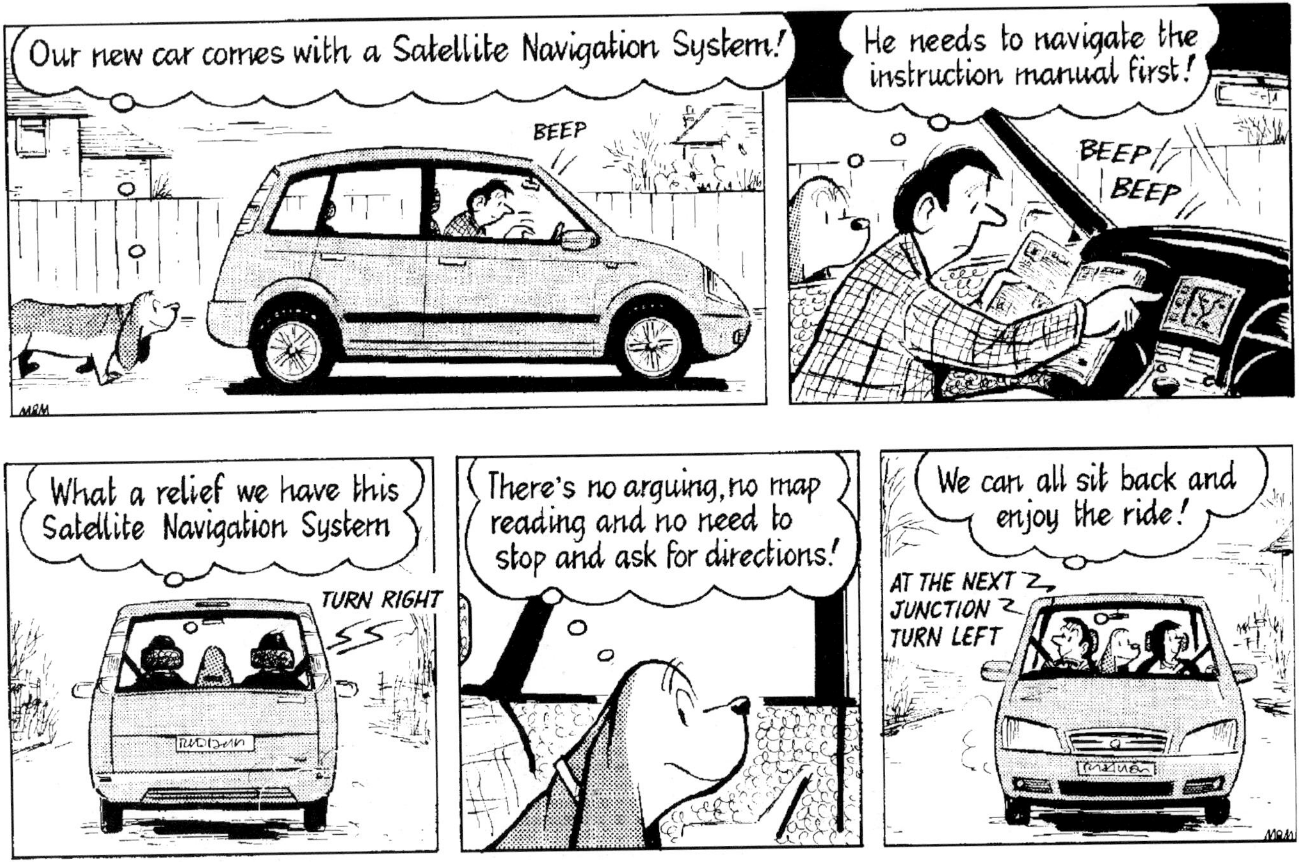
Our new car comes with a Satellite Navigation System!
BEEP
He needs to navigate the instruction manual first!
BEEP
BEEP
What a relief we have this Satellite Navigation System
TURN RIGHT
There's no arguing, no map reading and no need to stop and ask for directions!
We can all sit back and enjoy the ride!
AT THE NEXT JUNCTION TURN LEFT

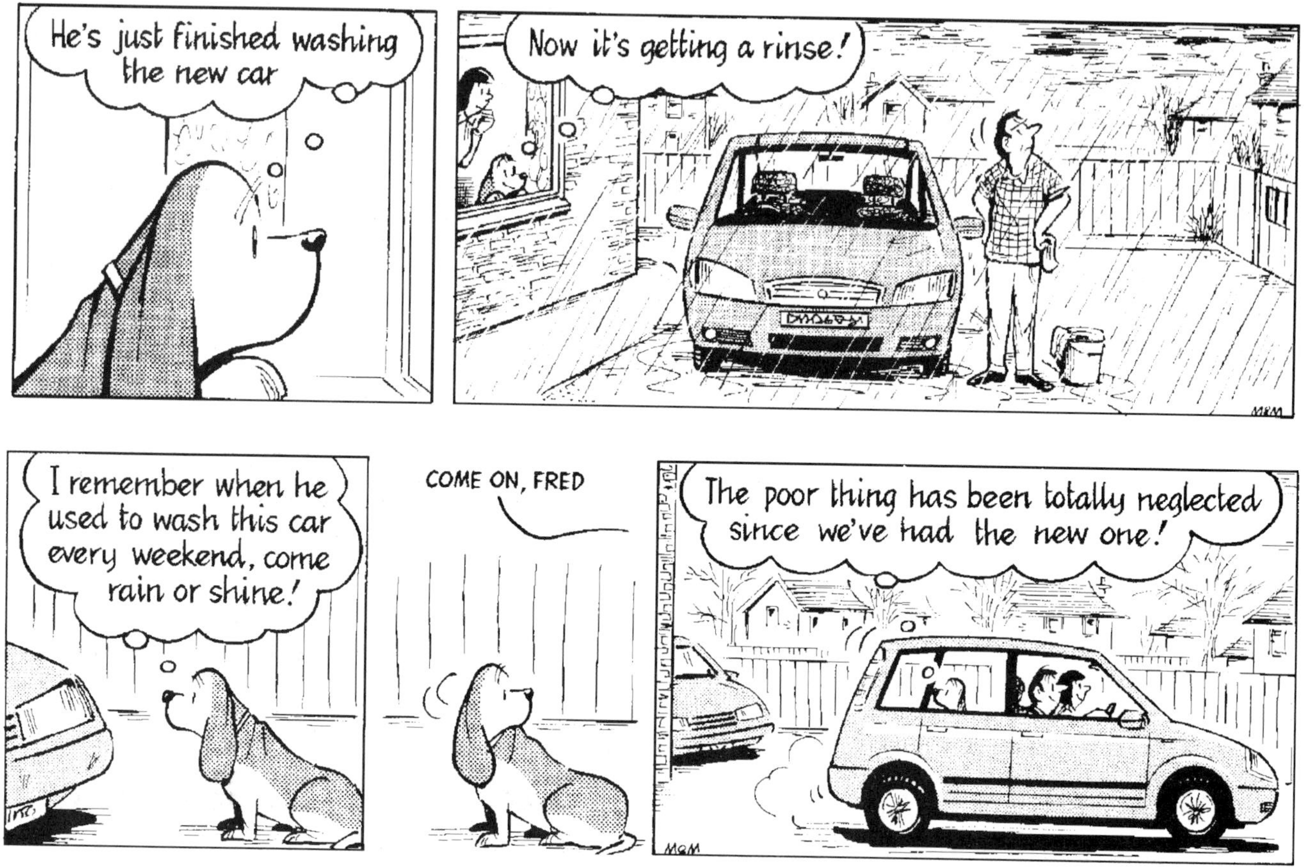
He's just finished washing the new car
Now it's getting a rinse!
I remember when he used to wash this car every weekend, come rain or shine!
COME ON, FRED
The poor thing has been totally neglected since we've had the new one!

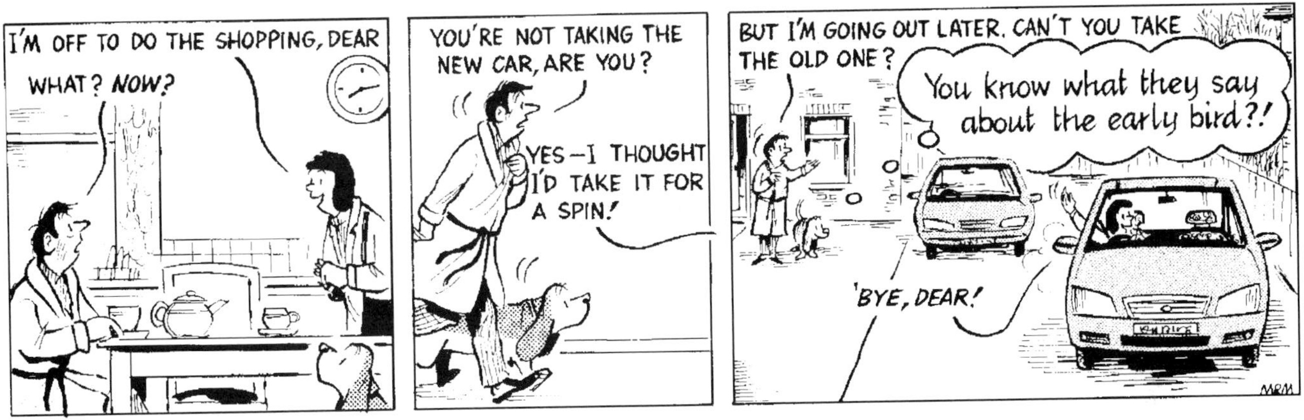
I'M OFF TO DO THE SHOPPING, DEAR
WHAT? *NOW*?
YOU'RE NOT TAKING THE NEW CAR, ARE YOU?
YES—I THOUGHT I'D TAKE IT FOR A SPIN!
BUT I'M GOING OUT LATER. CAN'T YOU TAKE THE OLD ONE?
You know what they say about the early bird?!
'BYE, DEAR!

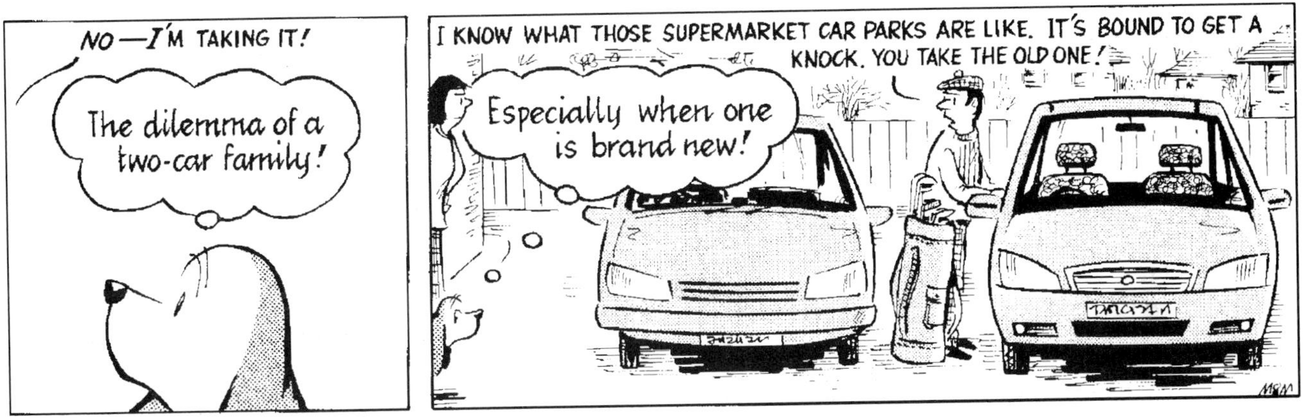
NO—*I*'M TAKING IT!
The dilemma of a two-car family!
I KNOW WHAT THOSE SUPERMARKET CAR PARKS ARE LIKE. IT'S BOUND TO GET A KNOCK. YOU TAKE THE OLD ONE!
Especially when one is brand new!

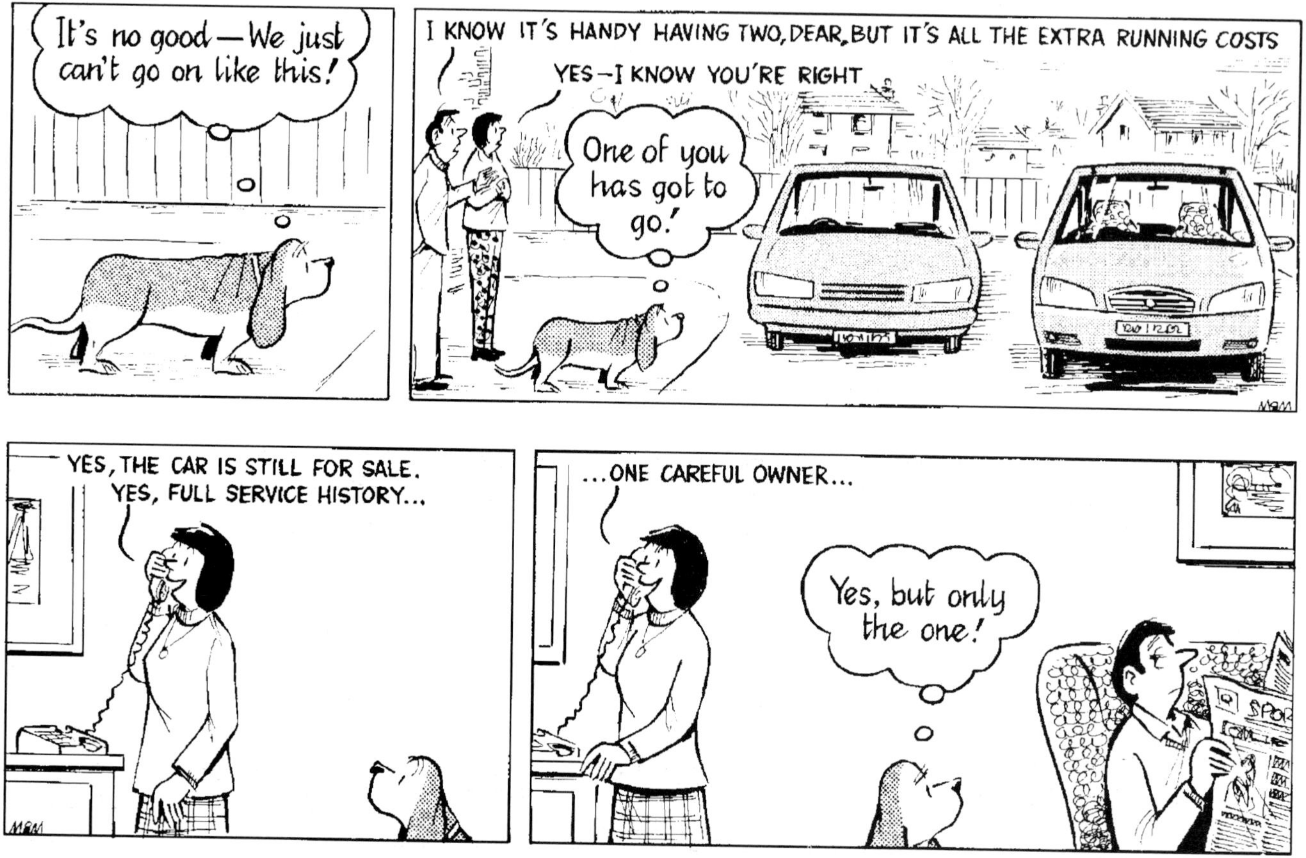
It's no good — We just can't go on like this!
I KNOW IT'S HANDY HAVING TWO, DEAR, BUT IT'S ALL THE EXTRA RUNNING COSTS
YES — I KNOW YOU'RE RIGHT
One of you has got to go!
YES, THE CAR IS STILL FOR SALE. YES, FULL SERVICE HISTORY...
...ONE CAREFUL OWNER...
Yes, but only the one!

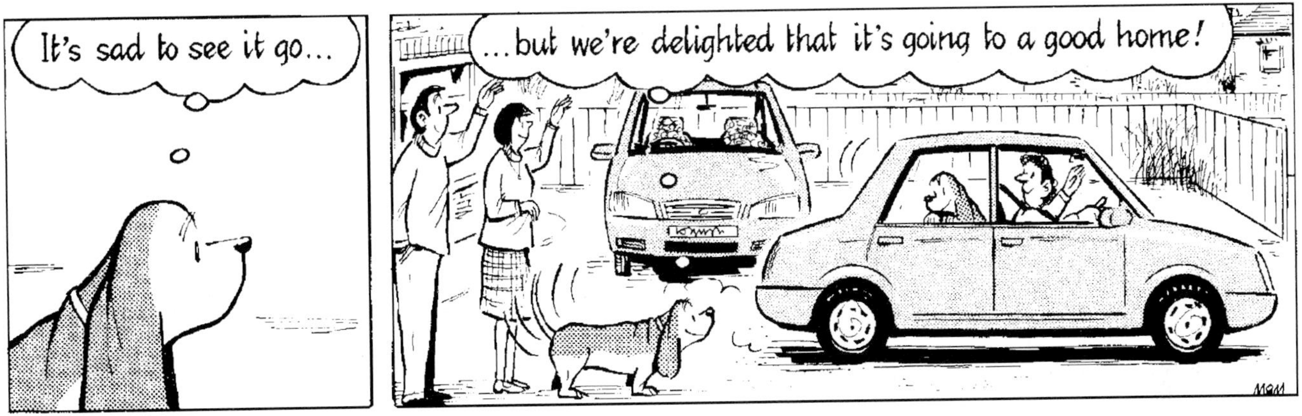
It's sad to see it go...
...but we're delighted that it's going to a good home!

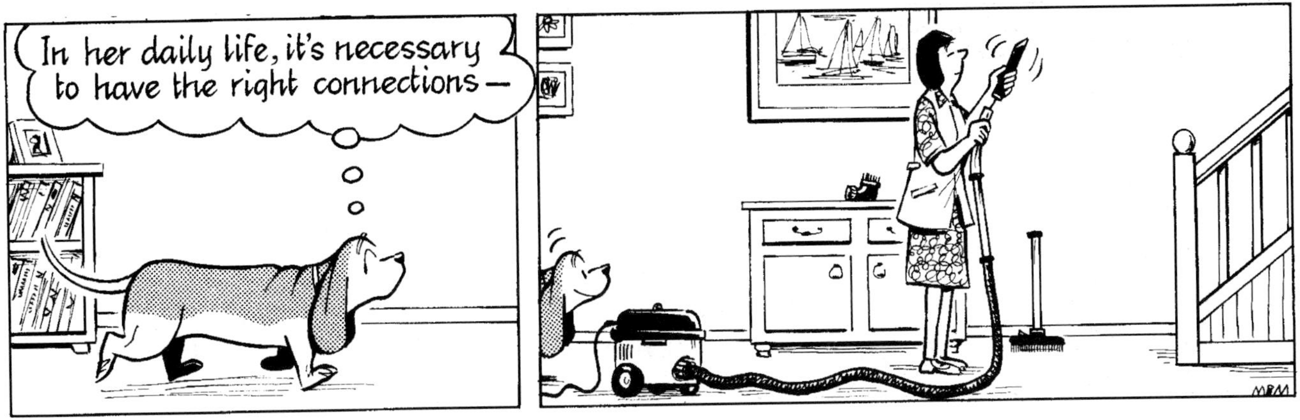
In her daily life, it's necessary to have the right connections –

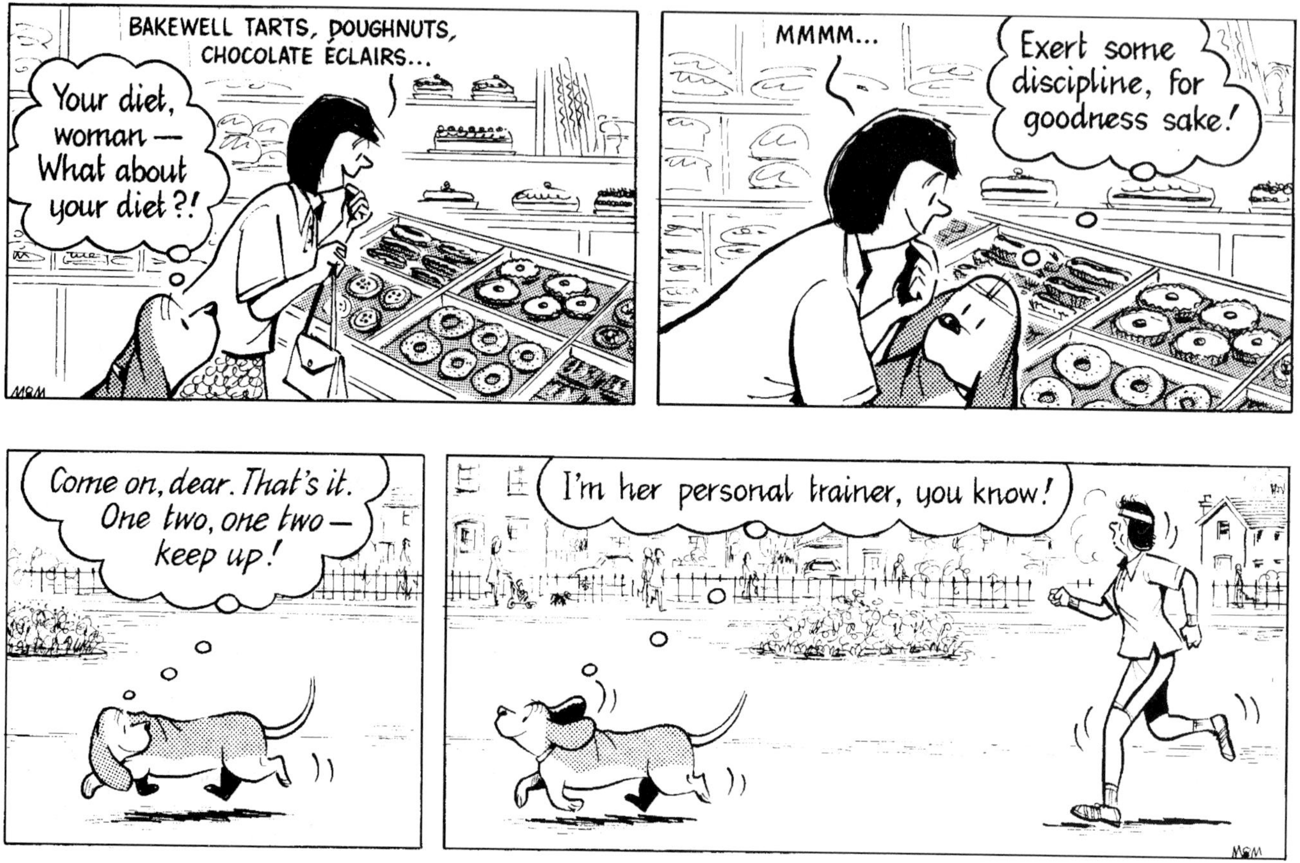
BAKEWELL TARTS, DOUGHNUTS, CHOCOLATE ÉCLAIRS...
Your diet, woman — What about your diet?!
MMMM...
Exert some discipline, for goodness sake!
Come on, dear. That's it. One two, one two — keep up!
I'm her personal trainer, you know!
MGM

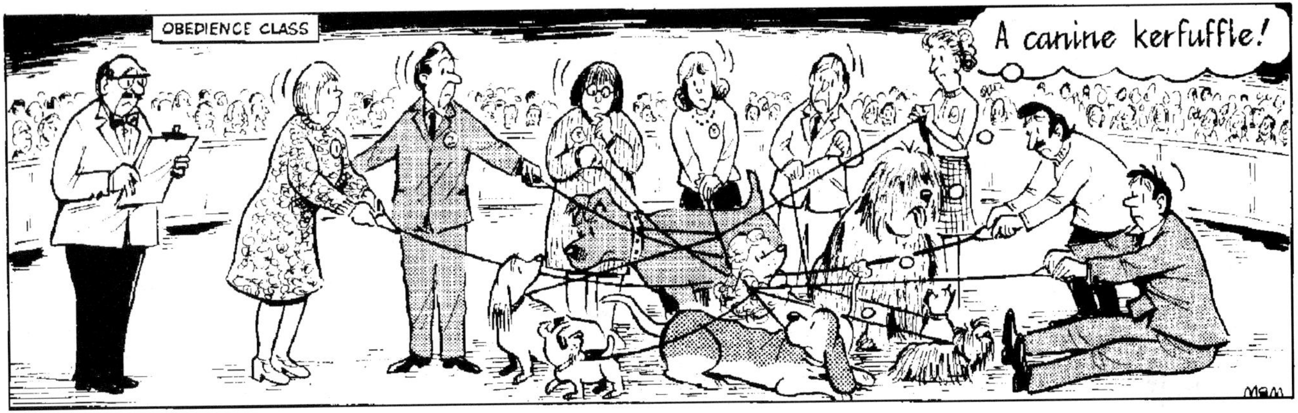
OBEDIENCE CLASS
A canine kerfuffle!

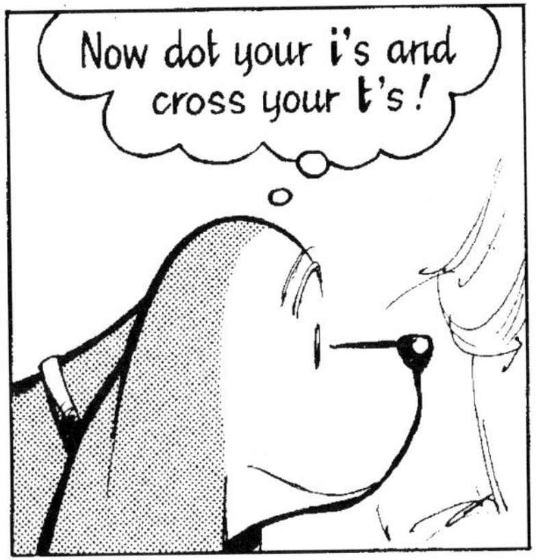
Now dot your i's and cross your t's!

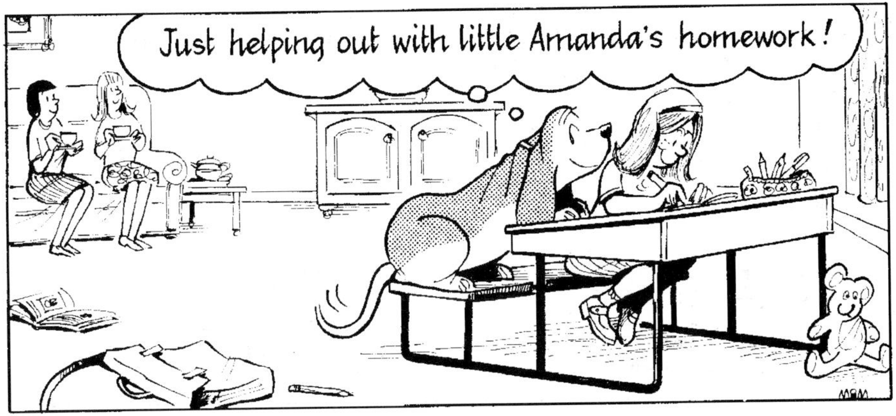
Just helping out with little Amanda's homework!

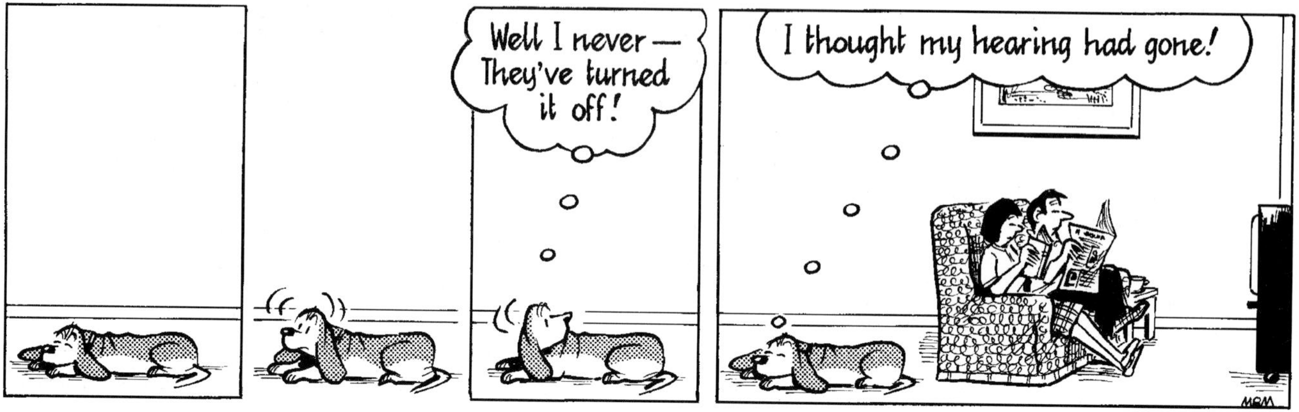
Well I never — They've turned it off!
I thought my hearing had gone!

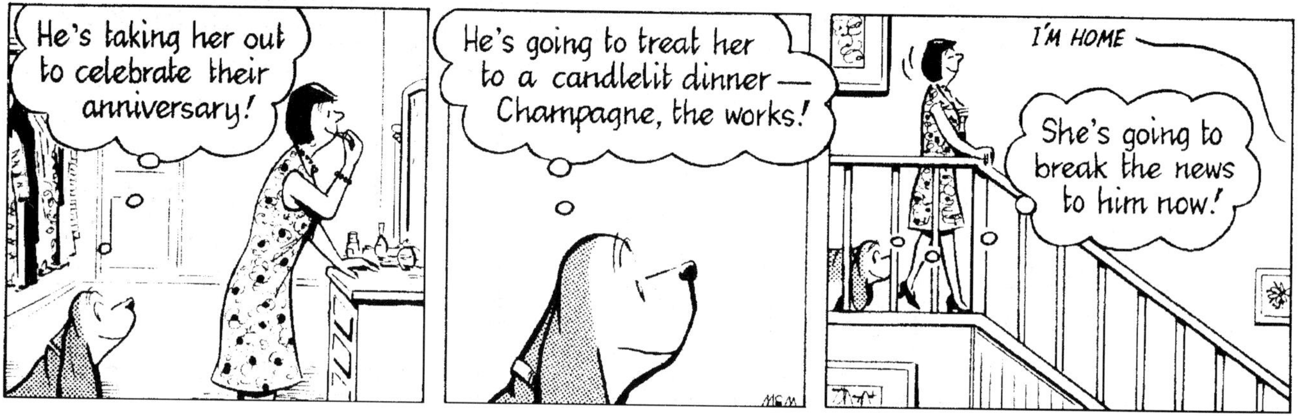
He's taking her out to celebrate their anniversary!
He's going to treat her to a candlelit dinner — Champagne, the works!
I'M HOME
She's going to break the news to him now!

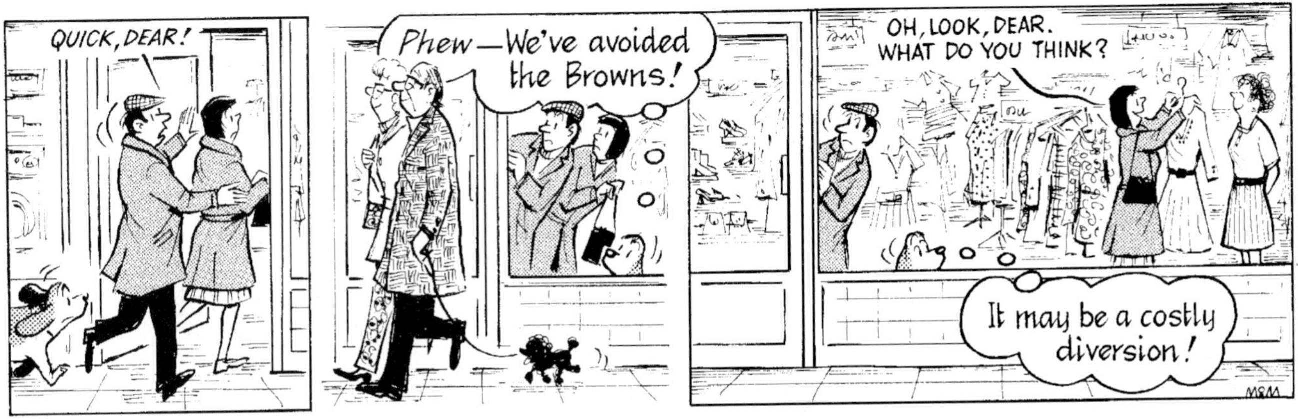
QUICK, DEAR!
Phew—We've avoided the Browns!
OH, LOOK, DEAR. WHAT DO YOU THINK?
It may be a costly diversion!

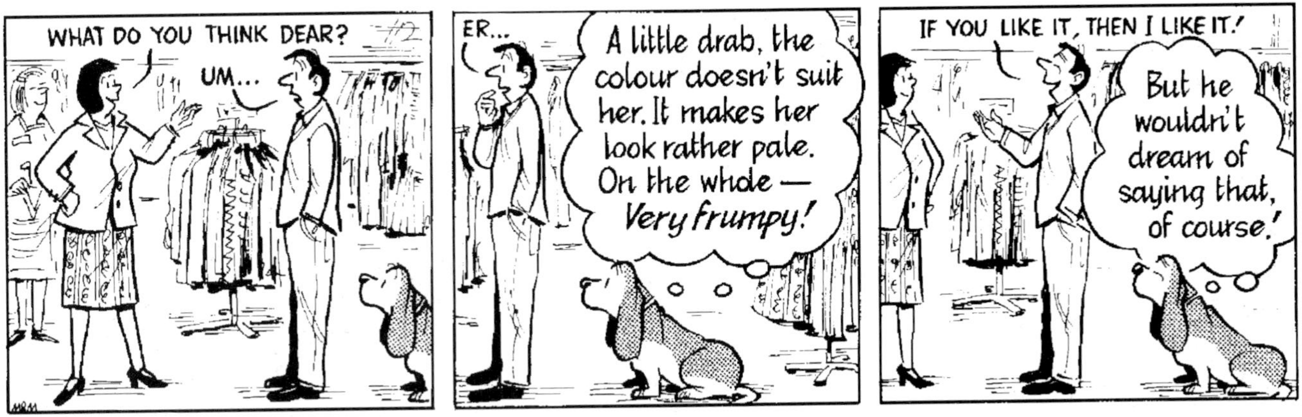
WHAT DO YOU THINK DEAR?
UM...
ER...
A little drab, the colour doesn't suit her. It makes her look rather pale. On the whole — Very frumpy!
IF YOU LIKE IT, THEN I LIKE IT!
But he wouldn't dream of saying that, of course!

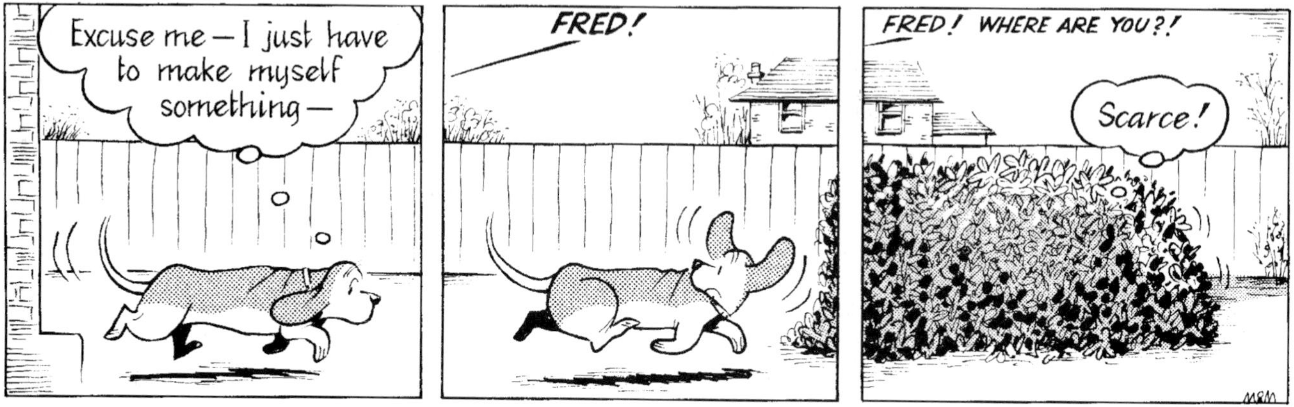
Excuse me – I just have to make myself something –
FRED!
FRED! WHERE ARE YOU?!
Scarce!
MGM

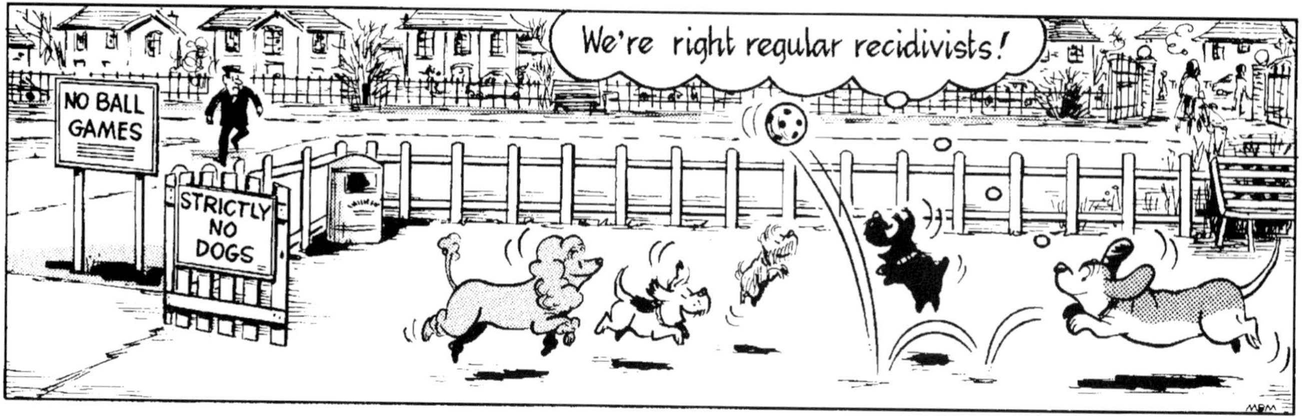
NO BALL GAMES
STRICTLY NO DOGS
We're right regular recidivists!
MGM

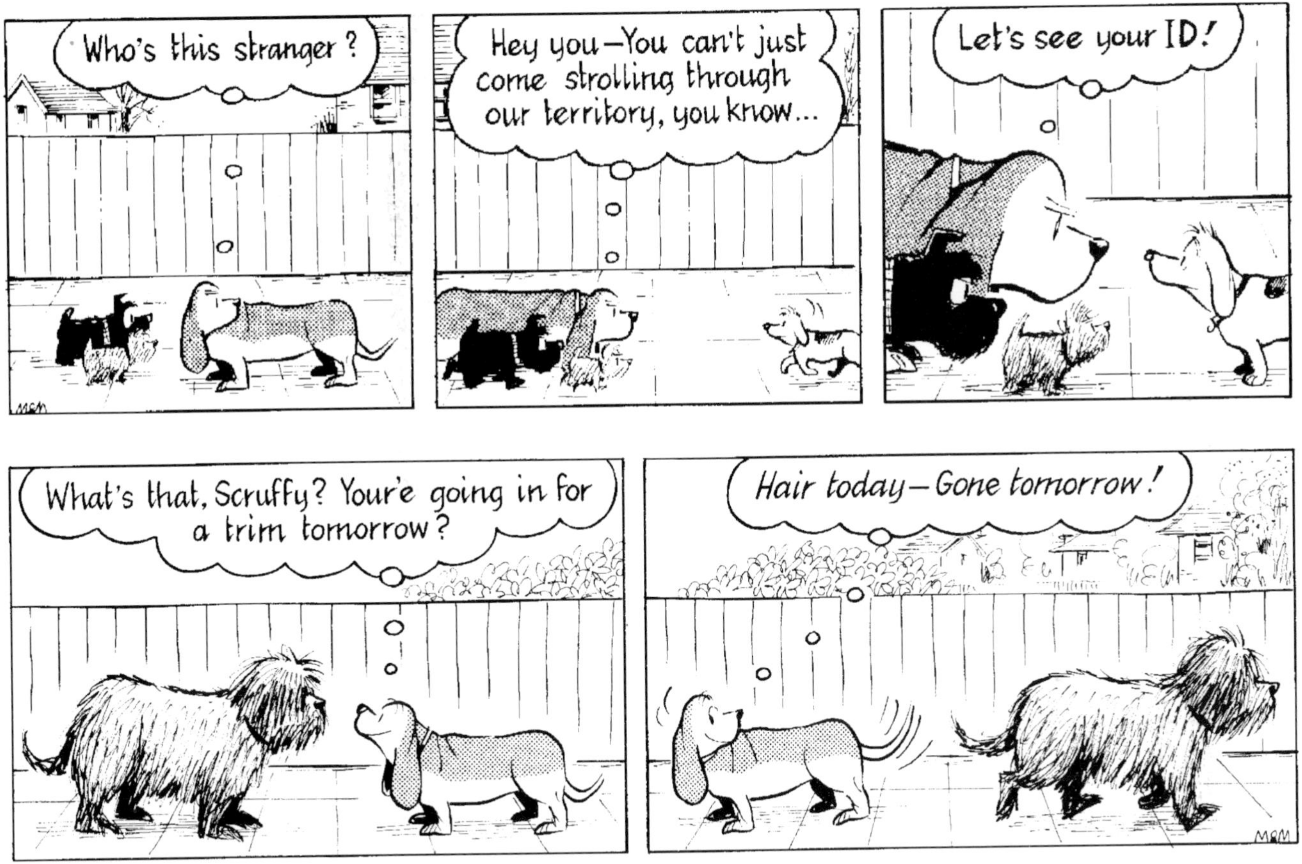
Who's this stranger?
Hey you—You can't just come strolling through our territory, you know...
Let's see your ID!
What's that, Scruffy? Your'e going in for a trim tomorrow?
Hair today—Gone tomorrow!
MGM

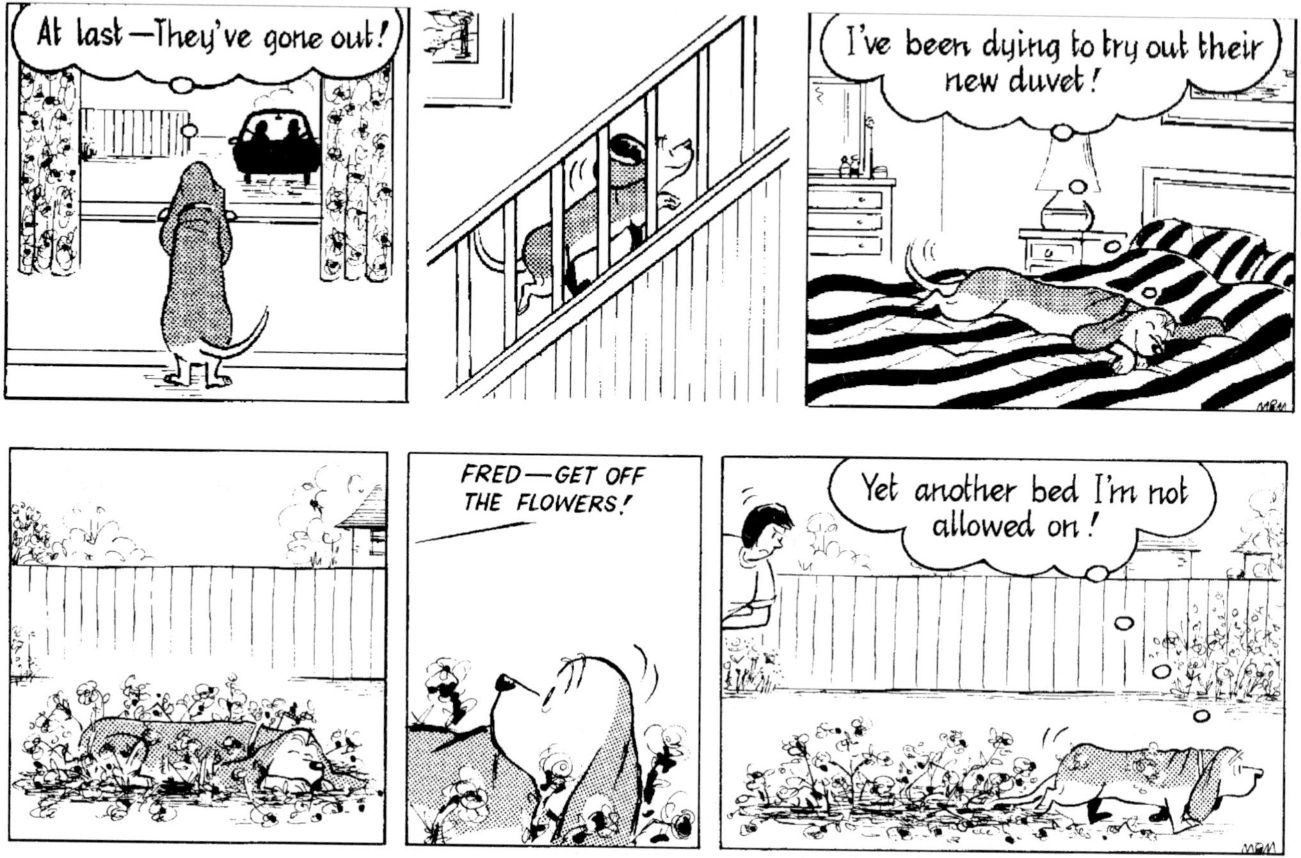
At last—They've gone out!
I've been dying to try out their new duvet!
FRED—GET OFF THE FLOWERS!
Yet another bed I'm not allowed on!

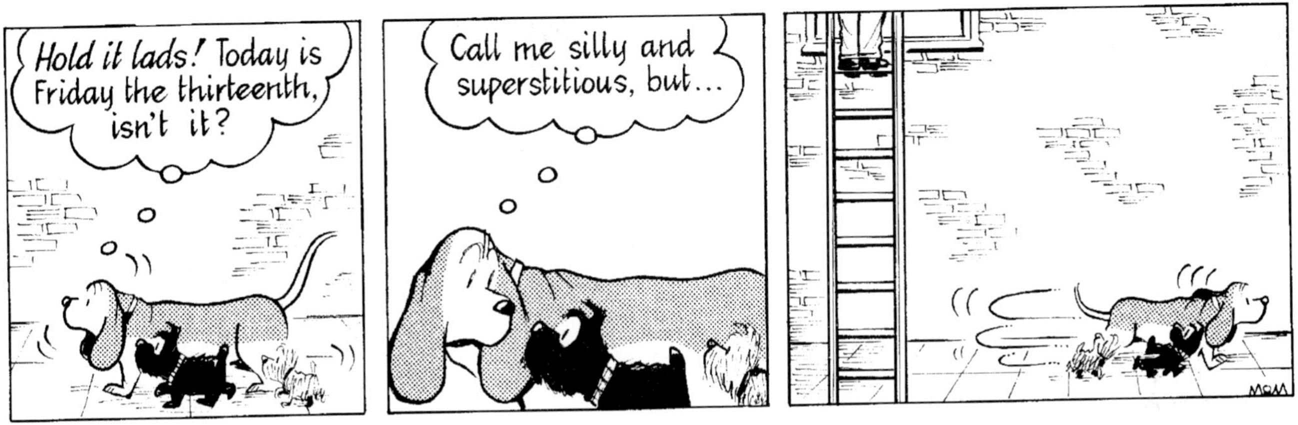
Hold it lads! Today is Friday the thirteenth, isn't it?
Call me silly and superstitious, but...

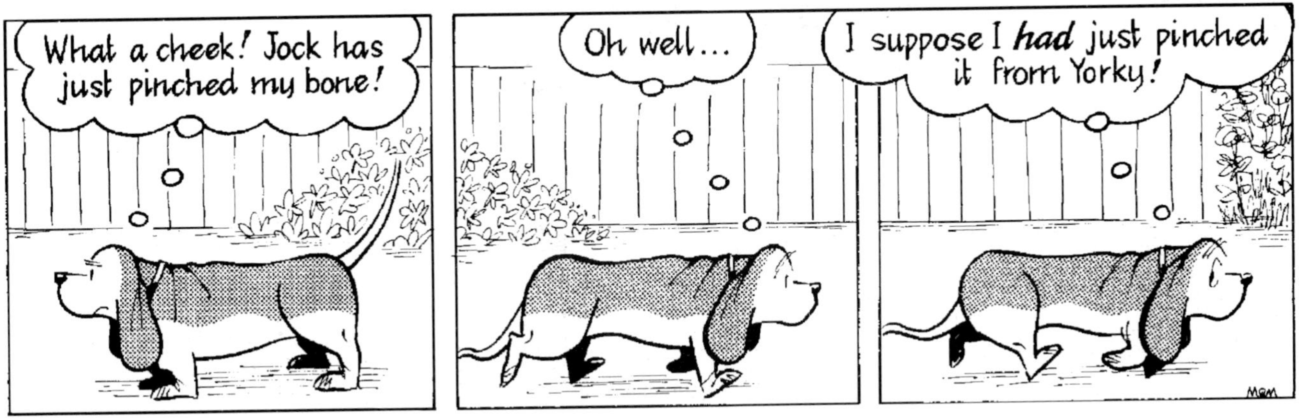
What a cheek! Jock has just pinched my bone!
Oh well...
I suppose I ***had*** just pinched it from Yorky!

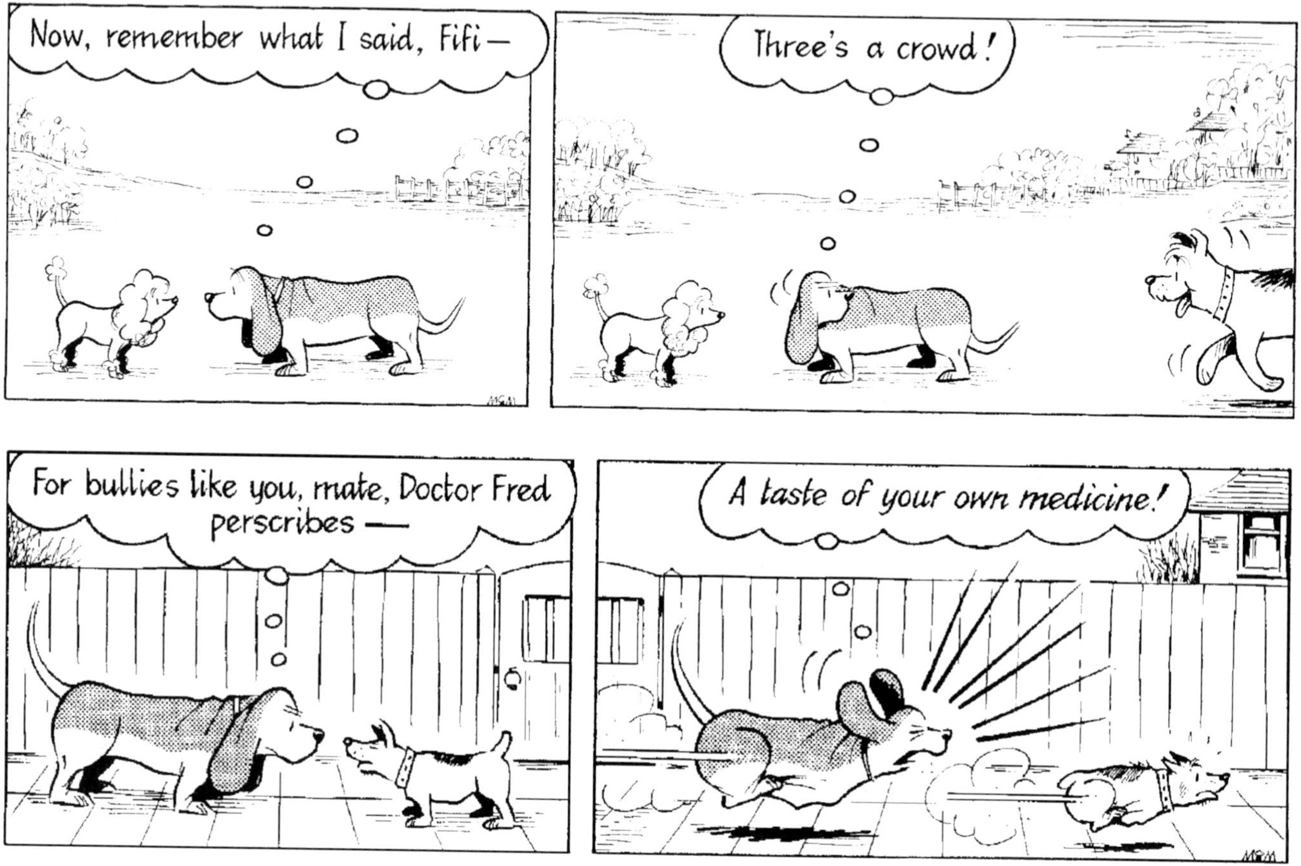
Now, remember what I said, Fifi—
Three's a crowd!
For bullies like you, mate, Doctor Fred perscribes —
A taste of your own medicine!

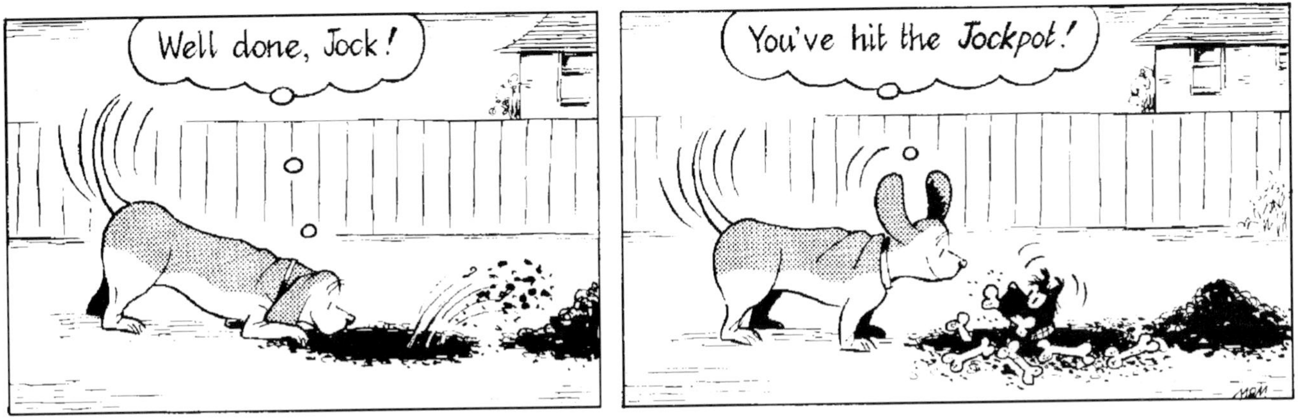
Well done, Jock!
You've hit the *Jockpot!*

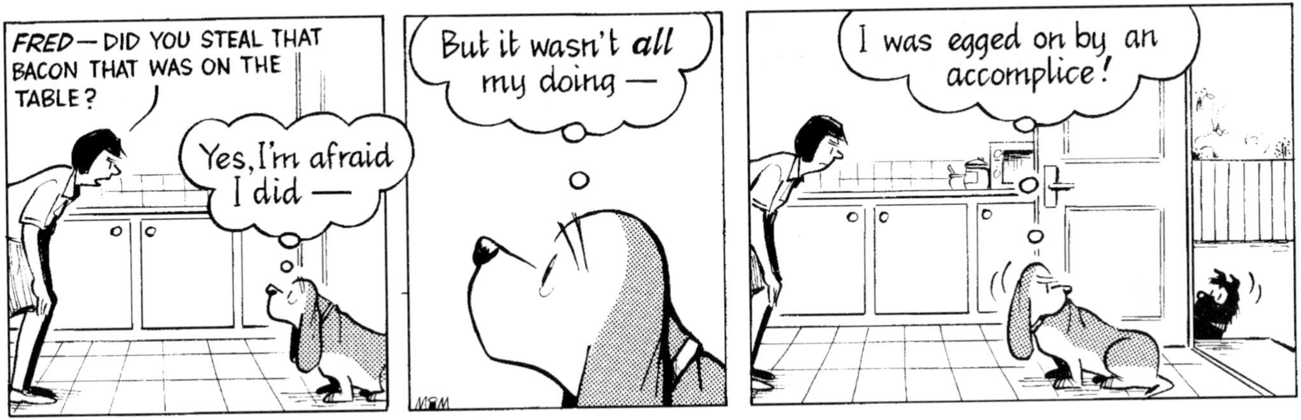
FRED—DID YOU STEAL THAT BACON THAT WAS ON THE TABLE?
Yes, I'm afraid I did —
But it wasn't **all** my doing —
I was egged on by an accomplice!

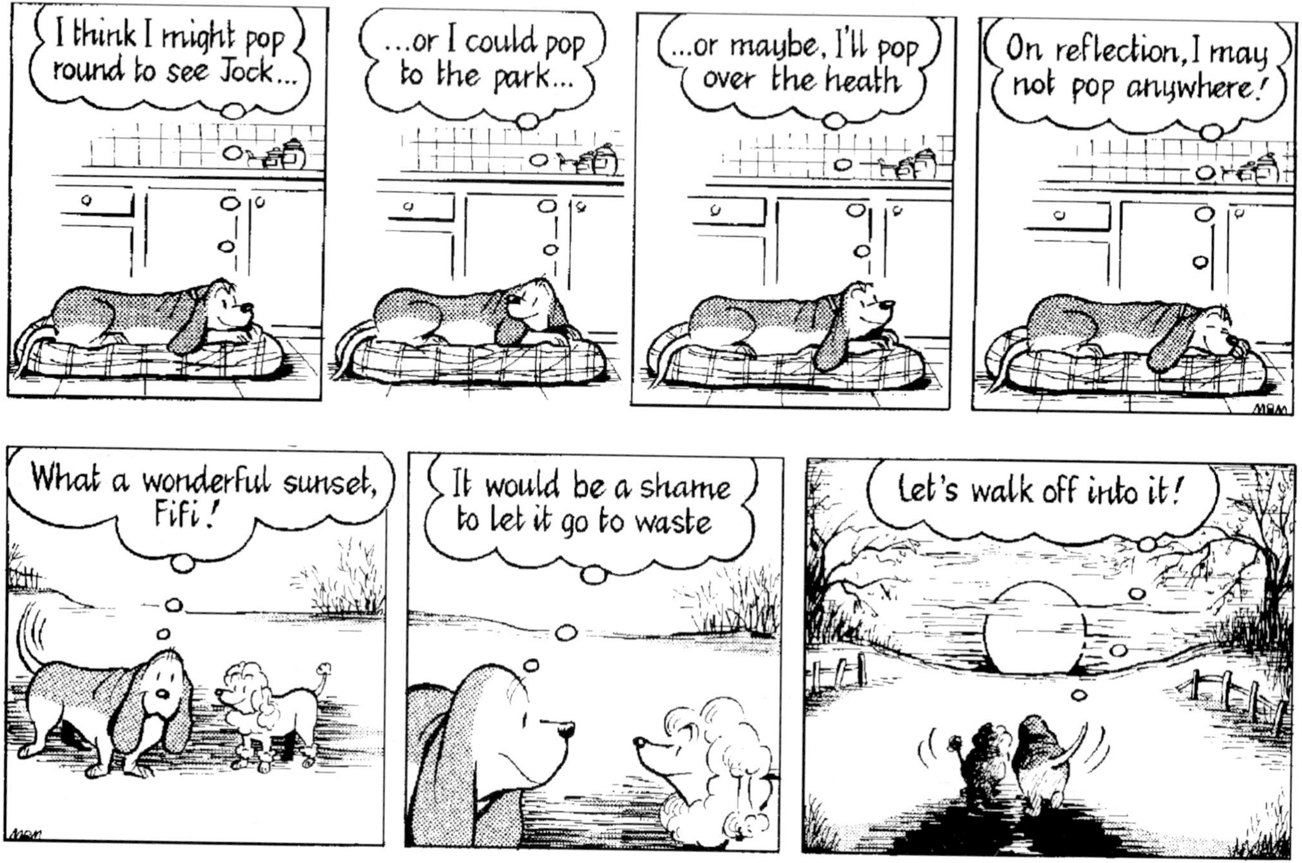
I think I might pop round to see Jock...
...or I could pop to the park...
...or maybe, I'll pop over the heath
On reflection, I may not pop anywhere!
MGM
What a wonderful sunset, Fifi!
MGM
It would be a shame to let it go to waste
Let's walk off into it!

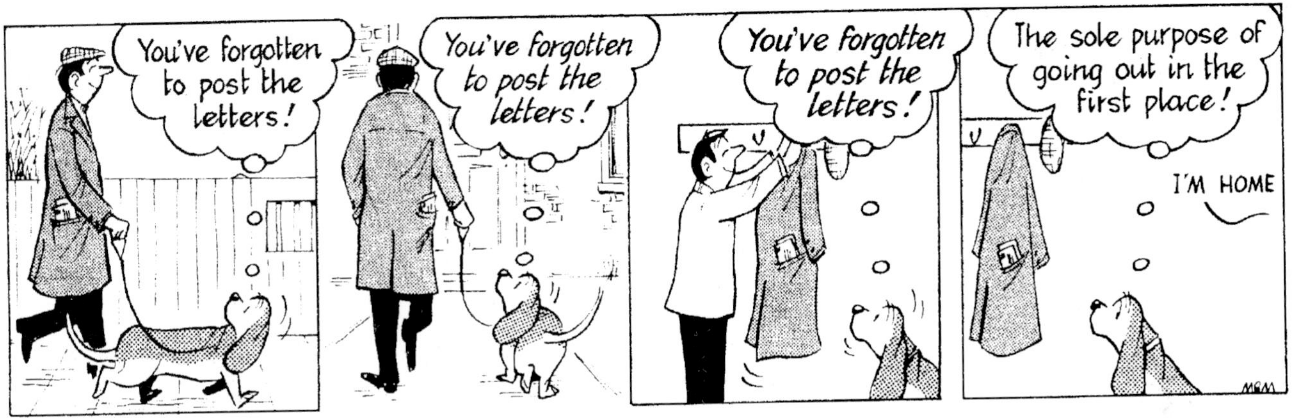
You've forgotten to post the letters!
You've forgotten to post the letters!
You've forgotten to post the letters!
The sole purpose of going out in the first place!
I'M HOME

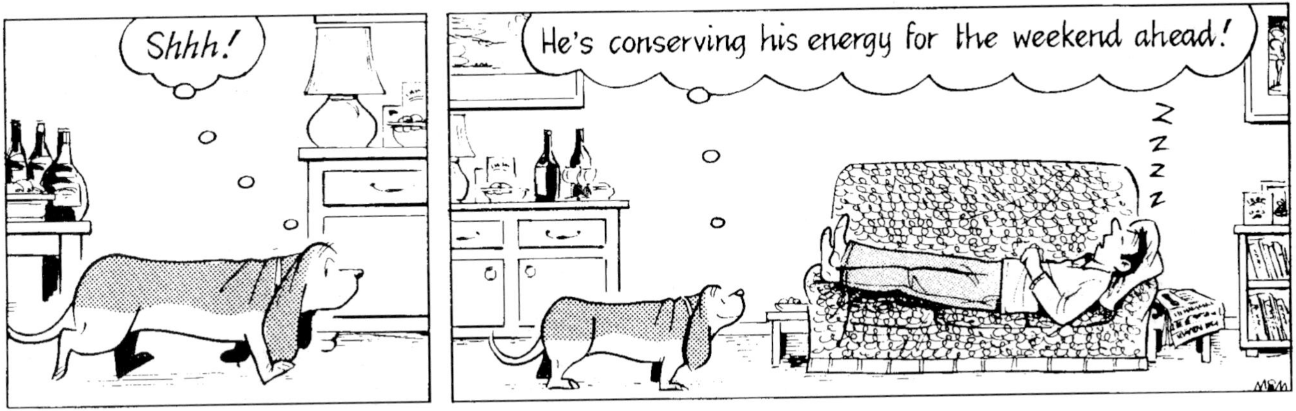
Shhh!
He's conserving his energy for the weekend ahead!
Z Z Z Z

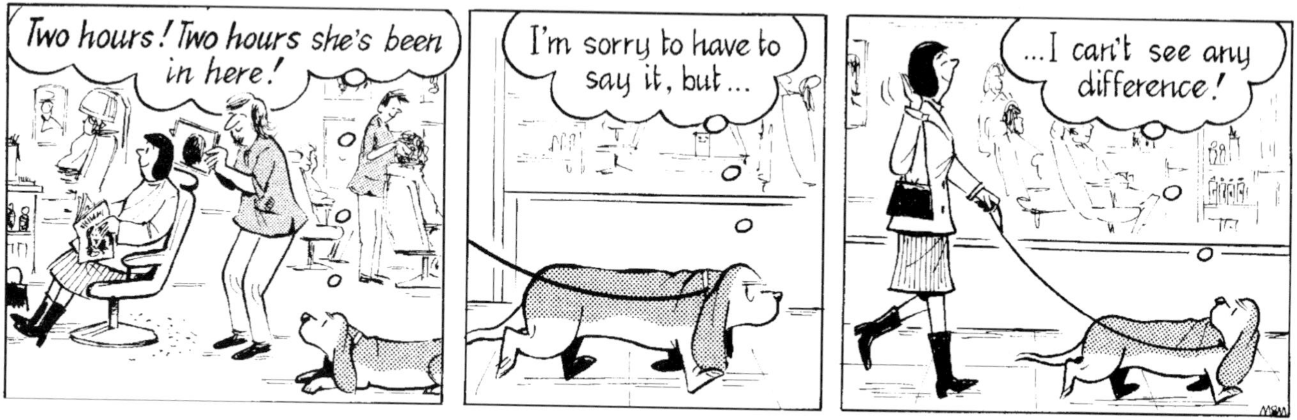
Two hours! Two hours she's been in here!
I'm sorry to have to say it, but...
...I can't see any difference!

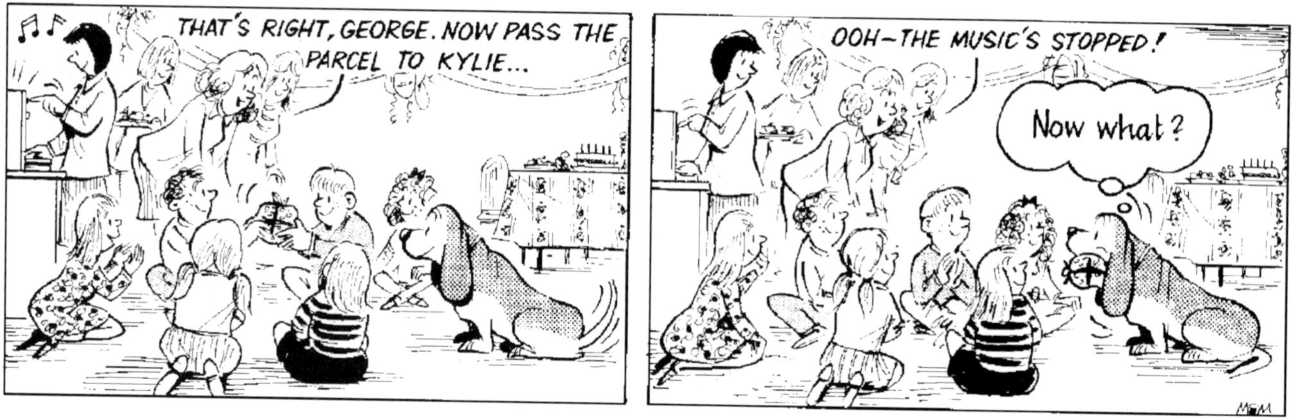
THAT'S RIGHT, GEORGE. NOW PASS THE PARCEL TO KYLIE...
OOH–THE MUSIC'S STOPPED!
Now what?

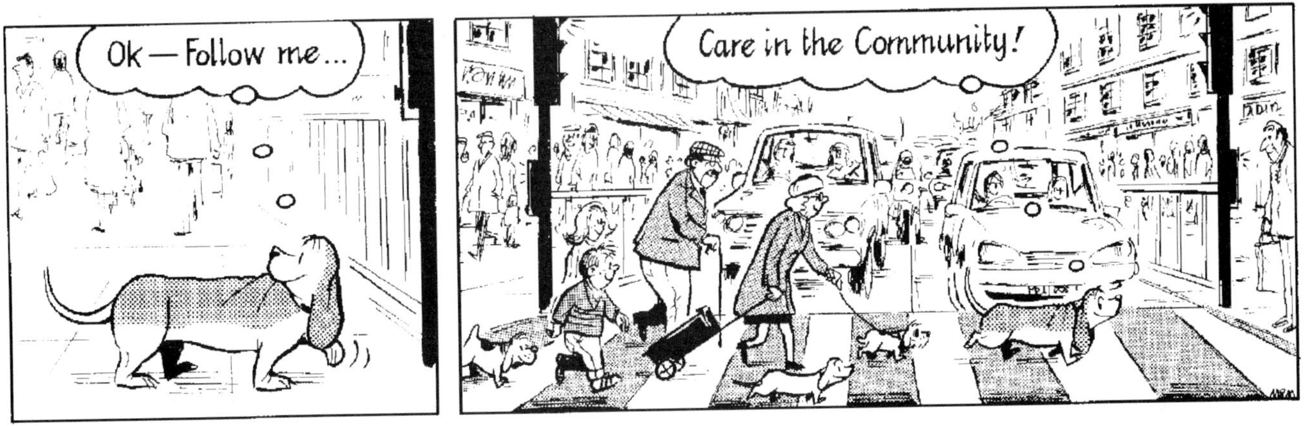
Ok — Follow me...
Care in the Community!

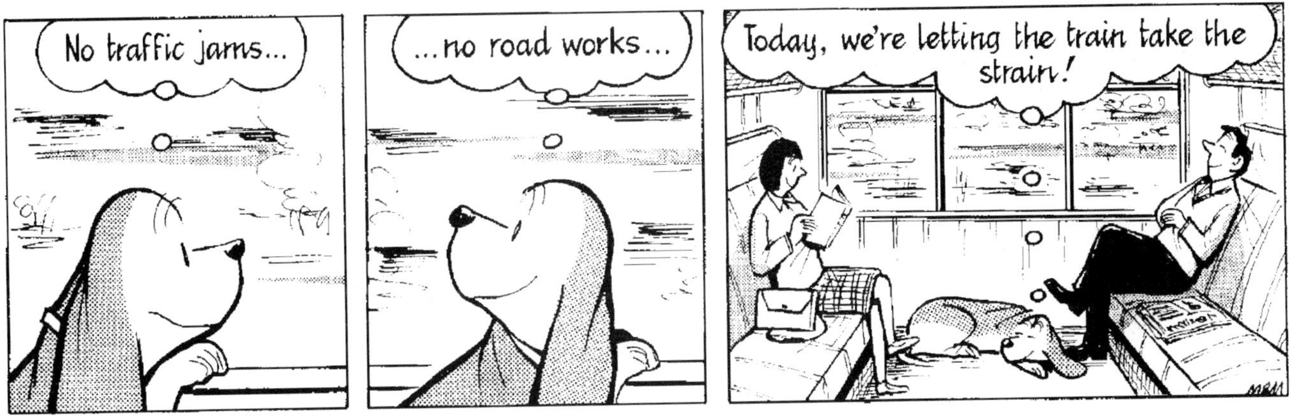
No traffic jams...
...no road works...
Today, we're letting the train take the strain!

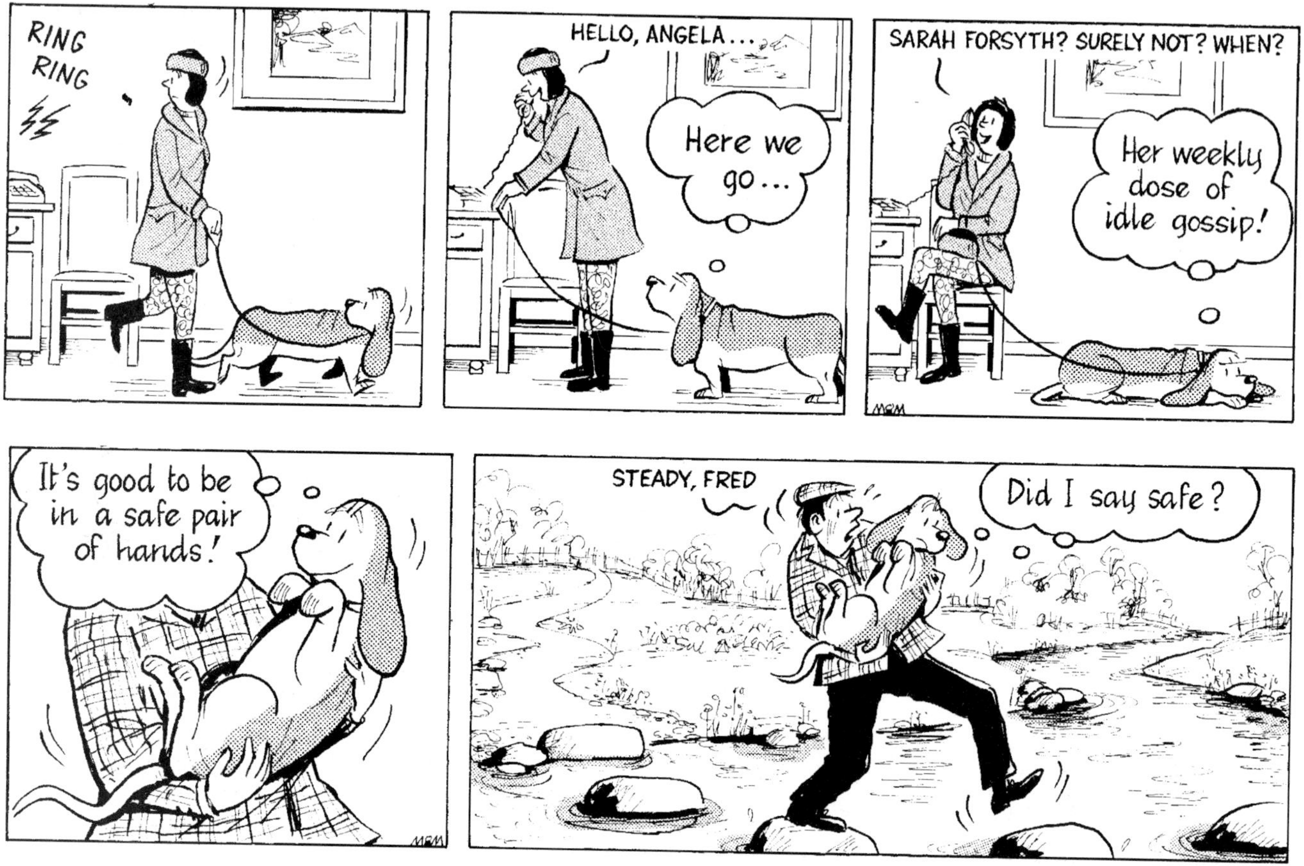
RING RING
HELLO, ANGELA...
Here we go...
SARAH FORSYTH? SURELY NOT? WHEN?
Her weekly dose of idle gossip!
MGM
It's good to be in a safe pair of hands!
MGM
STEADY, FRED
Did I say safe?

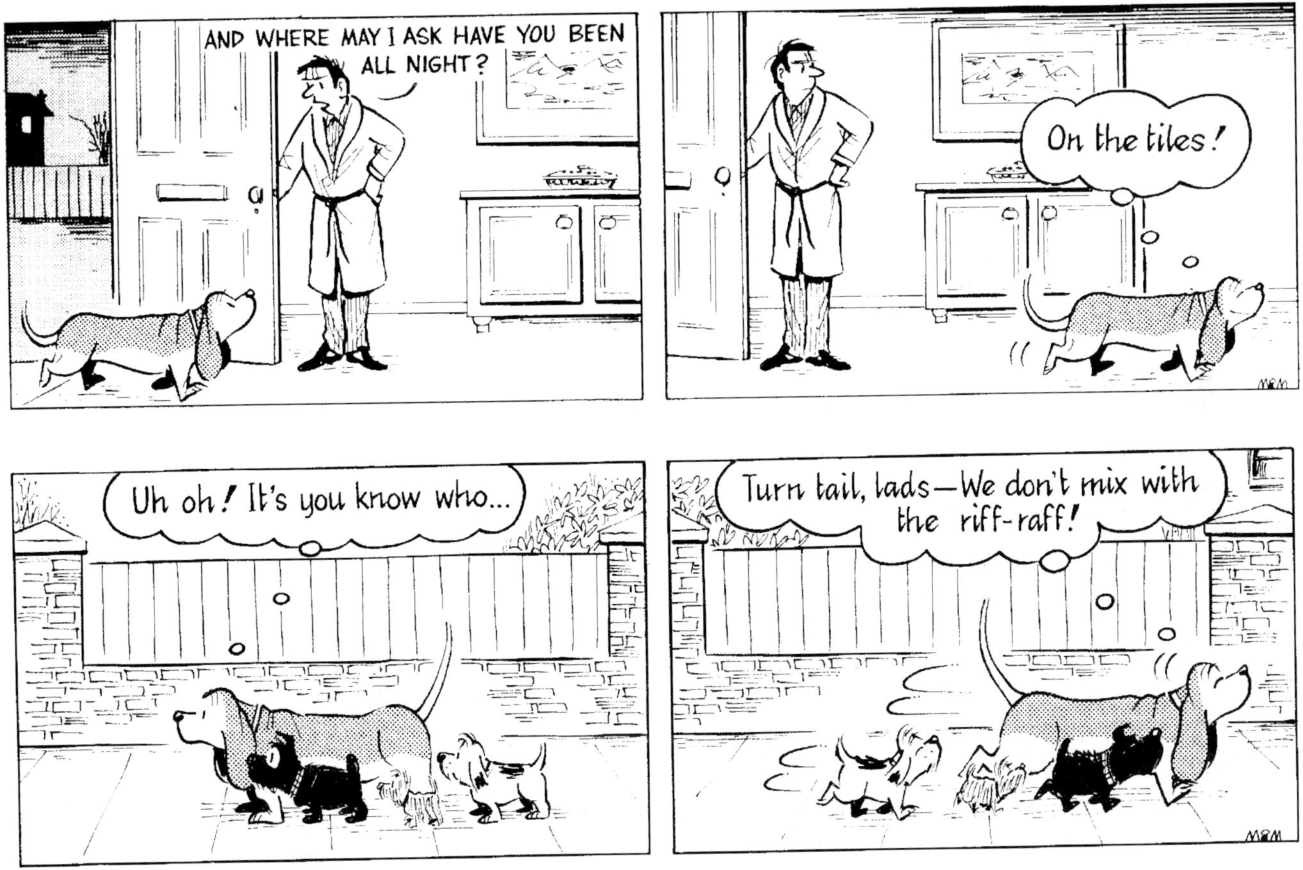
AND WHERE MAY I ASK HAVE YOU BEEN ALL NIGHT?
On the tiles!
Uh oh! It's you know who...
Turn tail, lads—We don't mix with the riff-raff!

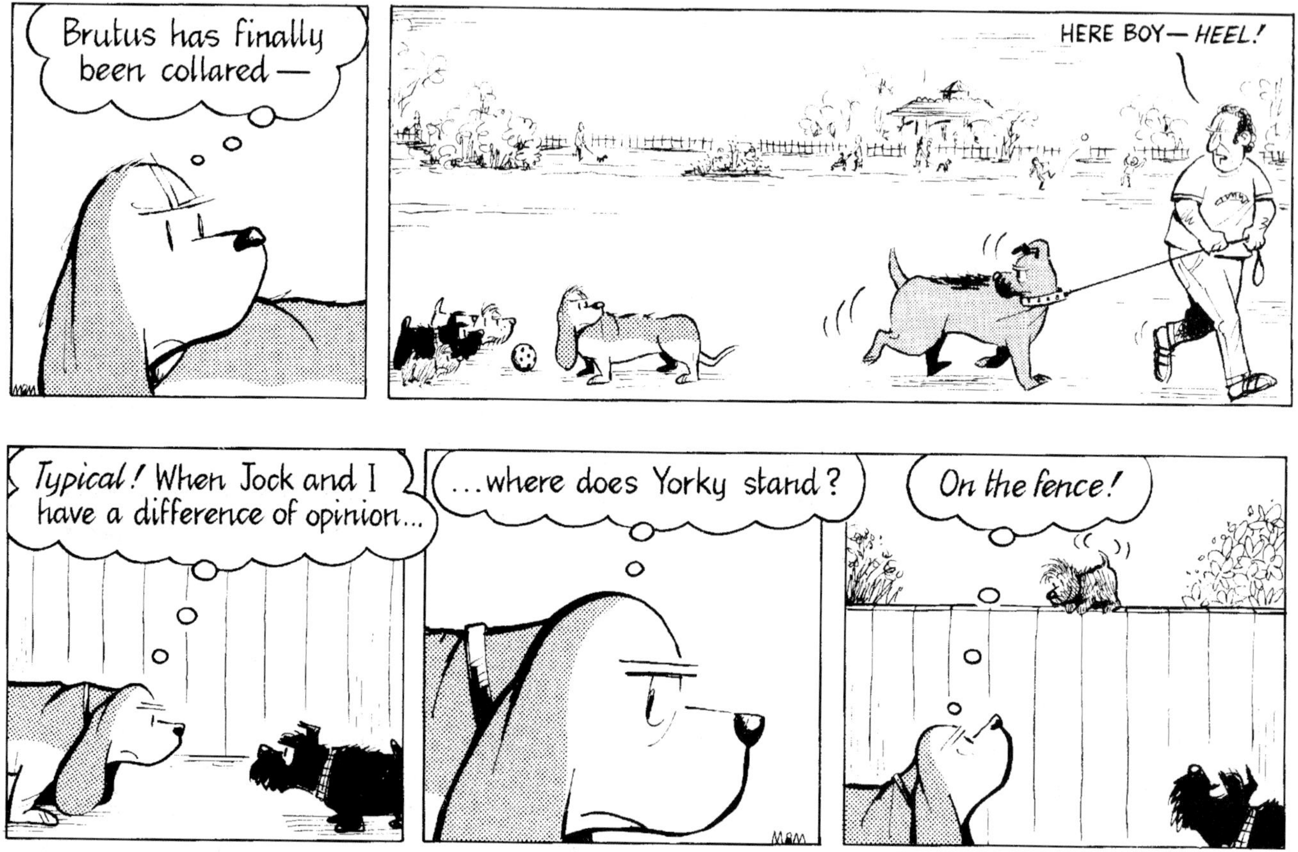
Brutus has finally been collared —
HERE BOY — HEEL!
Typical! When Jock and I have a difference of opinion...
...where does Yorky stand?
On the fence!

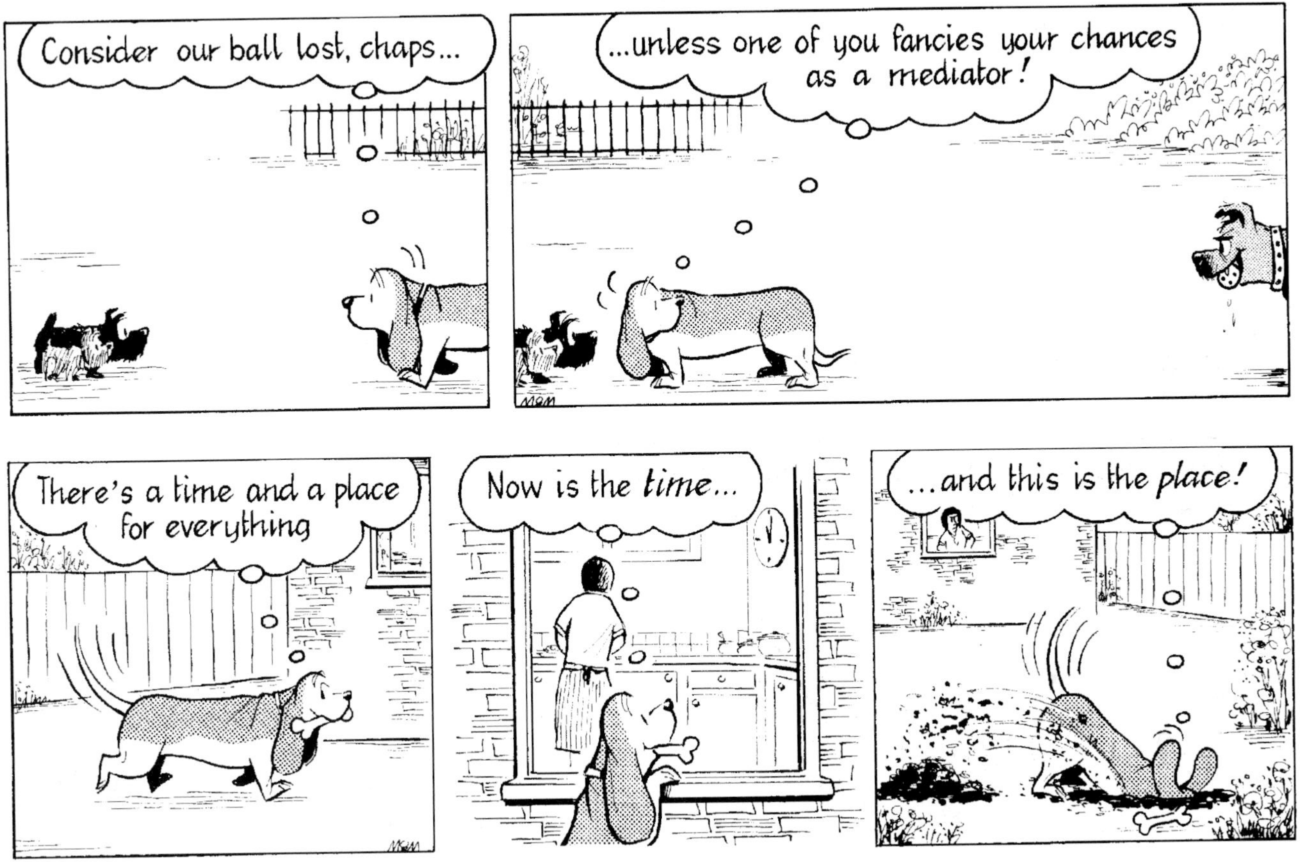
Consider our ball lost, chaps...
...unless one of you fancies your chances as a mediator!
There's a time and a place for everything
Now is the *time*...
...and this is the *place*!

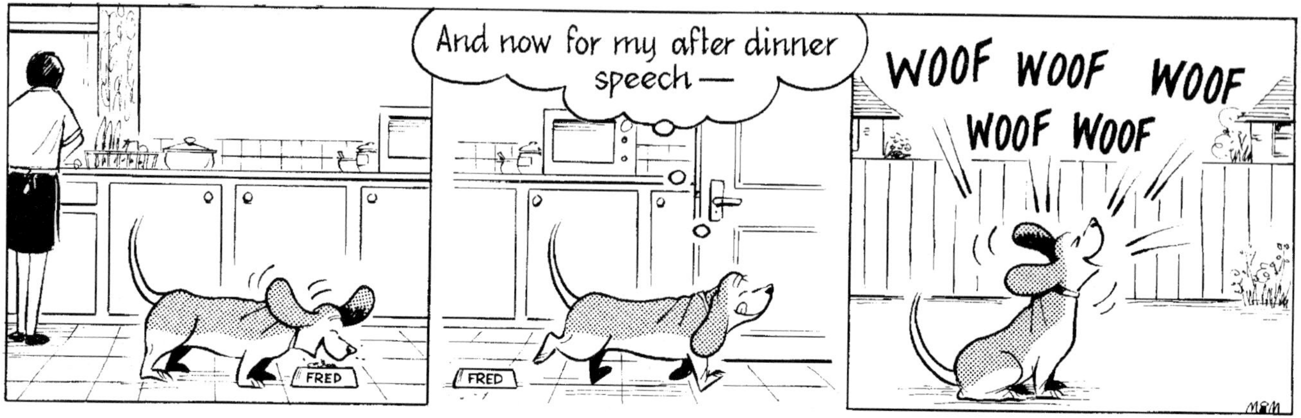
FRED
And now for my after dinner speech —
FRED
WOOF WOOF WOOF
WOOF WOOF
M&M

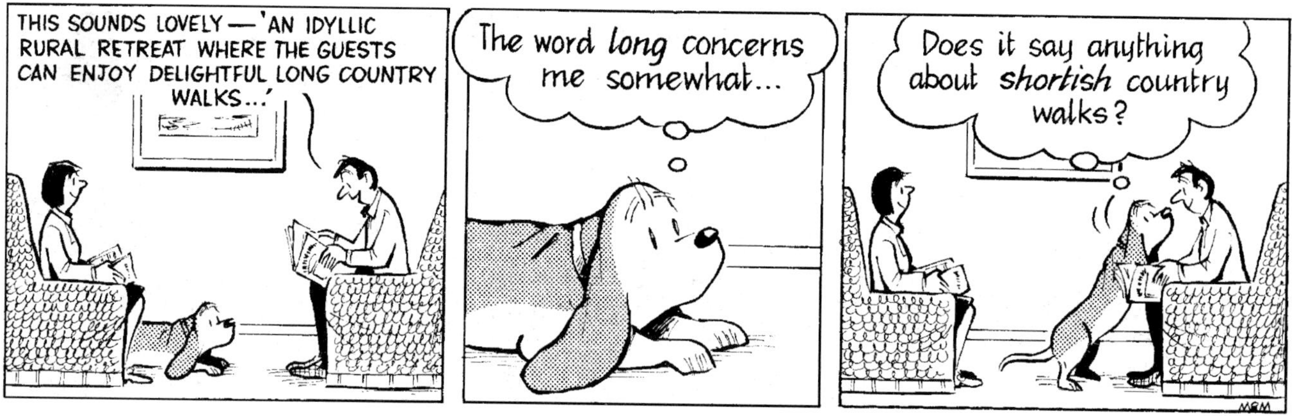
THIS SOUNDS LOVELY — 'AN IDYLLIC RURAL RETREAT WHERE THE GUESTS CAN ENJOY DELIGHTFUL LONG COUNTRY WALKS...'
The word *long* concerns me somewhat...
Does it say anything about *shortish* country walks?
M&M

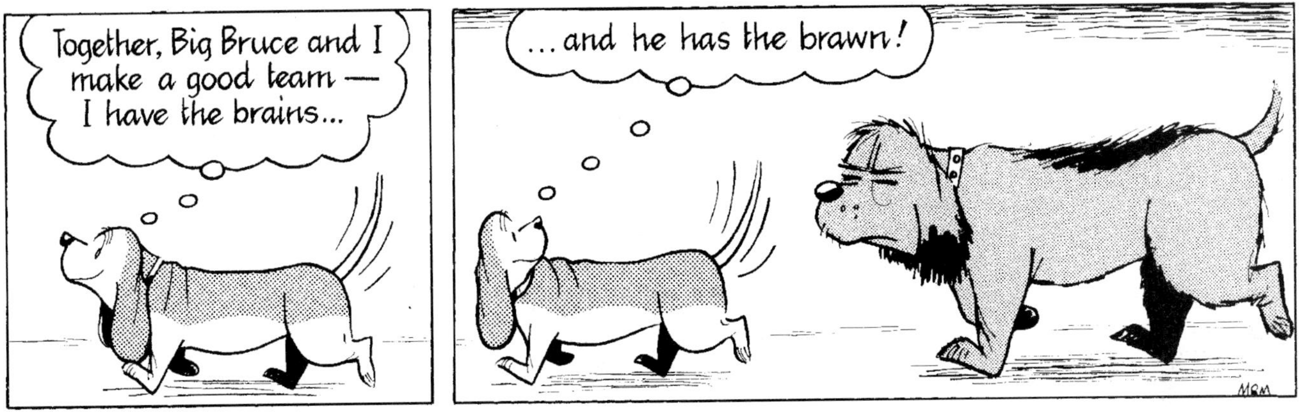
Together, Big Bruce and I make a good team — I have the brains...
... and he has the brawn!

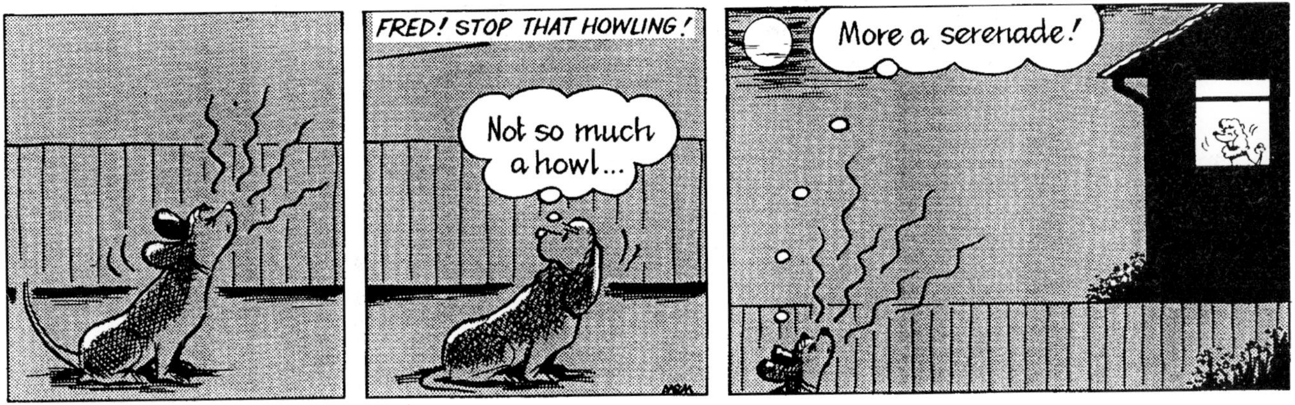
FRED! STOP THAT HOWLING!
Not so much a howl...
More a serenade!

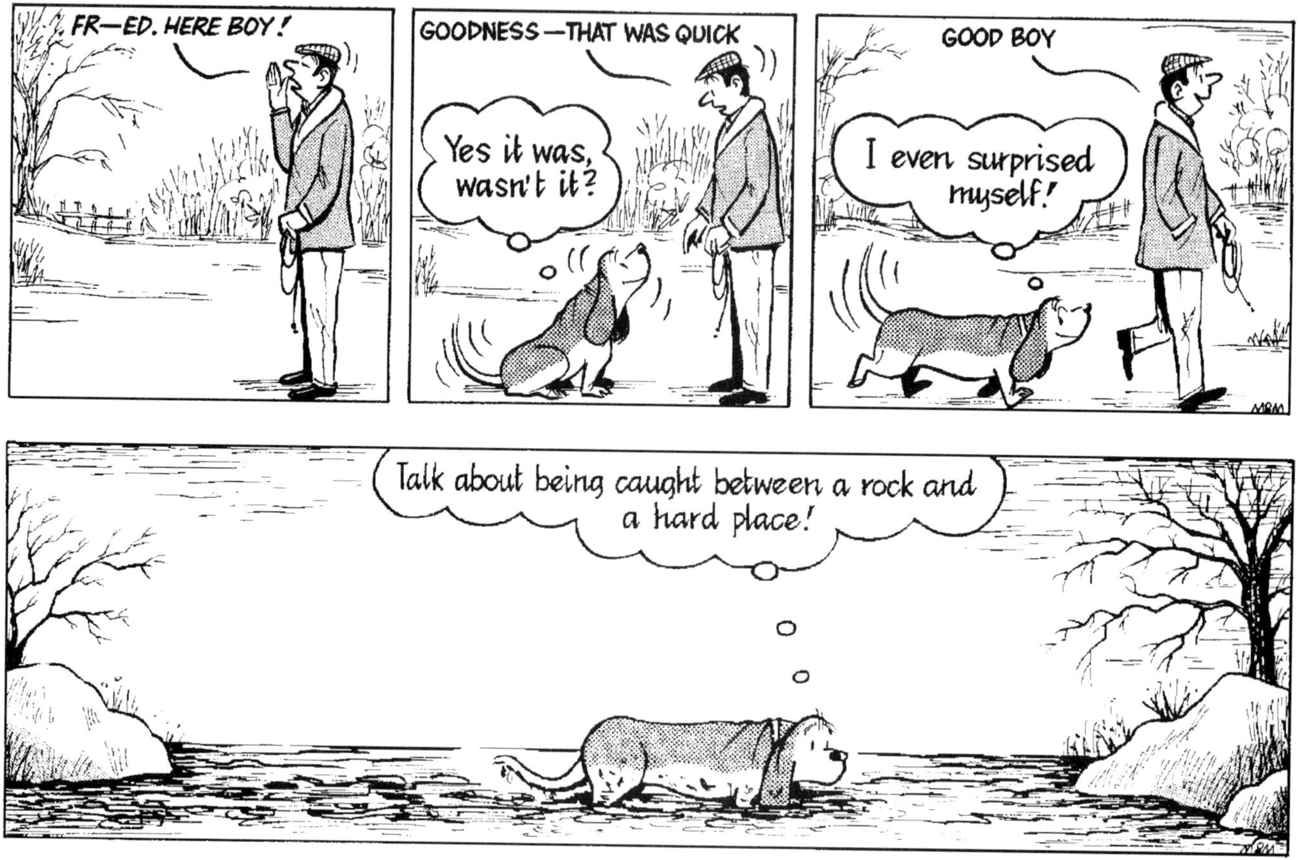
FR—ED. HERE BOY!
GOODNESS—THAT WAS QUICK
Yes it was, wasn't it?
GOOD BOY
I even surprised myself!
Talk about being caught between a rock and a hard place!

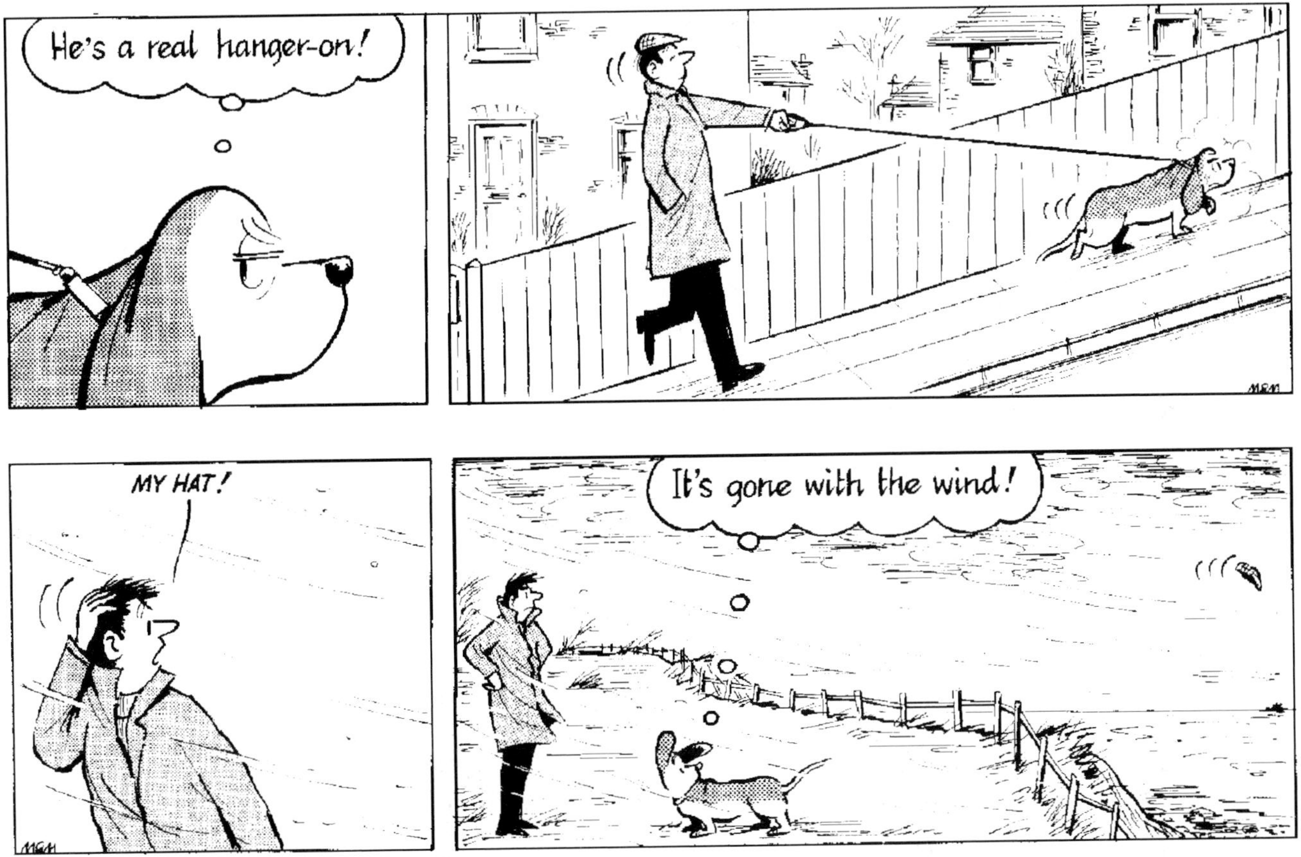
He's a real hanger-on!
MY HAT!
It's gone with the wind!

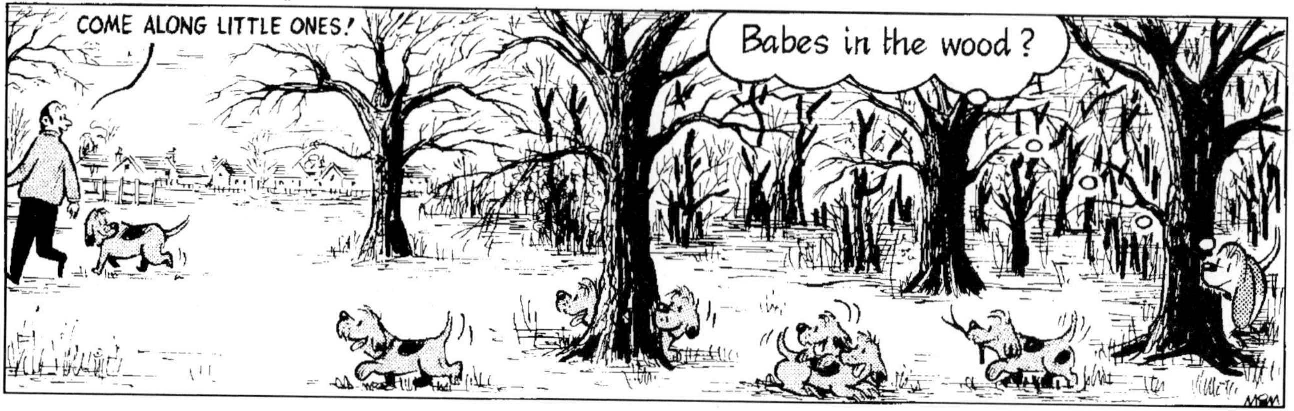
COME ALONG LITTLE ONES!
Babes in the wood?

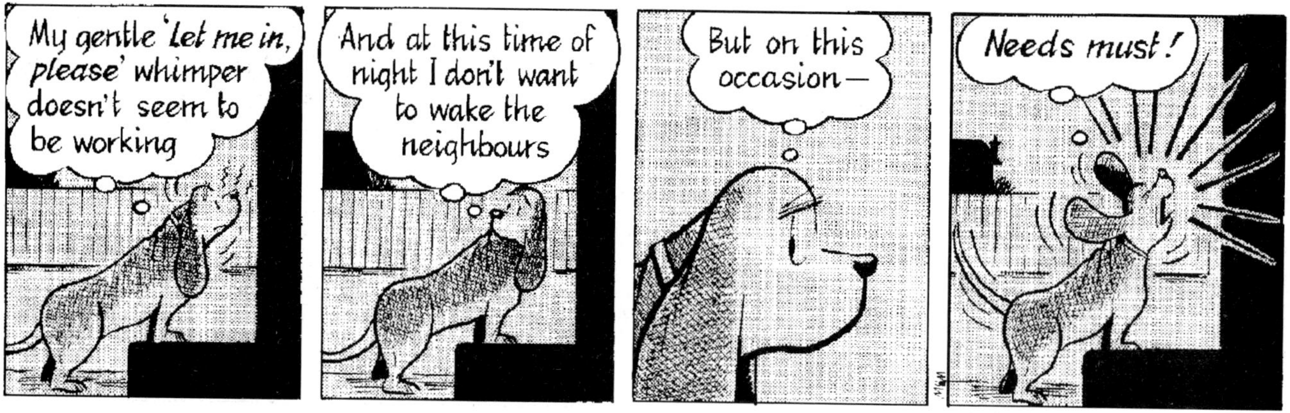
My gentle 'let me in, please' whimper doesn't seem to be working
And at this time of night I don't want to wake the neighbours
But on this occasion—
Needs must!

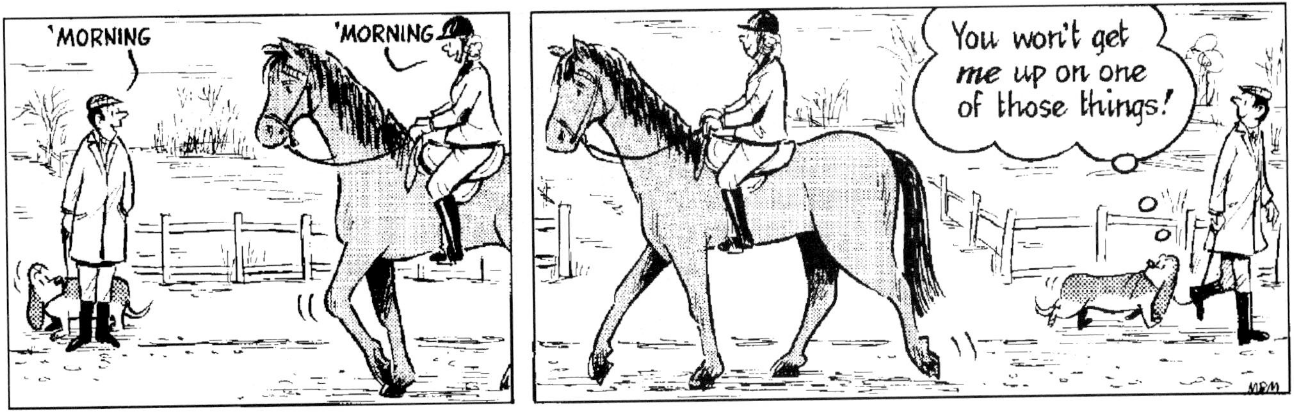
'MORNING
'MORNING
You won't get *me* up on one of those things!

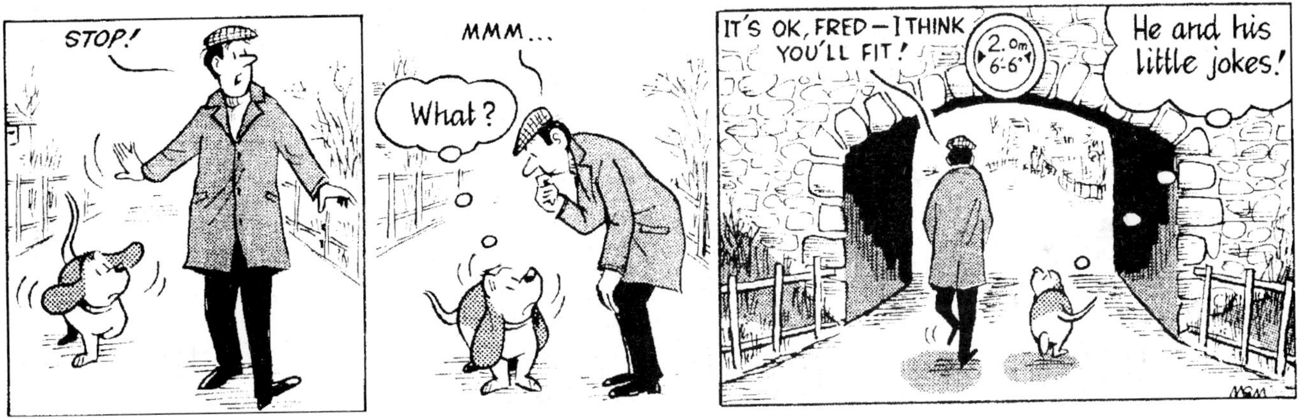
STOP!
MMM...
What?
IT'S OK, FRED — I THINK YOU'LL FIT!
2.0m
6'6"
He and his little jokes!

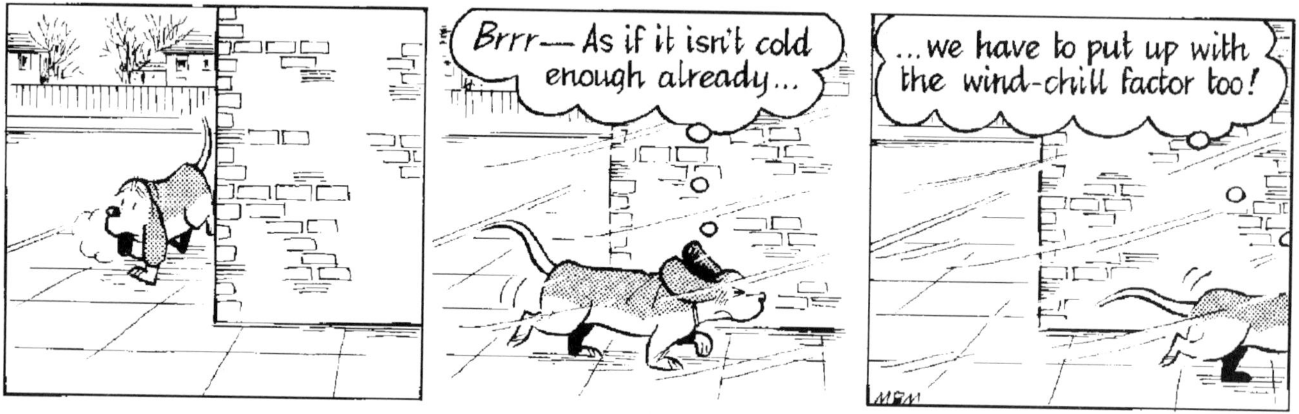
Brrr— As if it isn't cold enough already...
...we have to put up with the wind-chill factor too!

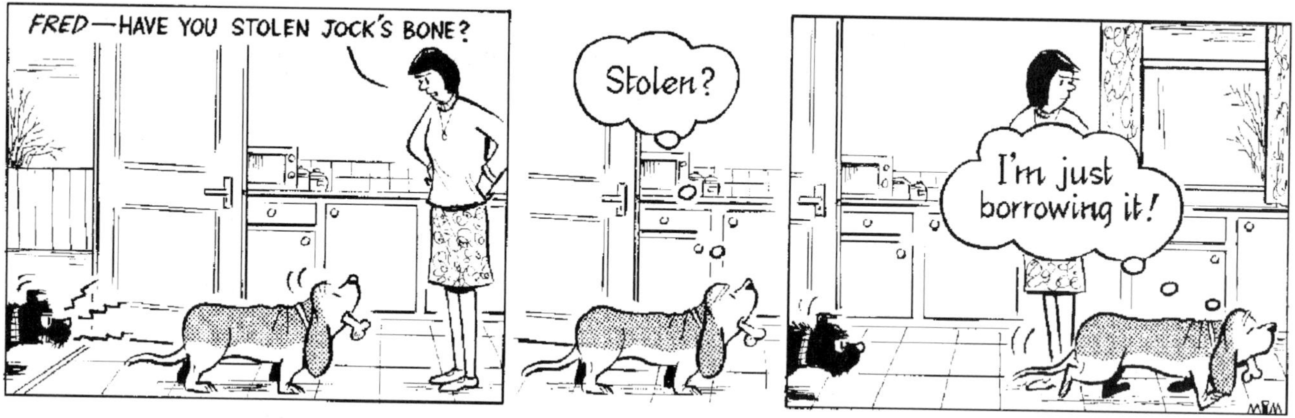
FRED—HAVE YOU STOLEN JOCK'S BONE?
Stolen?
I'm just borrowing it!

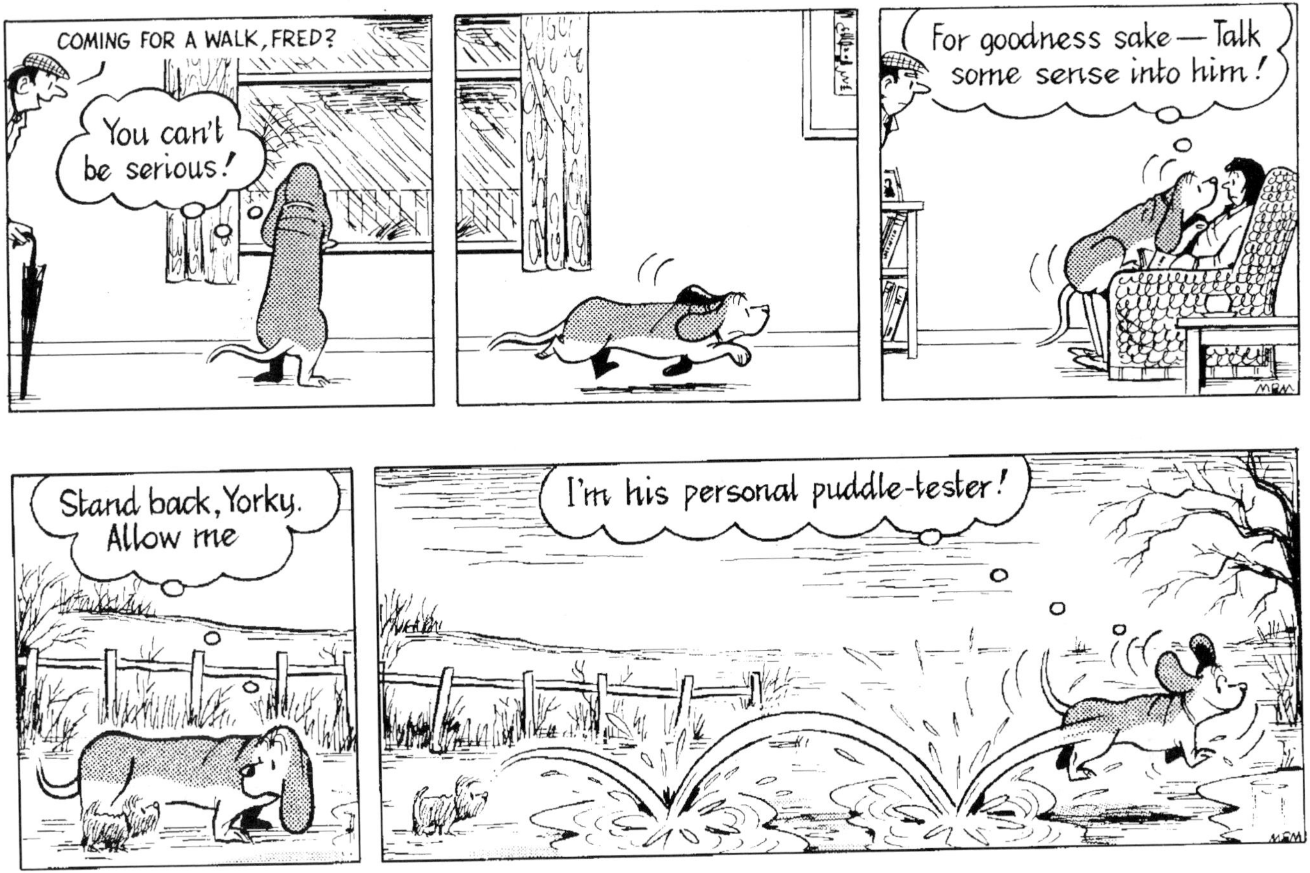
COMING FOR A WALK, FRED?
You can't be serious!
For goodness sake — Talk some sense into him!
Stand back, Yorky. Allow me
I'm his personal puddle-tester!

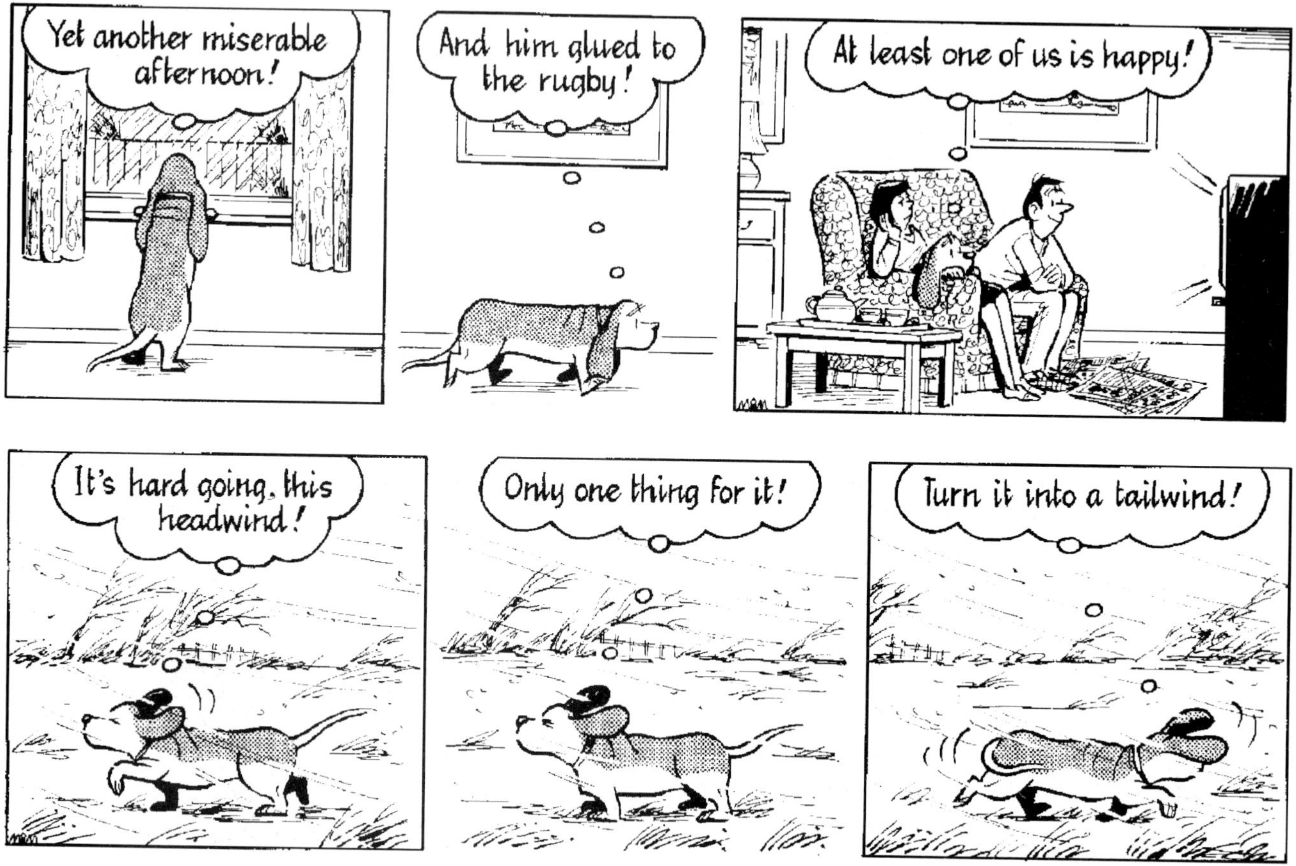
Yet another miserable afternoon!
And him glued to the rugby!
At least one of us is happy!
It's hard going, this headwind!
Only one thing for it!
Turn it into a tailwind!

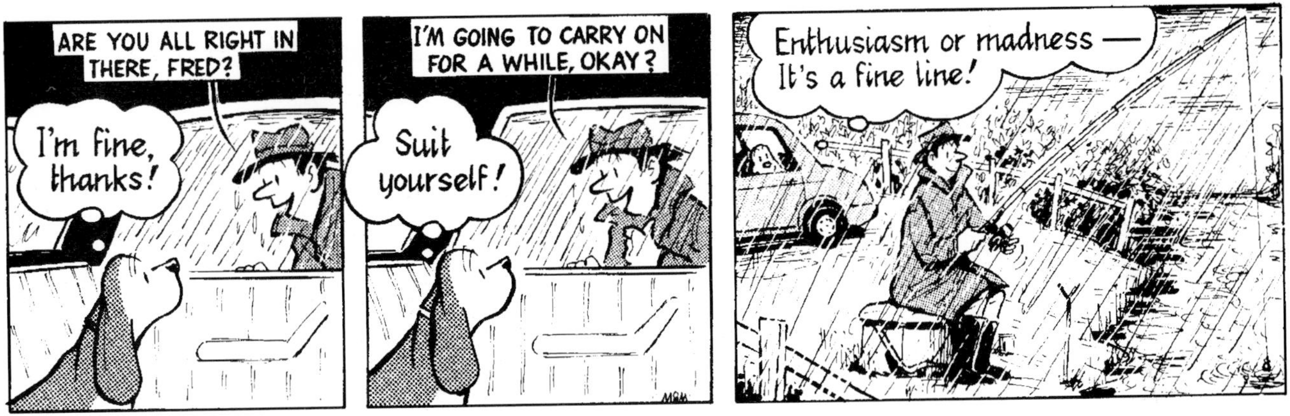
ARE YOU ALL RIGHT IN THERE, FRED?
I'm fine, thanks!
I'M GOING TO CARRY ON FOR A WHILE, OKAY?
Suit yourself!
Enthusiasm or madness — It's a fine line!

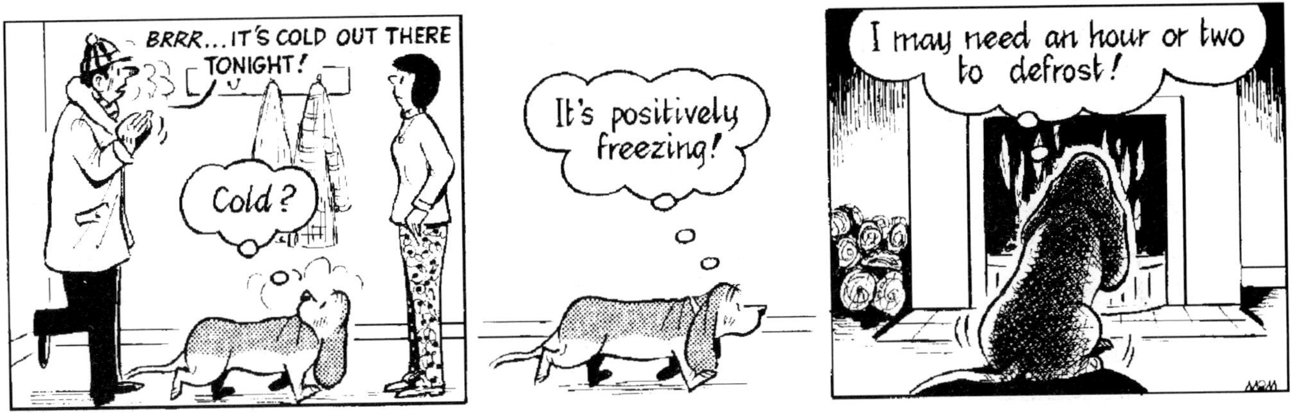
BRRR... IT'S COLD OUT THERE TONIGHT!
Cold?
It's positively freezing!
I may need an hour or two to defrost!

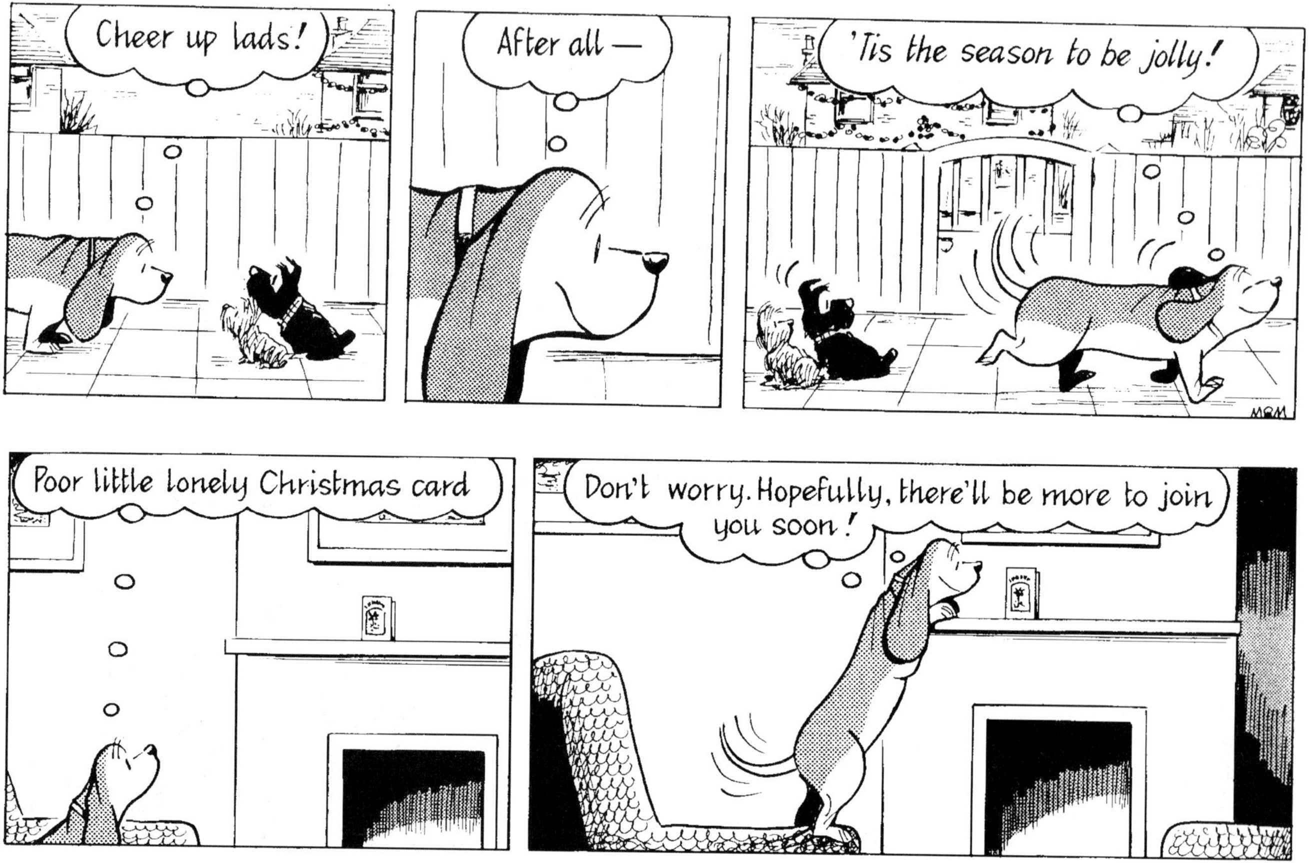
Cheer up lads!
After all —
'Tis the season to be jolly!
MGM
Poor little lonely Christmas card
Don't worry. Hopefully, there'll be more to join you soon!

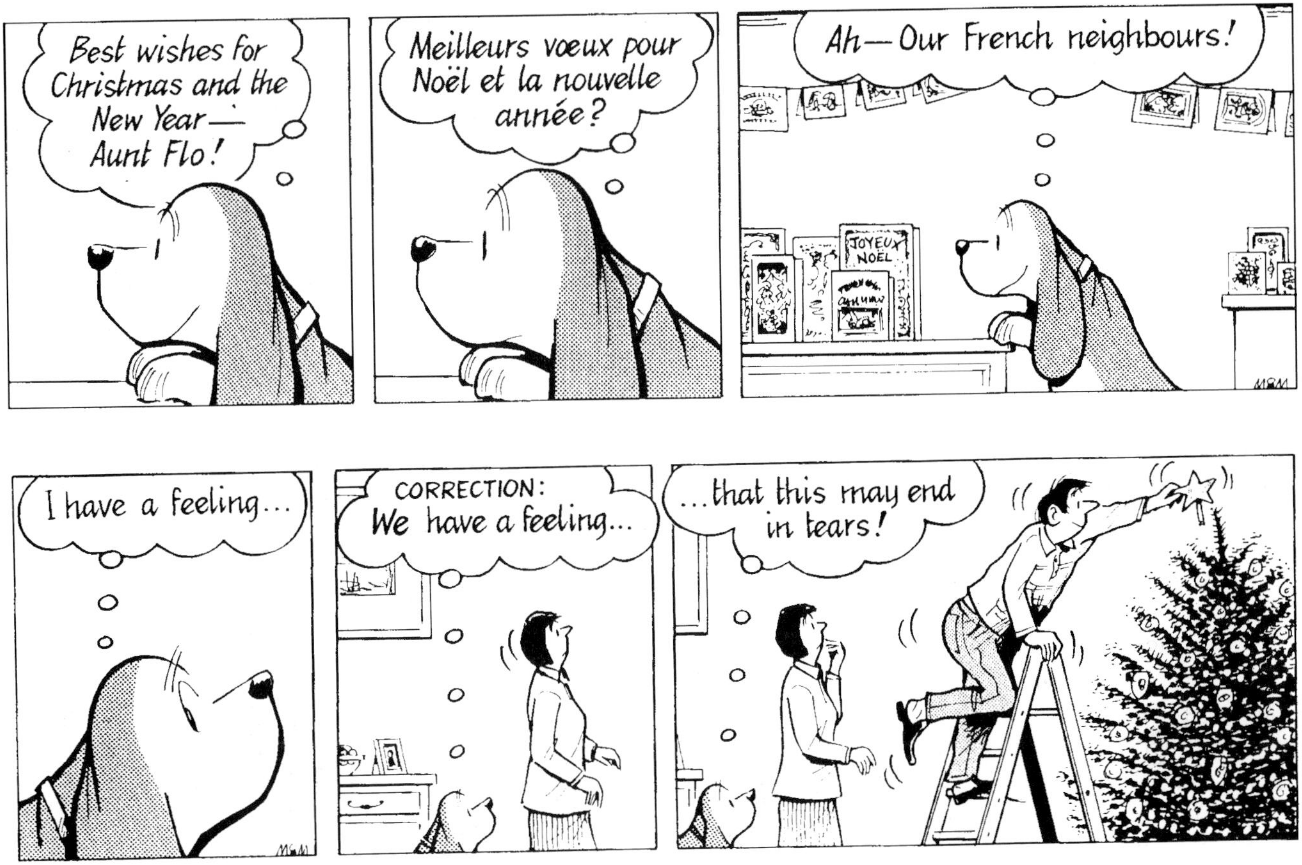
Best wishes for Christmas and the New Year— Aunt Flo!
Meilleurs voeux pour Noël et la nouvelle année?
Ah—Our French neighbours!
JOYEUX NOËL
I have a feeling...
CORRECTION: We have a feeling...
...that this may end in tears!

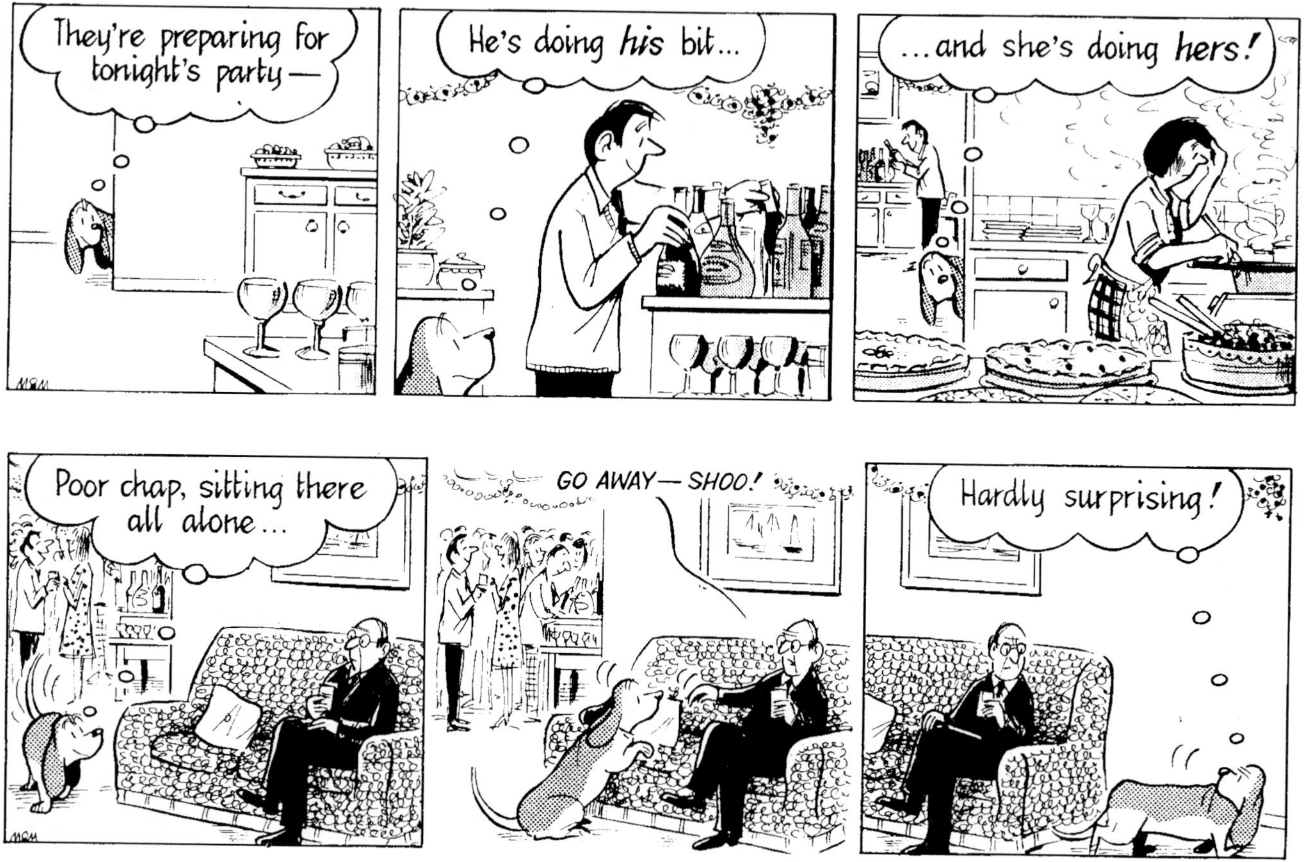
They're preparing for tonight's party —
He's doing *his* bit...
...and she's doing *hers!*
Poor chap, sitting there all alone...
GO AWAY — SHOO!
Hardly surprising!

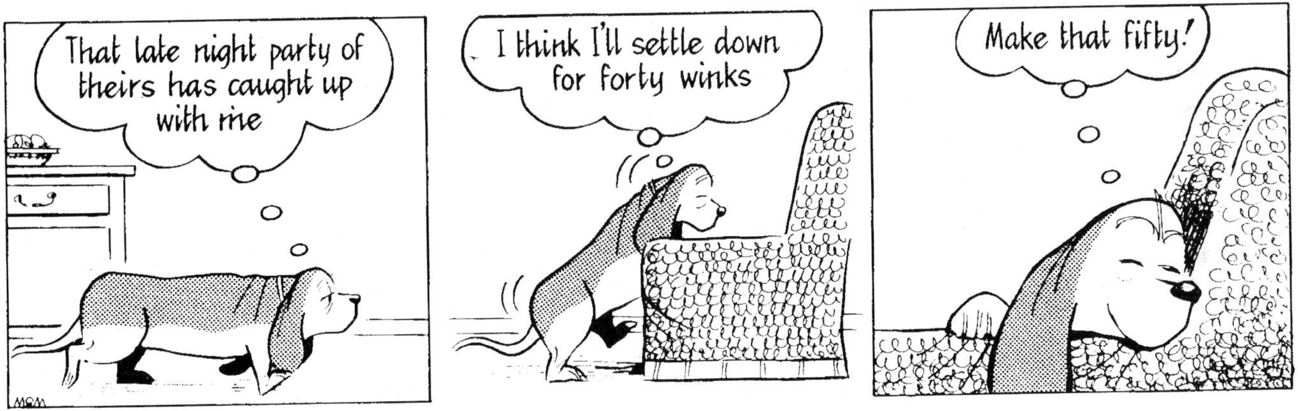
That late night party of theirs has caught up with me
I think I'll settle down for forty winks
Make that fifty!

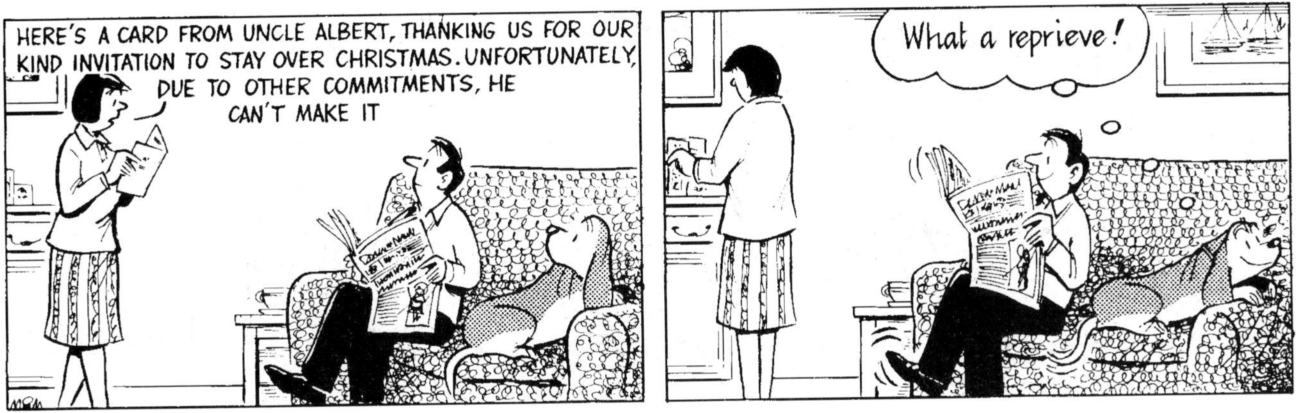
HERE'S A CARD FROM UNCLE ALBERT, THANKING US FOR OUR KIND INVITATION TO STAY OVER CHRISTMAS. UNFORTUNATELY, DUE TO OTHER COMMITMENTS, HE CAN'T MAKE IT
What a reprieve!

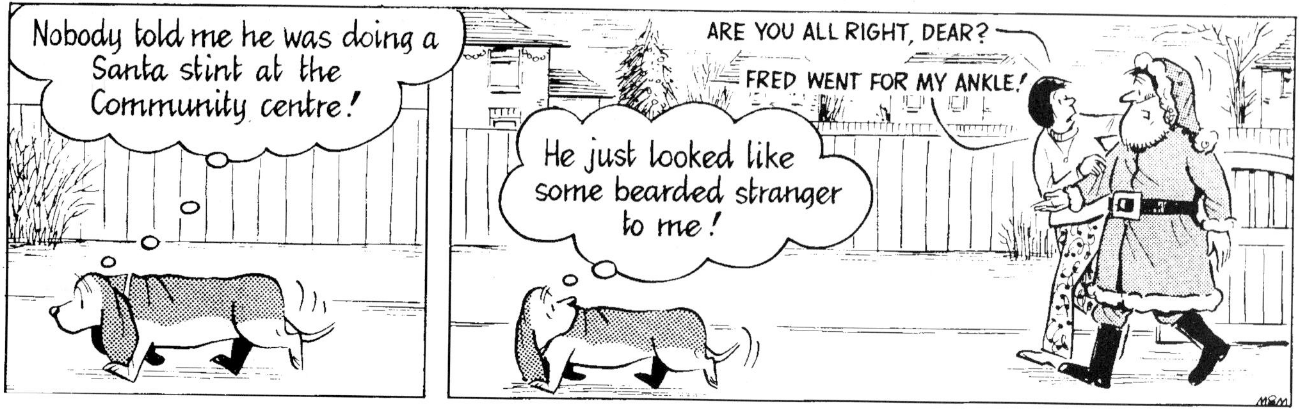
Nobody told me he was doing a Santa stint at the Community centre!
ARE YOU ALL RIGHT, DEAR?
FRED WENT FOR MY ANKLE!
He just looked like some bearded stranger to me!

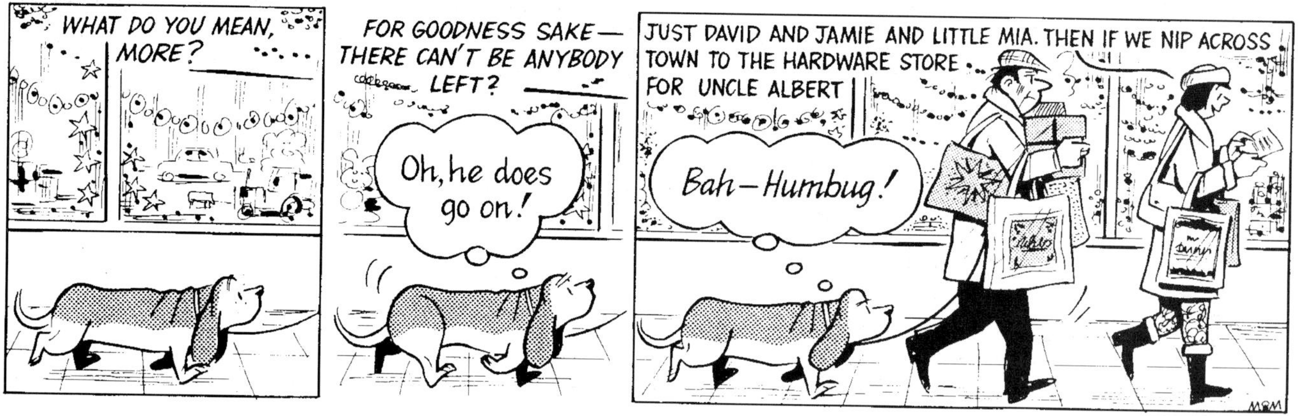
WHAT DO YOU MEAN, MORE?
FOR GOODNESS SAKE— THERE CAN'T BE ANYBODY LEFT?
Oh, he does go on!
JUST DAVID AND JAMIE AND LITTLE MIA. THEN IF WE NIP ACROSS TOWN TO THE HARDWARE STORE FOR UNCLE ALBERT
Bah–Humbug!

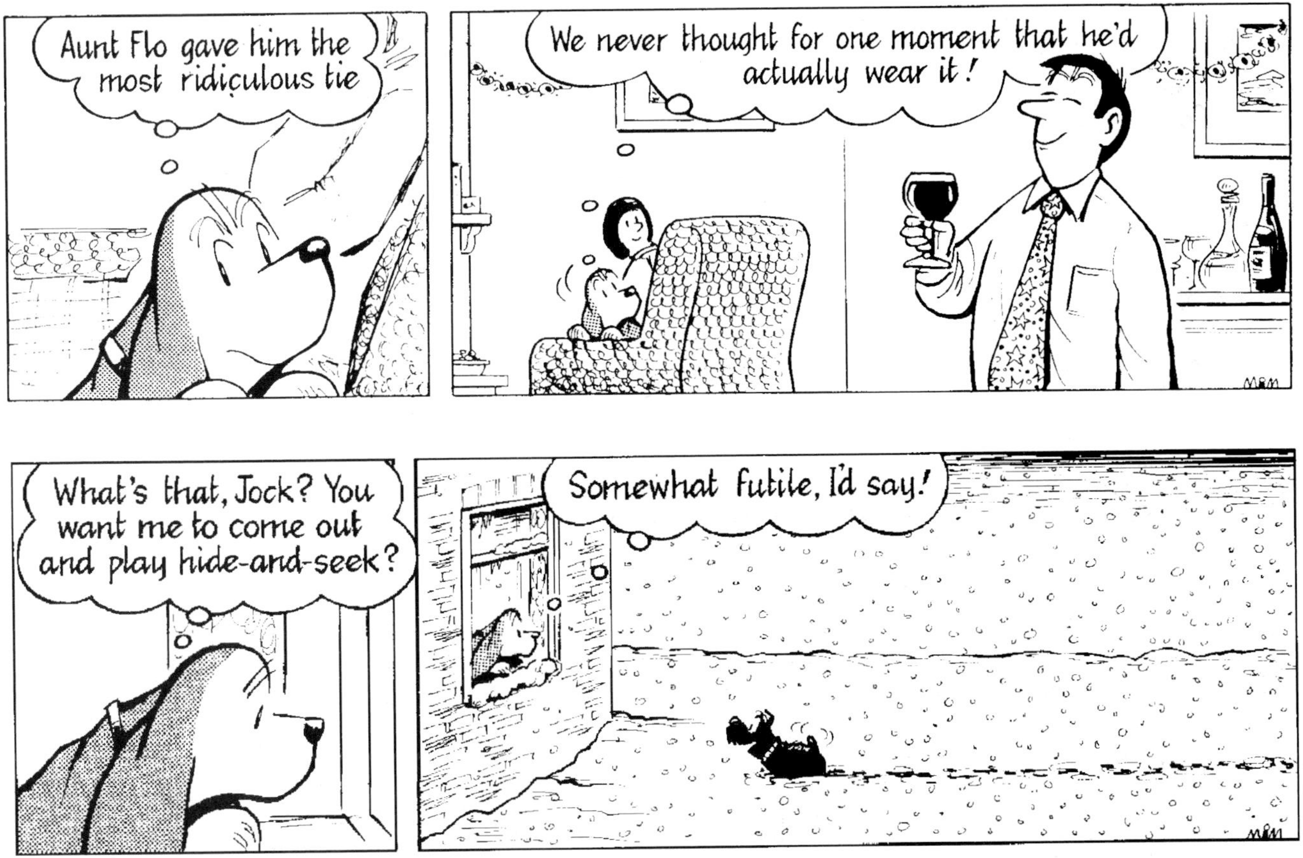
Aunt Flo gave him the most ridiculous tie
We never thought for one moment that he'd actually wear it!
What's that, Jock? You want me to come out and play hide-and-seek?
Somewhat futile, I'd say!

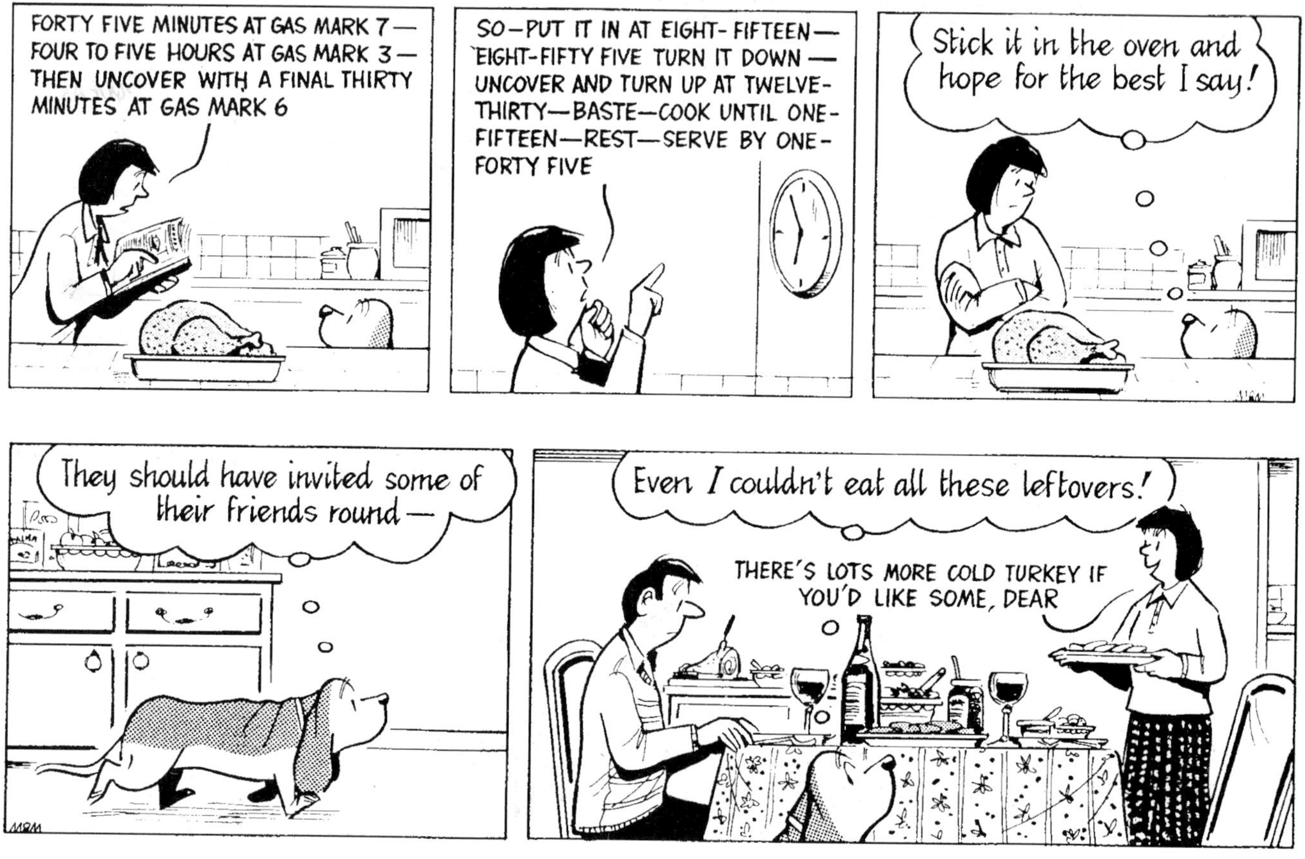

FORTY FIVE MINUTES AT GAS MARK 7— FOUR TO FIVE HOURS AT GAS MARK 3— THEN UNCOVER WITH A FINAL THIRTY MINUTES AT GAS MARK 6
SO—PUT IT IN AT EIGHT-FIFTEEN— EIGHT-FIFTY FIVE TURN IT DOWN— UNCOVER AND TURN UP AT TWELVE-THIRTY—BASTE—COOK UNTIL ONE-FIFTEEN—REST—SERVE BY ONE-FORTY FIVE
Stick it in the oven and hope for the best I say!
They should have invited some of their friends round—
Even *I* couldn't eat all these leftovers!
THERE'S LOTS MORE COLD TURKEY IF YOU'D LIKE SOME, DEAR

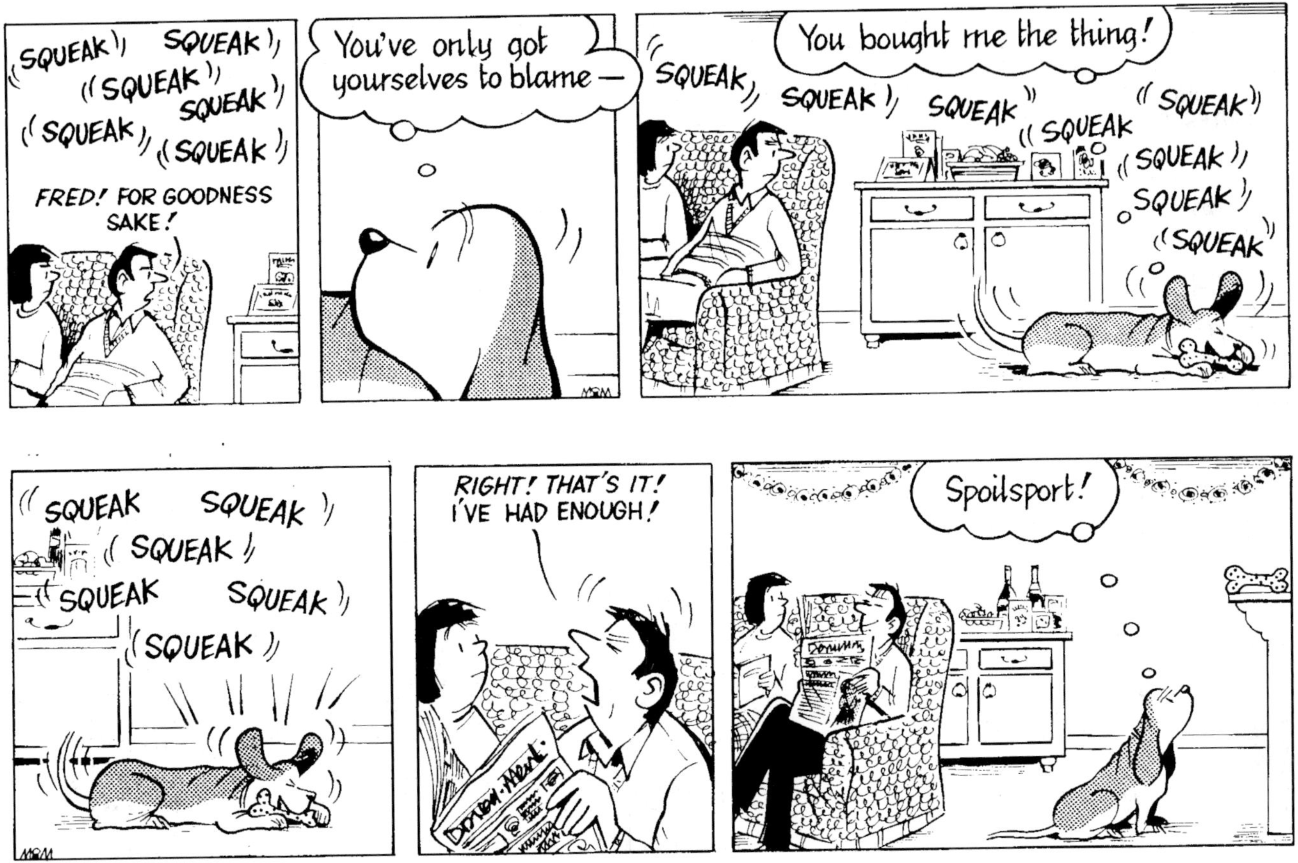
SQUEAK SQUEAK SQUEAK SQUEAK SQUEAK SQUEAK
FRED! FOR GOODNESS SAKE!
You've only got yourselves to blame —
SQUEAK SQUEAK SQUEAK
You bought me the thing!
SQUEAK SQUEAK SQUEAK SQUEAK SQUEAK
SQUEAK SQUEAK SQUEAK SQUEAK SQUEAK SQUEAK
RIGHT! THAT'S IT! I'VE HAD ENOUGH!
Spoilsport!

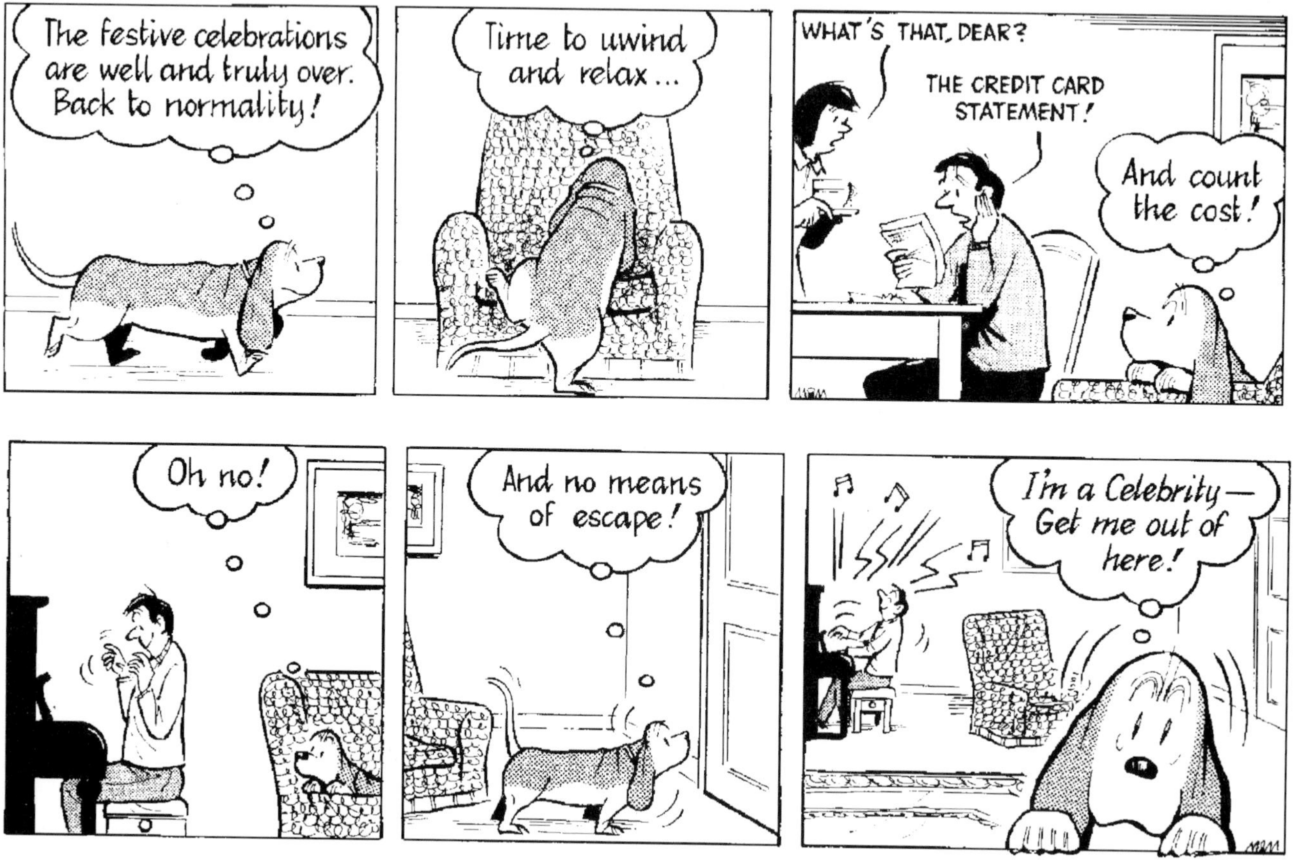
The festive celebrations are well and truly over. Back to normality!
Time to uwind and relax...
WHAT'S THAT, DEAR?
THE CREDIT CARD STATEMENT!
And count the cost!
Oh no!
And no means of escape!
I'm a Celebrity— Get me out of here!